STUDENT'S BOOK
with Digital Pack

Leslie Anne Hendra, Mark Ibbotson, and Kathryn O'Dell

3

Shaftesbury Road, Cambridge CB2 8EA, United Kingdom

One Liberty Plaza, 20th Floor, New York, NY 10006, USA

477 Williamstown Road, Port Melbourne, VIC 3207, Australia

314–321, 3rd Floor, Plot 3, Splendor Forum, Jasola District Centre, New Delhi – 110025, India

103 Penang Road, #05-06/07, Visioncrest Commercial, Singapore 238467

Cambridge University Press & Assessment is a department of the University of Cambridge.

We share the University's mission to contribute to society through the pursuit of education, learning and research at the highest international levels of excellence.

www.cambridge.org
Information on this title: www.cambridge.org/9781009231824

© Cambridge University Press & Assessment 2019, 2022

This publication is in copyright. Subject to statutory exception and to the provisions of relevant collective licensing agreements, no reproduction of any part may take place without the written permission of Cambridge University Press & Assessment.

First published with Digital Pack 2022

20 19 18 17 16 15 14 13 12 11 10 9 8 7

Printed in Malaysia by Vivar Printing

A catalogue record for this publication is available from the British Library

ISBN 978-1-009-23173-2 Student's Book with eBook
ISBN 978-1-009-23182-4 Student's Book with Digital Pack
ISBN 978-1-009-23183-1 Student's Book with Digital Pack A
ISBN 978-1-009-23184-8 Student's Book with Digital Pack B
ISBN 978-1-108-40900-1 Workbook with Audio
ISBN 978-1-108-40872-1 Workbook with Audio A
ISBN 978-1-108-41193-6 Workbook with Audio B
ISBN 978-1-108-40517-1 Teacher's Edition with Test Generator
ISBN 978-1-108-41068-7 Presentation Plus
ISBN 978-1-108-41203-2 Class Audio CDs
ISBN 978-1-108-40793-9 Video Resource Book with DVD
ISBN 978-1-009-23155-8 Full Contact with Digital Pack

Additional resources for this publication at www.cambridge.org/evolve

Cambridge University Press & Assessment has no responsibility for the persistence or accuracy of URLs for external or third-party internet websites referred to in this publication, and does not guarantee that any content on such websites is, or will remain, accurate or appropriate. Information regarding prices, travel timetables, and other factual information given in this work is correct at the time of first printing but Cambridge University Press & Assessment does not guarantee the accuracy of such information thereafter.

ACKNOWLEDGMENTS

The *Evolve* publishers would like to thank the following individuals and institutions who have contributed their time and insights into the development of the course:

Rosario Aste Rentería, **Instituto De Emprendedores USIL**, Peru; Kayla M. Briggs, **Hoseo University**, South Korea; Aslı Derin Anaç, **Bilgi University**, Turkey; Roberta Freitas, **IBEU**, Brazil; Luz Libia Rey G., **Centro Colombo Americano**, Colombia; Antonio Machuca Montalvo, **Organización The Institute TITUELS**, Mexico; Daniel Martin, **CELLEP**, Brazil; Ivanova Monteros A., **Universidad Tecnológica Equinoccial (UTE)**, Ecuador; Verónica Nolivos Arellano, Language Coordinator, Quito, Ecuador; Daniel Nowatnick, **Embassy English**, USA; Ray Purdy, **ELS Educational Services**, USA; Claudia Piccoli Díaz, **Harmon Hall**, Mexico City; Paola Romero C., **UDLA Quito**, Ecuador; Heidi Vande Voort Nam, **Chongshin University**, South Korea; Jason Williams, **Notre Dame Seishin University**, Japan; Matthew Wilson, **Miyagi University**, Japan.

To our student contributors, who have given us their ideas and their time, and who appear throughout this book:

Angie Melissa González Chaverra, Colombia; Andres Ramírez, Mexico; Celeste María Erazo Flores, Honduras; Brenda Tabora Melgar, Honduras; Andrea Vásquez Mota, Mexico.

Authors' Acknowledgments:

The authors would like to thank the whole team at Cambridge University Press. Special thanks go to Katie La Storia for overseeing the project, and to editors Cathy Yost and Kate Powers for encouraging and supporting us during the writing of this book.

Leslie Anne Hendra would like to thank Michael Stuart Clark and her sisters Valeria, Dariel, and Omanie.

Mark Ibbotson would like to thank Nathalie, Aimy and Tom.

Kathryn O'Dell would like to thank her family, including her sister Dionne, nephew Toby, and niece Miranda for keeping her up-to-date on current trends.

The authors and publishers acknowledge the following sources of copyright material and are grateful for the permissions granted. While every effort has been made, it has not always been possible to identify the sources of all the material used, or to trace all copyright holders. If any omissions are brought to our notice, we will be happy to include the appropriate acknowledgements on reprinting and in the next update to the digital edition, as applicable.

Photographs

Key: BG = Background, BC = Below Centre, BL = Below Left, BR = Below Right, CL = Centre Left, CR = Centre Right, TL = Top Left, TR = Top Right.

The following photographs are sourced from Getty Images.

p. xvi: Peter Muller/Cultura; p. xvi, p. 27 (lab), p. 82 (TR): Hill Street Studios/Blend Images; p. 1: ViewApart/iStock/Getty Images Plus; p. 2 (man), p. 82 (list): Steve Debenport/E+; p. 2 (BL): DGLimages/iStock/Getty Images Plus; p. 2 (BC): Jose Luis Pelaez Inc/Blend Images; p. 2 (BR): JGI/Jamie Grill/Blend Images; p. 3, p. 122: monkeybusinessimages/iStock/Getty Images Plus; p. 4: Thomas Barwick/Taxi; p. 5: Kevin Hagen/Getty Images News; p. 6: Alistair Berg/DigitalVision; p. 7: Eugenio Marongiu/Cultura; p. 8: Reimphoto/iStock Editorial/Getty Images Plus; p. 9: Soren Hald/Cultura; pp. 10, 20, 30, 42, 52, 62, 74, 84, 94, 106, 116, 126: Tom Merton/Caiaimage; p. 10 (Jack Ma): FABRICE COFFRINI/AFP; p. 10 (Carmen Aristegui): BERNARDO MONTOYA/AFP; p. 10 (Indira Gandhi): Laurent MAOUS/Gamma-Rapho; p. 10 (Nelson Mandela): PIERRE VERDY/AFP; p. 10 (Serena Williams): Gabriel Rossi/LatinContent; p. 11: Johnrob/E+; p. 12, p. 35: Maskot; p. 13: Ashley Gill/OJO Images; p. 14: Betsie Van Der Meer/Taxi; p. 15, p. 126 (TR): vgajic/E+; p. 16 (TR), p. 47: Westend61; p. 16 (BR): Dave and Les Jacobs/Blend Images; p. 17: Image Source; p. 18, p. 76 (Min-hee): Inti St Clair/Blend Images; p. 19 (light): Chris Collins/Corbis; p. 19 (signs): fotog; p. 20: MarioGuti; p. 21: Bruce Yuanyue Bi/Lonely Planet Images; p. 22: Chan Srithaweeporn/Moment Open; p. 23: John McCabe/Moment; p. 24: Chris Hondros/Getty Images News; p. 25: Rudi Von Briel/Photolibrary; p. 26: PhotoAlto/Ale Ventura; p. 27 (reception): moodboard/Cultura; p. 27 (restroom): EntropyWorkshop/iStock/Getty Images Plus; p. 27 (cafeteria): Michael Gottschalk/Photothek; p. 27 (meeting): alvarez/E+; p. 27 (library): Alberto Guglielmi/Blend Images; p. 28 (BG): Chris Cheadle/All Canada Photos; p. 28 (TR), p. 68: Robert Daly/Caiaimage; p. 29: drbimages/iStock/Getty Images Plus; p. 30 (TL): Iksung Nah/LOOP IMAGES/Corbis Documentary; p. 30 (TR): AFP; p. 32: pixelfit/E+; p. 33: PeopleImages/E+; p. 34: Ljupco/iStock/Getty Images Plus; p. 36: Michael Bollino/Moment; p. 37: R9_RoNaLdO/E+; p. 38: andresr/iStock/Getty Images Plus; p. 39: kali9/E+; p. 40: monkeybusinessimages/iStock Getty Images Plus; p. 42, p. 72, p. 84 (hiking), p. 90 (TR), p. 102 (woman): Hero Images; p. 44 (diver): MaFelipe/iStock/Getty Images Plus; p. 45: Snap Decision/Photographer's Choice RF; p. 46: alffoto/iStock Editorial/Getty Images Plus; p. 48: Carlo A/Moment; p. 49: David Madison/Moment Mobile; p. 50 (painting): Friedrich Schmidt/Photographer's Choice; p. 50 (woman): valentinrussanov/E+; p. 51: Doug Armand/Photographer's Choice; p. 52: ilbusca/E+; p. 53: xavierarnau/E+; p. 54 (BG): Chavalit Likitratcharoen/EyeEm; p. 54 (TR): Kevork Djansezian/Getty Images News; p. 55: Clover No.7 Photography/Moment; p. 56: Daria Botieva/EyeEm; p. 58: DarthArt/iStock Editorial/Getty Images Plus; p. 59: tovfla/iStock/Getty Images Plus; p. 60: sarawuth702/iStock/Getty Images Plus; p. 61: CliqueImages/Photodisc; p. 62: Holly Hildreth/Moment; p. 64: ImagesBazaar; p. 65, p. 88: PeopleImages/DigitalVision; p. 66: Fuse/Corbis; p. 67: John Shearer/TAS18/Getty Images Entertainment; p. 69: fredmantel/iStock/Getty Images Plus; p. 70: Caiaimage/Sam Edwards; p. 71: lisegagne/E+; p. 73: ajr_images/iStock/Getty Images Plus; p. 74 (TL): JohnGollop/E+; p. 74 (TR): Coprid/iStock/Getty Images Plus; p. 74 (CL): DrPAS/iStock/Getty Images Plus; p. 74 (CR): PetlinDmitry/iStock/Getty Images Plus; p. 75: Elizabethsalleebauer/RooM; p. 76 (Vanessa): Yuri_Arcurs/iStock/Getty Images Plus; p. 76 (Rodney): xavierarnau/iStock/Getty Images Plus; p. 77: MOHAMMED ABED/AFP; p. 78: lovro77/E+; p. 79: eclipse_images/E+; p. 80: fstop123/iStock/Getty Images Plus; p. 81: Tempura/E+; p. 82 (TL): Rawpixel/iStock/Getty Images Plus; p. 83: Sidekick/E+; p. 84 (reading): Jupiterimages/Creatas/Getty Images Plus; p. 84 (gym): LUNAMARINA/iStock/Getty Images Plus; p. 84 (kitchen): antonio arcos aka fotonstudio photography/Moment; p. 84 (picnic), p. 118: Mint Images; p. 84 (planning): skynesher/E+; p. 85: Simon Ritzmann/The Image Bank; p. 86: TommasoT/E+; p. 87: Andrew Smith/EyeEm; p. 89: Joos Mind/Stone; p. 90 (TL): miljko/E+; p. 90 (BR): hxdyl/iStock/Getty Images Plus; p. 91: Thomas Barwick/DigitalVision; p. 94: kupicoo/E+; p. 96: Paul; p. 97: White Packert/The Image Bank; p. 98: Alexander Spatari/Moment; p. 99 (cotton): SM Rafiq Photography./Moment; p. 99 (glass): Buena Vista Images/DigitalVision; p. 99 (plastic): Thanatham Piriyakarnjanakul/EyeEm; p. 99 (wood): Yevgen Romanenko/Moment; p. 100: Wavebreakmedia/iStock/Getty Images Plus; p. 101: AleksandarGeorgiev/E+; p. 102 (TL): John_Kasawa/iStock/Getty Images Plus; p. 102 (TC): AnikaSalsera/iStock/Getty Images Plus; p. 102 (TR): fcafotodigital/E+; p. 103: Mark de Leeuw; p. 104 (TL): fcafotodigital/iStock/Getty Images Plus; p. 104 (TR): Siphotography/iStock/Getty Images Plus; p. 105: Richard Newstead/Moment; p. 107: Henn Photography/Cultura; p. 108: Brad Barket/Getty Images Entertainment; p. 109: Klaus Vedfelt/DigitalVision; p. 110: Douglas Sacha/Moment; p. 111: Christoph Jorda/Corbis; p. 112: altrendo images/Juice Images; p. 113 (CR): Philippe TURPIN/Photononstop; p. 114: Markus Gann/EyeEm; p. 115 (TR): Irin Na-Ui/EyeEm; p. 115 (TL): Emiliano Granado; p. 116 (Indra Nooyi): Monica Schipper/Getty Images Entertainment; p. 116 (Lin-Manuel): Dia Dipasupil/Getty Images Entertainment; p. 116 (Angela Merkel): Xander Heinl/Photothek; p. 116 (Neil): Ilya S. Savenok/Getty Images Entertainment; 116 (Misty): Vincent Sandoval/Getty Images Entertainment; p. 117: sturti/E+; p. 119: sawaddee3002/iStock/Getty Images Plus; p. 120: JodiJacobson/E+; p. 121: Trevor Williams/Taxi Japan; p. 123: Adie Bush/Cultura; p. 124 (TL): Nick David/Taxi; p. 124 (TR): PJB/Photodisc; p. 125: Brand X Pictures/DigitalVision; p. 126 (TL): Ascent Xmedia/Stone; p. 126 (CL): Paul Bradbury/OJO Images; p. 126 (CR): Peter Cade/The Image Bank; p. 128: Thomas Northcut/DigitalVision; p. 158: Neustockimages/E+; p. 160: Jon Feingersh/Blend Images.

Below photographs are sourced from other libraries:

p. 43: © Cecilia Wessels; p. 44 (ring): © Bell Media Inc.

Front cover photography by Orbon Alija/E+.

Illustrations by Gergely Forizs (Beehive illustration) p. 72; Ana Djordjevic (Astound US) p. 106.

Audio production by CityVox, New York.

EVOLVE

SPEAKING MATTERS

EVOLVE is a six-level American English course for adults and young adults, taking students from beginner to advanced levels (CEFR A1 to C1).

Drawing on insights from language teaching experts and real students, EVOLVE is a general English course that gets students speaking with confidence.

This student-centered course covers all skills and focuses on the most effective and efficient ways to make progress in English.

Confidence in teaching.
Joy in learning.

Better Learning WITH EVOLVE

Better Learning is our simple approach where insights we've gained from research have helped shape content that drives results. Language evolves, and so does the way we learn. This course takes a flexible, student-centered approach to English language teaching.

Meet our student contributors ▶

Videos and ideas from real students feature throughout the Student's Book.

Our student contributors describe themselves in three words.

ANDRES RAMÍREZ
Friendly, happy, funny
Instituto Tecnológico de Morelia, México

BRENDA TABORA MELGAR
Honest, easygoing, funny
Centro Universitario Tecnológico, Honduras

ANGIE MELISSA GONZÁLEZ CHAVERRA
Intelligent, creative, passionate
Centro Colombo Americano, Colombia

ANDREA VÁSQUEZ MOTA
Creative, fun, nice
The Institute, Boca del Rio, México

CELESTE MARÍA ERAZO FLORES
Happy, special, friendly
Unitec (Universidad Tecnológica Centroamericana), Honduras

Student-generated content

EVOLVE is the first course of its kind to feature real student-generated content. We spoke to over 2,000 students from all over the world about the topics they would like to discuss in English and in what situations they would like to be able to speak more confidently.

The ideas are included throughout the Student's Book and the students appear in short videos responding to discussion questions.

INSIGHT	CONTENT	RESULT
Research shows that achievable speaking role models can be a powerful motivator.	Bite-sized videos feature students talking about topics in the Student's Book.	Students are motivated to speak and share their ideas.

"It's important to provide learners with interesting or stimulating topics."

Teacher, Mexico (Global Teacher Survey, 2017)

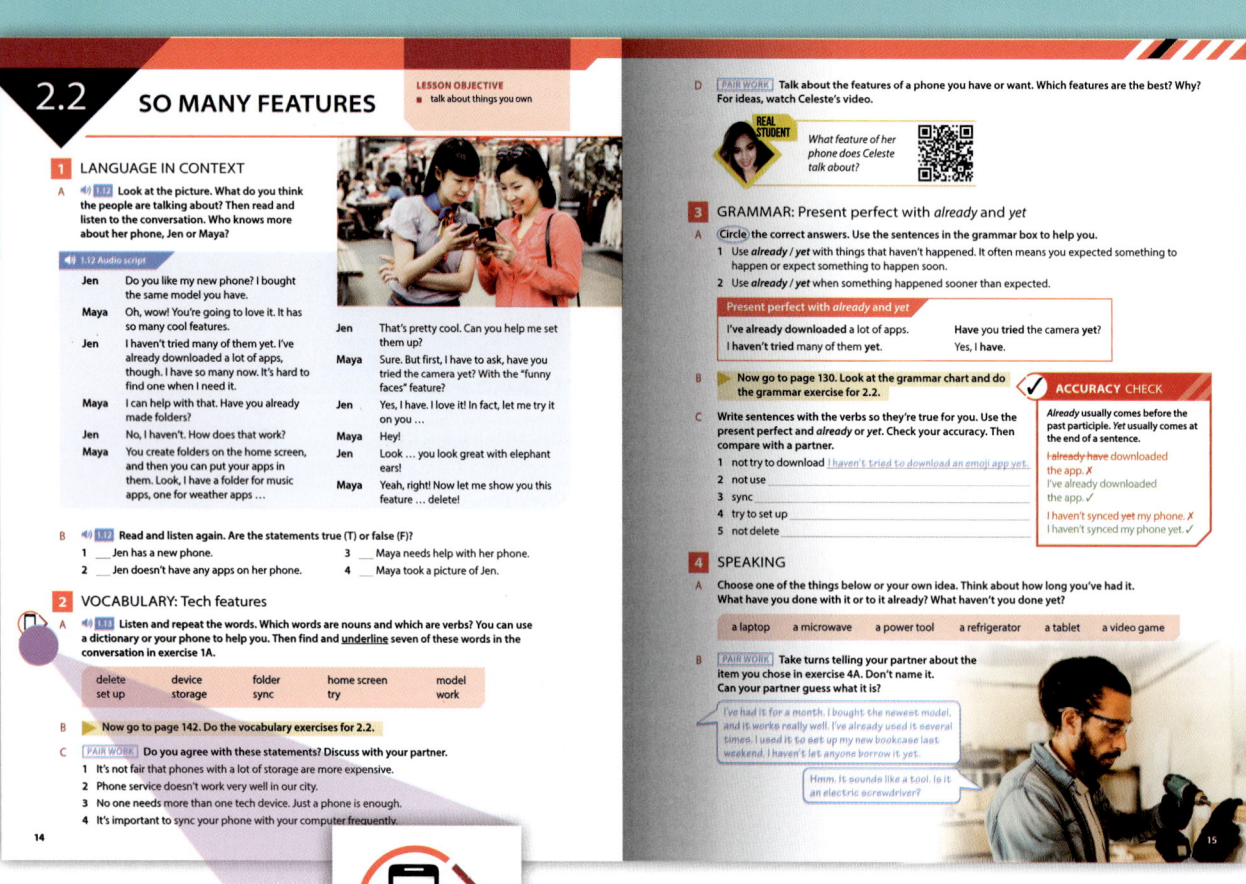

Find it

INSIGHT
Research with hundreds of teachers and students across the globe revealed a desire to expand the classroom and bring the real world in.

CONTENT
Find it are smartphone activities that allow students to bring live content into the class and personalize the learning experience with research and group activities.

RESULT
Students engage in the lesson because it is meaningful to them.

Designed for success

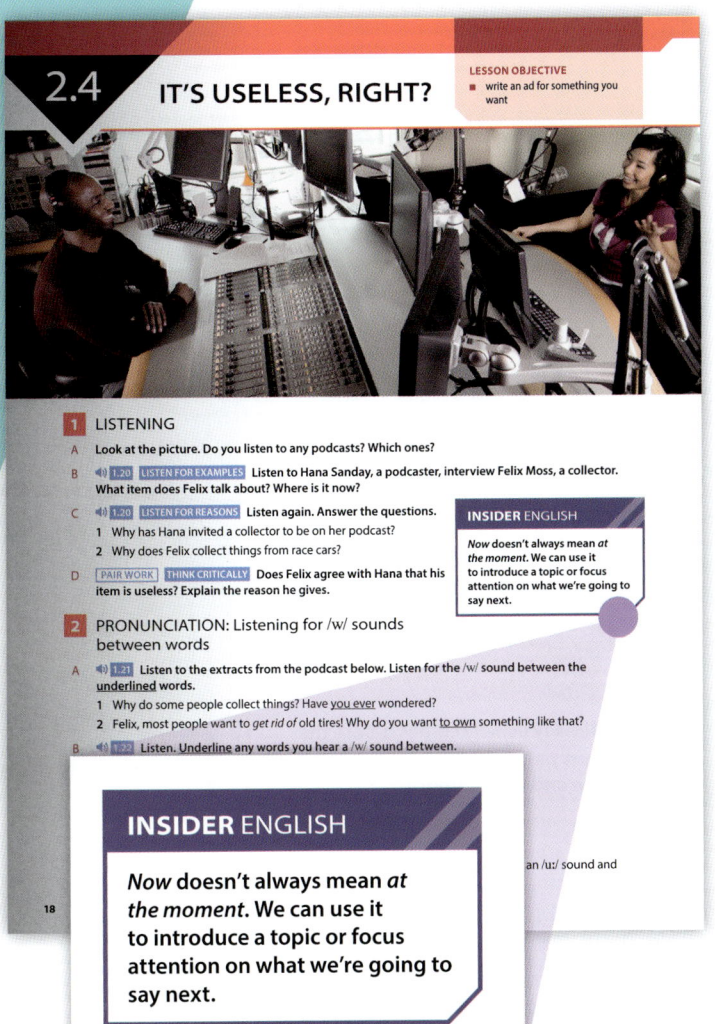

Pronunciation

INSIGHT
Research shows that only certain aspects of pronunciation actually affect comprehensibility and inhibit communication.

CONTENT
EVOLVE focuses on the aspects of pronunciation that most affect communication.

RESULT
Students understand more when listening and can be clearly understood when they speak.

Insider English

INSIGHT
Even in a short exchange, idiomatic language can inhibit understanding.

CONTENT
Insider English focuses on the informal language and colloquial expressions frequently found in everyday situations.

RESULT
Students are confident in the real world.

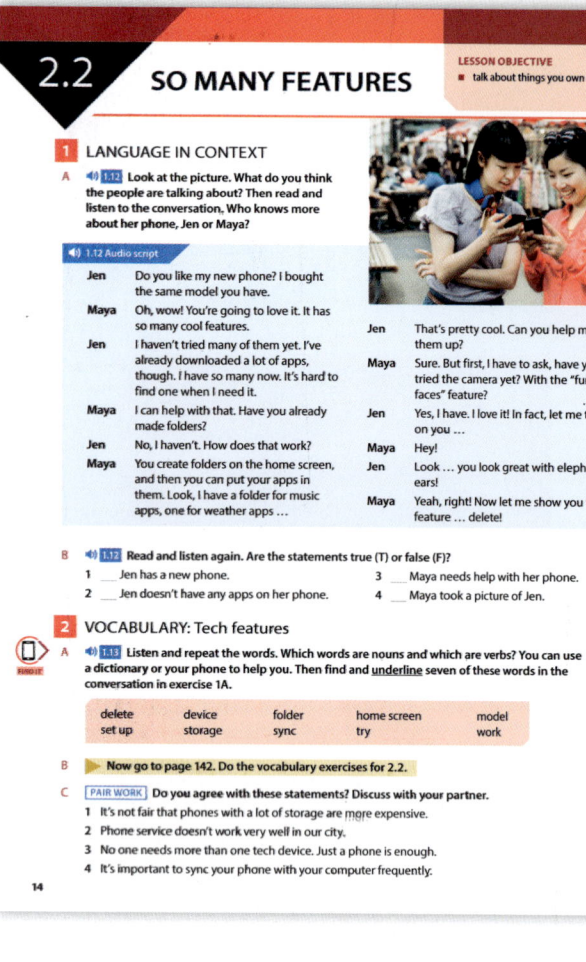

Accuracy check

INSIGHT
Some common errors can become fossilized if not addressed early on in the learning process.

CONTENT
Accuracy check highlights common learner errors (based on unique research into the Cambridge Learner Corpus) and can be used for self-editing.

RESULT
Students avoid common errors in their written and spoken English.

"The presentation is very clear and there are plenty of opportunities for student practice and production."

Jason Williams, Teacher, Notre Dame Seishin University, Japan

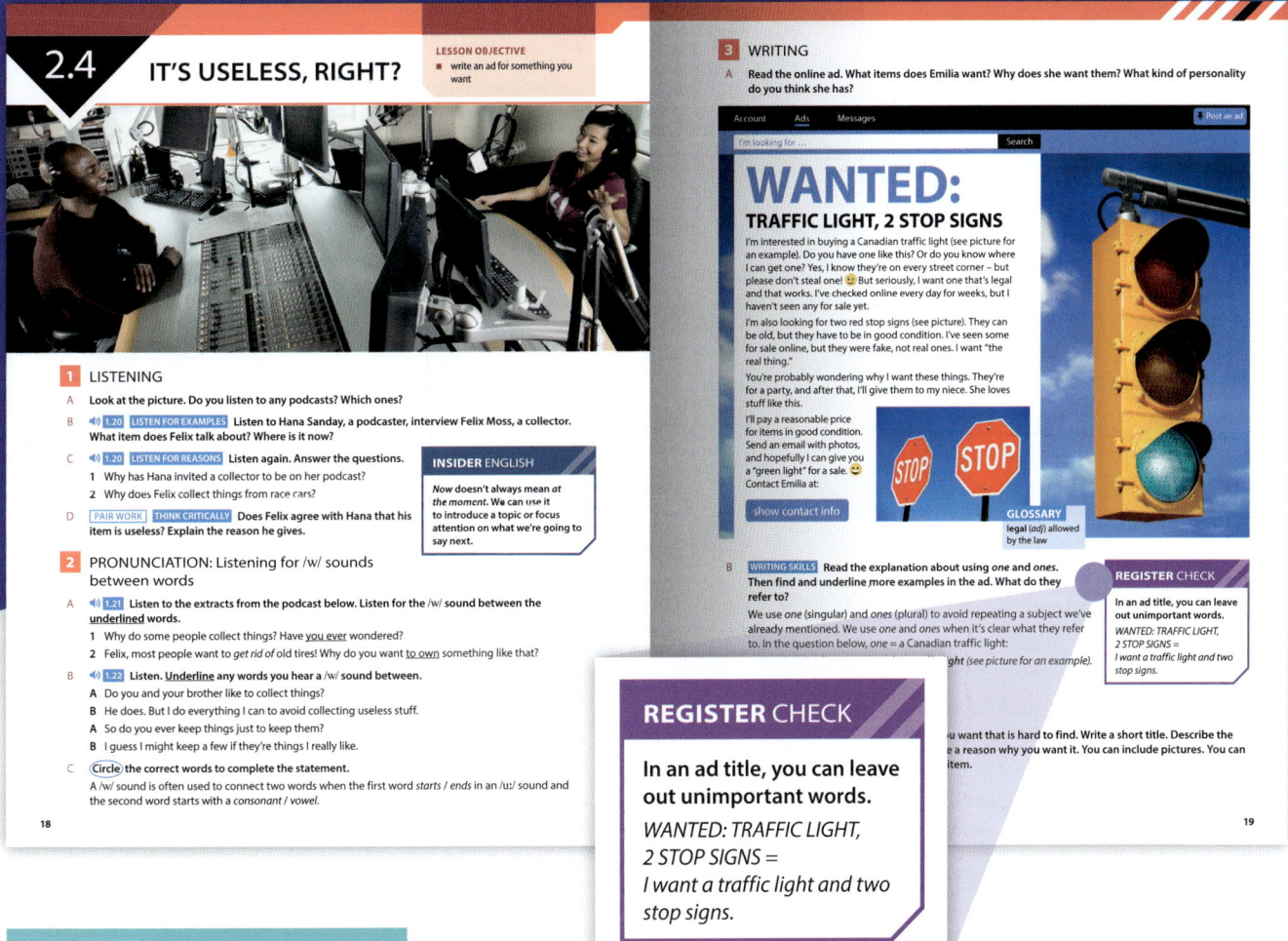

Register check

INSIGHT
Teachers report that their students often struggle to master the differences between written and spoken English.

CONTENT
Register check draws on research into the Cambridge English Corpus and highlights potential problem areas for learners.

RESULT
Students transition confidently between written and spoken English and recognize different levels of formality as well as when to use them appropriately.

You spoke. We listened.

Students told us that speaking is the most important skill for them to master, while teachers told us that finding speaking activities which engage their students and work in the classroom can be challenging.

That's why EVOLVE has a whole lesson dedicated to speaking: Lesson 5, *Time to speak*.

Time to speak

INSIGHT
Speaking ability is how students most commonly measure their own progress, but is also the area where they feel most insecure. To be able to fully exploit speaking opportunities in the classroom, students need a safe speaking environment where they can feel confident, supported, and able to experiment with language.

CONTENT
Time to Speak is a unique lesson dedicated to developing speaking skills and is based around immersive tasks which involve information sharing and decision making.

RESULT
Time to speak lessons create a buzz in the classroom where speaking can really thrive, evolve, and take off, resulting in more confident speakers of English.

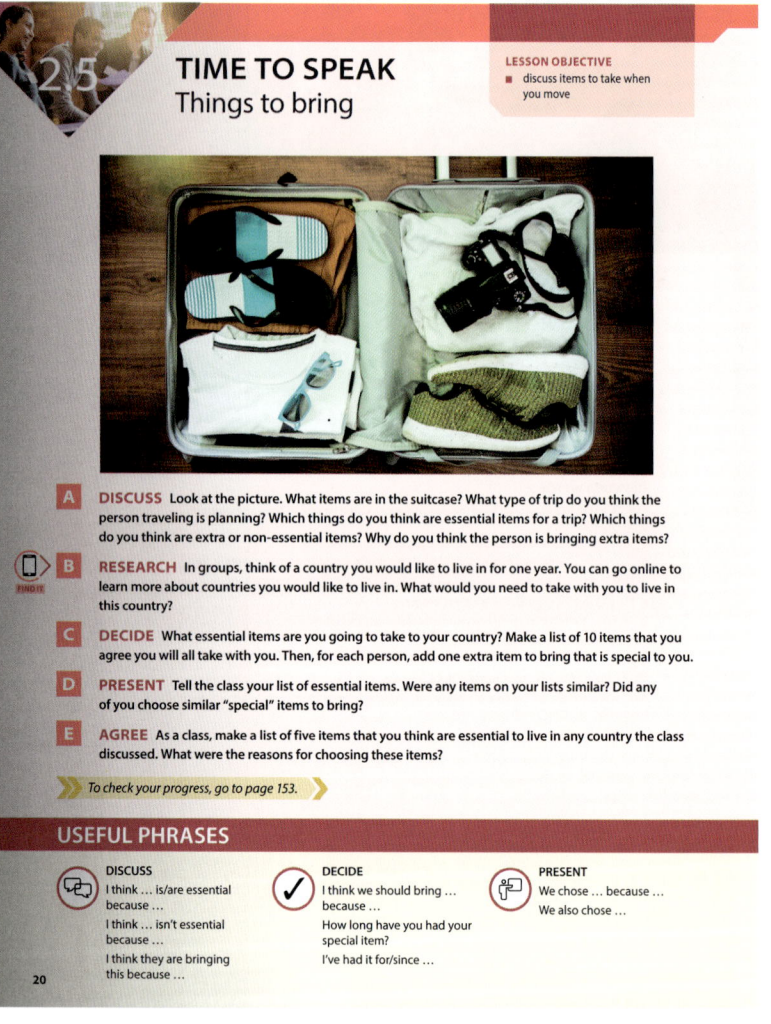

Experience Better Learning with EVOLVE: a course that helps both teachers and students on every step of the language learning journey.

Speaking matters. Find out more about creating safe speaking environments in the classroom.

EVOLVE unit structure

Unit opening page
Each unit opening page activates prior knowledge and vocabulary and immediately gets students speaking.

Lessons 1 and 2
These lessons present and practice the unit vocabulary and grammar in context, helping students discover language rules for themselves. Students then have the opportunity to use this language in well-scaffolded, personalized speaking tasks.

Lesson 3
This lesson is built around a functional language dialogue that models and contextualizes useful fixed expressions for managing a particular situation. This is a real world strategy to help students handle unexpected conversational turns.

Lesson 4
This is a combined skills lesson based around an engaging reading or listening text. Each lesson asks students to think critically and ends with a practical writing task.

Lesson 5
Time to speak is an entire lesson dedicated to developing speaking skills. Students work on collaborative, immersive tasks which involve information sharing and decision making.

CONTENTS

		Learning objectives	Grammar	Vocabulary	Pronunciation
Unit 1	Who we are	■ Talk about people's personalities ■ Ask and answer questions about people ■ Make introductions and get to know people ■ Write an email to get to know someone ■ Ask questions to test a leader's personality	■ Information questions ■ Indirect questions	■ Describing personality ■ Giving personal information	■ Stressing new information
Unit 2	So much stuff	■ Talk about things you've had for a while ■ Talk about things you own ■ Switch from one topic to another ■ Write an ad for something you want ■ Discuss items to take when you move	■ Present perfect with *ever, never, for,* and *since* ■ Present perfect with *already* and *yet*	■ Describing possessions ■ Tech features	■ Saying /t/ at the start of words ■ Listening for /w/ sounds
Unit 3	Smart moves	■ Ask and answer questions about your city ■ Talk about how to get from one place to another ■ Ask for and give directions in a building ■ Write a personal statement for a job application ■ Give a presentation about a secret spot in your city	■ Articles ■ Modals for advice	■ City features ■ Public transportation	■ Saying consonant clusters at the start of a word
		Review 1 (Review of Units 1–3)			
Unit 4	Think first	■ Describe opinions and reactions ■ Make plans for a trip ■ Offer and respond to reassurance ■ Write an email describing plans for an event ■ Choose activities for different groups of people	■ *be going to* and *will* for predictions ■ *will* for sudden decisions; present continuous for future plans	■ Describing opinions and reactions ■ Making decisions and plans	■ Saying /p/ at the start of a word ■ Listening for linked sounds – final /n/
Unit 5	And then …	■ Talk about lost and found things ■ Talk about needing and giving help ■ Talk about surprising situations ■ Write a short story ■ Tell and compare stories	■ Simple past ■ Past continuous and simple past	■ Losing and finding things ■ Needing and giving help	■ Showing surprise
Unit 6	Impact	■ Talk about urban problems ■ Talk about problems and solutions ■ Express concern and relief in different situations ■ Write a post giving your point of view ■ Decide if a "green" plan will work	■ Quantifiers ■ Present and future real conditionals	■ Urban problems ■ Adverbs of manner	■ Unstressed vowels at the end of a word ■ Listening for weak words
		Review 2 (Review of Units 4–6)			

Functional language	Listening	Reading	Writing	Speaking
■ Make introductions; say how you know someone; end a conversation **Real-world strategy** ■ Meet someone you've heard about		We're family! ■ An email to a cousin in a different country	A message introducing yourself ■ An email to a relative in another country ■ Paragraphs	■ Talk about questions you ask new people ■ Ask and answer questions about famous people ■ Introduce yourself and ask questions ■ Describe someone's personality **Time to speak** ■ Decide what makes a good leader
■ Introduce new topics; change the subject; stay on track **Real-world strategy** ■ Use short questions to show interest	It's useless, right? ■ A podcast interview with a collector		An online advertisement ■ An ad requesting something you want ■ *one* and *ones*	■ Talk about the "history" of personal objects ■ Talk about how long you've had items ■ Talk about personal interests ■ Talk about someone's reasons for collecting **Time to speak** ■ Discuss things to take in a move
■ Ask for directions; give directions **Real-world strategy** ■ Repeat details to show you understand		Maybe you can help ■ An ad for volunteer jobs	A volunteer application ■ A personal statement for an application ■ Checking punctuation, spelling, and grammar	■ Ask and answer city questions ■ Talk about routes to places in your city ■ Give directions to places at school or work ■ Talk about a volunteer job **Time to speak** ■ Discuss "secret spots" in your city
■ Offer reassurance; respond to reassurance **Real-world strategy** ■ Use *at least* to point out the good side of a situation	Business and pleasure ■ Colleagues discussing plans for a fun event for students		An email with an event schedule ■ An email describing plans for an event ■ Linking words to show order	■ Talk about your plans for the week and weekend ■ Make plans for a weekend trip ■ Talk about difficult situations ■ Choose the best group activity **Time to speak** ■ Plan a "microadventure"
■ Give surprising news; react with surprise **Real-world strategy** ■ Repeat words to express surprise		Storytelling ■ An article about how to tell a good story	A true story ■ A story ■ Expressions for storytelling	■ Talk about things you have lost or found ■ Describe a time you helped someone ■ Talk about surprising personal news ■ Say what makes a story good **Time to speak** ■ Share "amazing but true" stories
■ Express concern; express relief **Real-world strategy** ■ Use *though* to give a contrasting idea	Beating the traffic ■ A podcast about drone deliveries		Online comment reacting to a podcast ■ Comment about a podcast ■ Using questions to make points	■ Discuss the impact of urban problems ■ Talk about city problems and solutions ■ Talk about worrisome situations ■ Evaluate someone's ideas **Time to speak** ■ Discuss making cities "green"

xiii

	Learning objectives	Grammar	Vocabulary	Pronunciation
Unit 7 Entertain us	■ Discuss your changing tastes in music ■ Talk about TV shows and movies ■ Refuse invitations and respond to refusals ■ Write a movie review ■ Talk about changing tastes	■ *used to* ■ Comparisons with *(not) as … as*	■ Music ■ TV shows and movies	■ Saying /m/ in *I'm*
Unit 8 Getting there	■ Talk about what you've been doing ■ Talk about progress ■ Catch up with people's news ■ Write a post about managing your time ■ Decide on better ways to use your time	■ Present perfect continuous ■ Present perfect vs. present perfect continuous	■ Describing experiences ■ Describing progress	■ Saying /ɑ/ and /æ/ vowel sounds ■ Listening for weak forms of *didn't*
Unit 9 Make it work	■ Talk about college subjects ■ Discuss rules for working and studying at home ■ Express confidence and lack of confidence ■ Write the main part of a résumé ■ Decide how to use your skills	■ Modals of necessity ■ Modals of prohibition and permission	■ College subjects ■ Employment	■ Grouping words

Review 3 (Review of Units 7–9)

	Learning objectives	Grammar	Vocabulary	Pronunciation
Unit 10 Why we buy	■ Say what things are made of ■ Talk about where things come from ■ Question or approve of someone's choices ■ Write feedback about company products ■ Design a commercial	■ Simple present passive ■ Simple past passive	■ Describing materials ■ Production and distribution	■ Saying /u/, /aʊ/, and /ʊ/ vowel sounds ■ Listening for contrastive stress
Unit 11 Pushing yourself	■ Talk about how to succeed ■ Talk about imaginary situations ■ Give opinions and ask for agreement ■ Write a personal story ■ Talk about a person you admire	■ Phrasal verbs ■ Present and future unreal conditionals	■ Succeeding ■ Opportunities and risks	■ Saying /ʃ/ and /dʒ/ sounds
Unit 12 Life's little lessons	■ Talk about accidents ■ Talk about extreme experiences ■ Describe and ask about feelings ■ Write an anecdote about a life lesson ■ Plan a fun learning experience	■ Indefinite pronouns ■ Reported speech	■ Describing accidents ■ Describing extremes	■ Saying *-ed* at the end of a word ■ Listening for *'ll*

Review 4 (Review of Units 10–12)

Grammar charts and practice, pages 129–140   Vocabulary exercises, pages 141–152

Functional language	Listening	Reading	Writing	Speaking
■ Refuse invitations; respond to a refusal **Real-world strategy** ■ Soften comments		**Animation for all ages** ■ An online article about animated movies and TV shows	**A review of an animated movie** ■ A movie review ■ Organizing ideas	■ Talk about how musical tastes have changed ■ Compare favorite movies/TV shows ■ Invite someone to an event and refuse an invitation ■ Talk about humor in animated movies **Time to speak** ■ Discuss changing tastes in entertainment
■ Say how long it's been; ask about someone's news; answer **Real-world strategy** ■ Use *that would be* to comment on something	**A time-saving tip** ■ A podcast interview about time management		**A post about a podcast** ■ A post about time management ■ Time expressions	■ Talk about what you've been doing recently ■ Explain what you've been spending time on ■ Talk to a friend you haven't seen for a while ■ Talk about someone's new habits **Time to speak** ■ Prioritize tasks to improve balance
■ Express confidence; express lack of confidence **Real-world strategy** ■ Focus on reasons		**A job search** ■ An online job ad and a résumé for the job	**A résumé** ■ Experiences and activities for a résumé ■ How to write a résumé	■ Talk about subjects in school that prepare you for the future ■ Present rules for working or studying at home ■ Discuss plans for doing challenging activities ■ Identify what job an ad is for **Time to speak** ■ Describe skills for an ideal job
■ Question someone's choices; approve someone's choices **Real-world strategy** ■ Change your mind	**Not just customers – fans** ■ A podcast about customers as fans		**Online customer feedback about products** ■ Feedback about products ■ *However* and *although* to contrast ideas	■ Describe how materials affect the environment ■ Share where things you own were produced ■ Talk about things you want to buy ■ Talk about companies you like **Time to speak** ■ Discuss reasons why people buy things
■ Ask for agreement; agree **Real-world strategy** ■ Soften an opinion		**Outside the comfort zone** ■ An online article about benefits of leaving your comfort zone	**A story about a challenging new activity** ■ A story about pushing yourself ■ Comparing facts	■ Talk about a failure and its effects ■ Discuss what you might risk for money ■ Express opinions about topics with two sides ■ Talk about pushing yourself **Time to speak** ■ Discuss what makes people successful
■ Describe your feelings; ask about or guess others' feelings **Real-world strategy** ■ End a story	**Lessons learned?** ■ An expert presentation about life lessons		**A story about learning a lesson** ■ An anecdote about a life lesson ■ Using different expressions with similar meanings	■ Talk about a small, amusing accident ■ Describe an extreme experience ■ Talk about emotions associated with an experience ■ Talk about learning from mistakes **Time to speak** ■ Talk about activities to learn new skills

CLASSROOM LANGUAGE

🔊 **1.02** PAIR WORK AND GROUP WORK

Choosing roles

- Do you want to go first?
- I'll be Student A, and you be Student B.
- Let's switch roles and do it again.

Eliciting opinions

- What do you think, _____?
- How about you, _____?

Asking for clarification or more information

- I'm not sure I understand. Can you say that again?
- Does anyone have anything to add?

Completing a task

- We're done.
- We're finished. What should we do now/next?

CHECKING YOUR WORK

Comparing answers

- Let's compare answers.
- What do you have for number … ?
- I have …
- I have the same thing.
- I have something different.
- I have a different answer.

Offering feedback

- Let's switch papers.
- I'm not quite sure what you mean here.
- I really like that you …
- It looks like you …
- I wondered about …
- Can you say this another way?
- I wanted to ask you about …
- Let's check this one again.

WHO WE ARE

1

UNIT OBJECTIVES
- talk about people's personalities
- ask and answer questions about people
- make introductions and get to know people
- write an email to get to know someone
- ask questions to test a leader's personality

START SPEAKING

A Where are these people? What are they doing?

B What do you think the people are like? Guess as much as you can about them.

C Imagine you're in this place talking to these people. What are you asking them? What are you telling them about yourself? For ideas, watch Andres's video.

REAL STUDENT *What does Andres say about himself?*

1.1 WHAT'S YOUR PERSONALITY?

LESSON OBJECTIVE
- talk about people's personalities

1 LANGUAGE IN CONTEXT

A **PAIR WORK** Do you meet new people often? Where do you meet them? Who have you met lately?

B Read the article. How does Kenneth say you can learn about someone?

What kind of person are you?
The answer is in your questions.

How do you get to know someone new? You can ask a lot of questions: *What's your name? Whose class are you in? Which neighborhood do you live in? Where did you go to school? What kind of work do you do?* But the answers don't tell you about someone's personality. I think it's best to *listen* to the questions that people ask you.

A **sociable** person, for example, will ask you a lot of questions. Quiet people don't ask you much. The same is true about **selfish** people – they show little interest in other people. Or imagine you're telling someone about a problem you have. A **generous** person might ask, "How can I help?" But if you ask someone for help first, and they agree, are you sure they're really helpful? Or are they just afraid to say "no"?

So, the next time you meet someone, ask less, and listen more. The questions people ask show more about their personalities than their answers do.

Kenneth Spears

C **PAIR WORK** Read the article again. Do you agree with Kenneth? Why or why not?

2 VOCABULARY: Describing personality

A 🔊 **1.03** Listen and repeat the words. Which words describe the people in the pictures? More than one answer is possible.

| brave | cheerful | easygoing | generous | helpful | honest |
| intelligent | nervous | reliable | selfish | serious | sociable |

B **GROUP WORK** Which three words in exercise 2A describe you best? Tell your group.

C ▶ Now go to page 141. Do the vocabulary exercises for 1.1.

D **PAIR WORK** Use the words in exercise 2A to talk about people you know. For ideas, watch Angie's video.

REAL STUDENT
Do you know anyone like the person Angie describes?

3 GRAMMAR: Information questions

A Circle the correct answers. Use the sentences in the grammar box to help you.
1 Use *what* / *which* to ask a general question.
2 Use *what* / *which* to ask about a specific group of people or things.
3 Use *whose* to ask **who someone is** / **who something belongs to**.
4 Use *how* to ask about **the way to do something** / **when to do something**.

> **Information questions**
>
> **Whose** class **are** you in?   **Where did** you **go** to school?
> **Which** neighborhood **do** you **live** in?   **How can** I help?
> **What are** you **doing** these days?

B Look at the words in the box. Complete the information questions with the correct words. Then ask and answer the questions with a partner.

| How | When | Where | Who | Whose | Why |

1 _____ do you usually meet your friends? At night or on the weekends?
2 _____ do you greet new people? With a smile?
3 _____ do you go with your friends to have fun?
4 _____ 's the most sociable person you know?
5 _____ are you learning English? For work?
6 Do you ever use someone else's computer? _____ computer do you use?

C ▶ Now go to page 129. Look at the grammar chart and do the grammar exercise for 1.1.

D Write information questions for the answers below.
1 _____ ?   I had eggs for breakfast.
2 _____ ?   I speak English and Spanish.
3 _____ ?   My keys are in my pocket.
4 _____ ?   I got here by bus.
5 _____ ?   I usually get up at 6:30.

E [PAIR WORK] Ask and answer the questions in exercise 3D with your own information.

4 SPEAKING

[GROUP WORK] What questions do you ask when you meet people for the first time? What do you think your questions say about you?

> I usually ask people, "What do you do for fun?" Sometimes we like the same things!

> What do you think that question says about you?

> I think it shows people that I am interested in them.

1.2 TRUE FRIENDS?

LESSON OBJECTIVE
- ask and answer questions about people

1 LANGUAGE IN CONTEXT

A 🔊 **1.04** Look at the picture. Do you think the people are good friends? Why or why not? Then read and listen to Jared interview Amber for his podcast. Why does Amber ask questions about his friend Scott?

B 🔊 **1.04** Read and listen again. What questions does Amber ask Scott? Can you answer these questions about your good friends?

🔊 **1.04 Audio script**

Jared	Today, I'm talking with Amber Crane, a friendship expert. So, Amber, you have some questions that show if someone is a true friend. Tell me more.
Amber	OK. I'm going to show you by example. Give me the name of one of your friends.
Jared	Um, Scott.
Amber	Let's see how well you know Scott. **Is** he **single** or **married**?
Jared	He**'s married**.
Amber	OK. Can you tell me where he **was born** and **raised**?
Jared	Yes. He was born in Chicago, but he **was raised** in Oswego.
Amber	Good. Now I'd like to know what sports or hobbies he**'s into**.
Jared	He**'s into** soccer, and he likes to paint. Hey, I'm answering harder questions. Does that mean Scott and I are true friends?
Amber	Well, no. You could know these things about anyone through social media.
Jared	True. So, what question can I answer that shows Scott is a *true* friend?
Amber	Try this one. Do you know if he likes broccoli?
Jared	I'll tell you after the break … and after I text Scott!

2 VOCABULARY: Giving personal information

A 🔊 **1.05** Complete the paragraph with the verbs in the box. Use the simple past. Then listen and check.

be born	be into	be married	be raised	be single
celebrate	live alone	live with my family	retire	

I ¹ _was born_ in Detroit, but I ² _____ in the country. I ³ _____ – my parents, brother, and sister – on a farm. My brother and I ⁴ _____ sports, especially baseball. After high school, I moved back to Detroit. I ⁵ _____ in a small apartment – I didn't have any roommates. And I ⁶ _____ – I didn't have a girlfriend at that time. But I have a wife now. Alicia and I ⁷ _____ five years ago, and we ⁸ _____ our anniversary last Wednesday. My parents took us out to dinner. They ⁹ _____ a year ago, so they have a lot of free time.

B ▶ Now go to page 141. Do the vocabulary exercises for 1.2.

C [PAIR WORK] Tell your partner about your life. Use expressions from exercise 2A.

> I was born and raised in Pisco, but now I live with my family in Lima.

4

3 GRAMMAR: Indirect questions

A Circle the correct answers. Use the sentences in the grammar box to help you.
1 In indirect questions, use **question word order** / **statement word order**.
2 Use **what** / **if** in an indirect *yes/no* question.
3 For indirect questions within statements, put a **period** / **question mark** at the end.

> **Indirect questions**
>
> **Can you tell me** where he was born and raised?
> **Do you know if** he likes broccoli?
> **I'd like to know** what sports or hobbies he's into.

> ! You can also use these words to form indirect questions:
> *Do you have any idea … ?*
> *I want to find out …*
> *I wonder …*

B Change the direct questions into indirect questions. Start with the phrases shown. Then check your accuracy.
1 Where were you raised? → Can you tell me _____ ?
2 When does your teacher want to retire? → Do you have any idea _____ ?
3 Are your friends into sports? → I wonder _____ .
4 When do your parents celebrate their anniversary? → Do you know _____ ?
5 Were your brothers and sisters born in this city? → I'd like to know _____ .

> ✓ **ACCURACY CHECK**
>
> In *yes/no* indirect questions, do **not** use *do* or *does* in the second part of the question.
> Do you know where ~~does~~ she work? ✗
> Do you know where she works? ✓

C PAIR WORK Ask and answer the indirect questions you wrote in exercise 3B.

D ▶ Now go to page 129. Look at the grammar chart and do the grammar exercise for 1.2.

4 SPEAKING

A Write three questions to ask a classmate about an actor, a singer, or a world leader. Use the verbs in exercise 2A or your own ideas.

Where was Justin Trudeau born?

B GROUP WORK Ask and answer your questions from exercise 4A. Use indirect questions. You can go online to find any answers you didn't know.

> Do you know where Justin Trudeau was born?
>
> No, I don't.
>
> I think he was born in Ottawa, Canada.

1.3 NICE TALKING TO YOU

LESSON OBJECTIVE
- make introductions and get to know people

1 FUNCTIONAL LANGUAGE

A When you meet someone for the first time, which of these things do you talk about?

people you both know	where you live
your classes	where you're from
your interests	your job

B 🔊 **1.06** Read and listen. Nina goes to a party at her coworker Jodi's home. Who does she talk to? What topics in exercise 1A do they talk about?

🔊 1.06 Audio script

A Hello. **I'm Nina.**

B Nice to meet you. **I'm Mia, Jodi's sister.** How **do you know Jodi**?

A **I work with her.** Actually, my desk is next to hers.

B Wow, I'd love to know what she's like at work! Is she really serious?

A No. She's really easygoing, actually. So, what kind of work do you do, Mia?

B I'm in sales. Do you know the company R&R Johnson? I work for them.

A few minutes later

B Well, **I should let you go.** It was really nice to **meet you**, Nina.

A Thanks. **It was nice talking to you.**

B Oh! Hold on a sec. There's Rafe. **This is Rafe**, **my husband.** And **this is Nina, Jodi's coworker.**

C Hi, Nina. Nice to meet you. So, you work with Jodi … What's she like at work?

C Complete the chart with the expressions in bold from the conversations.

Introductions	Saying how you know someone	Ending a conversation
¹_____ Nina.	How ⁵_____ Jodi?	I should ⁷_____ .
I'm Mia, Jodi's ²_____ .	I ⁶_____ her.	Sorry, I have to go now.
This is Rafe, ³_____ .	I'm her sister/friend/coworker.	It was really nice to ⁸_____ .
This is Nina, Jodi's ⁴_____ .		It was nice ⁹_____ to you.

D (Circle) the correct response to each sentence.
1 How do you know Yolanda?
   a I'm her brother.   **b** This is my sister.
2 This is Rosa, my sister. And this is Cal, my coworker.
   a It was nice talking to you.   **b** Nice to meet you.
3 I should let you go.
   a Sorry, I have to go now.   **b** OK. It was really nice to meet you.

INSIDER ENGLISH

We say *Hold on a sec* (sec = second) when we want someone to wait for a moment.

2 REAL-WORLD STRATEGY

A 🔊 **1.07** Listen to another conversation at Jodi's party. How are Ji-soo and Nathan related to Jodi?

B 🔊 **1.07** Read the information in the box about meeting someone you've heard about. Then listen to the conversation again. Which sentences from the box do Ji-soo and Nathan use?

> **MEETING SOMEONE YOU'VE HEARD ABOUT**
> When you meet someone you've heard about before, you can say, "I've heard a lot about you," or "I've heard good things about you." The responses can be, "Good things, I hope!" or "Oh, that's nice."
>
> It's great to meet you, Mia. **I've heard good things about you.**
> **Oh, that's nice.** So, how do you know Jodi?

C 🔊 **1.08** Complete another conversation with sentences from the box. Listen and check.

- **A** Hi. I'm Jessica, Nathan's sister.
- **B** Hello, Jessica. I'm Leo. I work with Nathan.
- **A** Nice to meet you, Leo. _____.
- **B** _____.

D ▶ PAIR WORK Student A: Go to page 157. Student B: Go to page 159. Follow the instructions.

3 PRONUNCIATION: Stressing new information

A 🔊 **1.09** Listen to the conversations. Notice that words containing new information are stressed.

1. **A** Hello. I'm **Nina**.   **B** I'm Mia, Jodi's **sister**.
2. **A** This is **Rafe**, my **husband**.   **B** Nice to meet you.

B 🔊 **1.10** PAIR WORK Underline the new information in the conversation below. Then listen. Do the speakers stress the words you underlined? Practice the conversation with a partner.

- **A** Hi, I'm Robert, Jessica's brother.
- **B** Hi, Robert. I'm Amaya.
- **A** So how do you know Jessica?
- **B** Oh, we work together. She's my boss.
- **A** Oh really? Is she a good boss?
- **B** Uh, I don't know yet. I just started.

4 SPEAKING

A PAIR WORK Imagine you are meeting for the first time. Introduce yourselves. Then ask questions to get to know each other. You can ask about the topics in exercise 1A and your own ideas.

> Hello. I'm Nick Martin.

> Nice to meet you, Nick. I'm Alexandra Clark.

> Nice you meet you, too. So, Alexandra, do you live here, in San Francisco?

B GROUP WORK Get together with another pair. One person in each pair: Introduce yourself and your partner. Everyone: Ask the other pair questions to get to know them.

1.4 WE'RE FAMILY!

LESSON OBJECTIVE
- write an email to get to know someone

1 READING

A **READ FOR GIST** Read Andrew's email to a cousin in Norway that he has never met. Which of these subjects does he mention?

| a farm | family members | his car | his college | movies | sports |

To: Elin Hansen <elin953Hansen@blinknet.com>
From: Andrew Bennett <and.bennett@mymail.org>
Subject: Your American cousin

Reply   Forward

Hi Elin,

I'm writing because I want to get in touch with the Norwegian side of the family. My Aunt Joan got your email address from your mom. Aunt Joan says you're one of my cousins, and you're about my age – 23. I just finished my degree in economics at North Dakota State University in Fargo. Fargo is the biggest city in North Dakota, and I live there with my parents.

I'd like to know about you and what you're interested in. Are you a student, or do you work? What kind of music do you like? Aunt Joan says you live in Oslo. Can you tell me what it's like? And is it true that everyone in Norway is really into winter sports? Sorry for all the questions, but this is an unusual situation – we're strangers, but we're also family. 😊

Our side of the family moved to North Dakota from Norway a long time ago. They had a farm in the Red River Valley in North Dakota, and the old house is still there (see attached photo).

Hope to hear from you soon.

Andrew

B **READ FOR DETAILS** Read again. Answer the questions.
1 How did Andrew hear about Elin?
2 What information does Andrew give about himself?
3 What information does he give about his family?

C **PAIR WORK** **THINK CRITICALLY** Which of these adjectives describe Andrew? Explain your ideas.

| brave | cheerful | helpful |
| nervous | selfish | sociable |

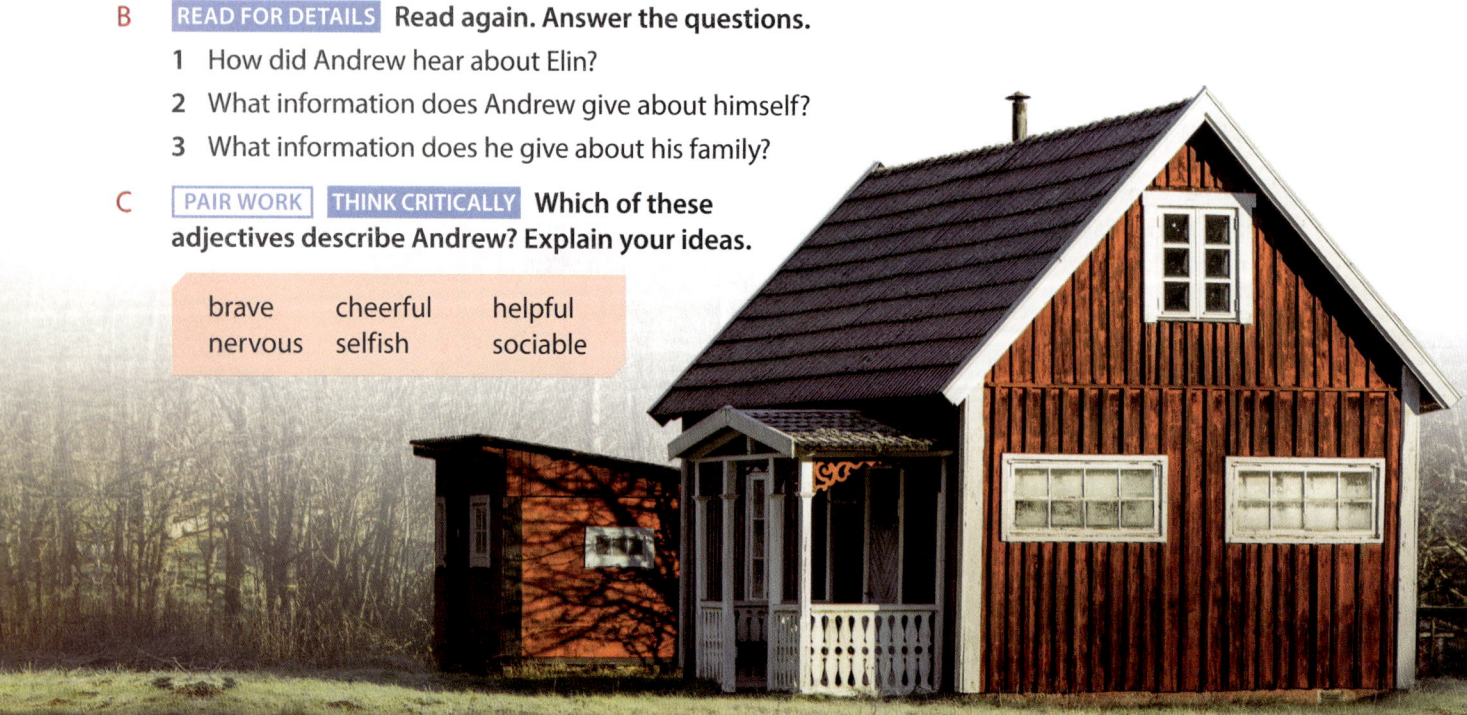

2 WRITING

A Read Elin's email to Andrew. Does she answer all his questions?

To: Andrew Bennett <and.bennett@mymail.org>
From: Elin Hansen <elin953Hansen@blinknet.com>
Subject: Re: Your American cousin

Hi Andrew,

¹ Thanks for your email. It's great to hear from you!

² You asked about me. Well, I'm 24, I graduated this spring, and I'm working in an architect's office now. In my free time, I get together with friends, go shopping, go hiking, and chat with family and friends online. Oh, and I like all kinds of music.

³ Oslo is the capital of Norway and is its biggest city. It's a nice place to live because people are friendly and sociable. It's full of great museums and restaurants, and people walk and ride bikes a lot around the city. I don't know if everyone in Norway is into winter sports, but it's true that a lot of us enjoy snowboarding, hockey, and skiing (see attached photo of me).

⁴ I'd love to hear about Fargo. I wonder what people do for fun there. Can you tell me more about your family? Do you have any brothers or sisters? What do you do in your free time?
Also, do you know who lives in the old house in the Red River Valley now?

⁵ This is so interesting! Let's stay in touch.

Elin

B **WRITING SKILLS** Read about paragraphs. Then match the paragraphs of Elin's email (1–5) to the topics she writes about (a–e).

A paragraph is a group of sentences. All of the sentences in a paragraph are about the same topic. Each paragraph is about a different topic. We often use opening and closing sentences in an email. These often have their own paragraphs and can be one or two lines.

a ___ closing sentences
b ___ questions about Andrew
c ___ opening sentences
d ___ information about Elin
e ___ information about Elin's country

REGISTER CHECK

We use different opening and closing sentences in informal and formal emails. For example:

Informal	Formal
It's great to hear from you.	It was a pleasure to hear from you.
Let's stay in touch.	I look forward to hearing from you again.

C Imagine you recently heard from a relative in another country. Choose the country. Write an email to the relative. Give information about yourself and ask questions about his/her life and country. Use paragraphs.

D **PAIR WORK** Read your partner's email. Did you learn anything new about your partner?

1.5 TIME TO SPEAK
What makes a leader?

LESSON OBJECTIVE
- decide what makes a good leader

A DISCUSS Look at the pictures of the leaders on this page. What do you know about these people? In what way are they leaders?

B RESEARCH In pairs, talk about leaders you know and that you admire. They could be leaders of a country, a company, or a sports team, for example. You can go online to learn more about current leaders. What qualities make these leaders great?

C DECIDE In groups, talk about the leaders that you know or learned about, and the qualities you think are important. Imagine that you are going to choose someone to be your class president. Decide who you would choose to lead your class and why.

D PRESENT As a group, present your choice for class president to the class. Explain why you chose this person and why you think he or she is best for the job.

E AGREE As a class, take a vote on who you want to choose for your class's president. What quality of this leader was the most important to you?

Jack Ma

Carmen Aristegui

Nelson Mandela

Serena Williams

To check your progress, go to page 153.

USEFUL PHRASES

DISCUSS
Do you know who this is?
Which one is he/she?
I think this is …
He/She is the …

DECIDE
Who did you learn about?
This person is a good leader because he/she is …
Who is the best one?
So, do we all agree?

PRESENT
We decided that … should be our president, because …
We chose him/her because …

UNIT OBJECTIVES
- talk about things you've had for a while
- talk about things you own
- switch from one topic to another
- write an ad for something you want
- discuss special items to take when you move

SO MUCH STUFF

2

START SPEAKING

A What do you see in the drawer? What else do you think is inside it?

B Why do a lot of homes have a place where people keep lots of different kinds of things?

C What do you keep in your "junk drawer"? For ideas, watch Andres's video.

REAL STUDENT

Do you and Andres keep the same things in your drawers?

11

2.1 MY GARAGE

LESSON OBJECTIVE
- talk about things you've had for a while

1 LANGUAGE IN CONTEXT

A Look at the picture. What are the people doing? Why do you think they're doing it?

B Read Ethan's social media post about what's in his garage. Check (✓) the things he mentions.

- ☐ bikes
- ☐ a bookcase
- ☐ clothes
- ☐ comic books
- ☐ dishes
- ☐ souvenirs
- ☐ toys
- ☐ computer games

Profile | Wall | Friends

It's time for a big cleanup! Have you ever felt that way? We've lived here since 2013, but a lot of our stuff is still in the garage. Our car has been outside for two years! 😉 So we've finally decided to do something with all of the stuff. But I've never sold anything in my life, so I'm not sure which things people will want to buy and which things are useless.

For example, we have two old bikes. We haven't ridden them for years. I have some boxes of comic books. I've had them since I was 12, but they're in good condition. I also found a box of outdated computer games. A friend gave them to me, but I've never actually played them. There's also a brand new bookcase in the garage. It's plain, but it's OK. And I've collected a lot of travel souvenirs over the years: pictures, plates, hats … They're all in a big box. I have no idea if anyone else would think they're special.

So, if you have any ideas about what I can sell – great! And if you want to buy something – even better!

👍 Like   💬 Comment   ➤ Share   👍 35   ❤ 35

GLOSSARY
collect (v) find and keep a particular kind of thing

C Read the social media post again. Which items do you think Ethan can sell? Why?

2 VOCABULARY: Describing possessions

A 🔊 **1.11** Find and underline the expressions (1–6) in Ethan's blog post in exercise 1B. Match the expressions (1–6) with their opposites (a–f). Then listen and check.

1	brand new	a	useful
2	in good condition	b	used
3	plain	c	common
4	outdated	d	modern
5	special	e	damaged
6	useless	f	fancy

B **PAIR WORK** Take turns asking and answering the questions.

1. When do you think it's important to buy something brand new? Why?
2. Do you have items at home that are damaged, outdated, or useless? Why do you keep them?
3. Can you think of any stores that sell used things? What do they sell? Are the items usually in good condition?

C ▶ Now go to page 142. Do the vocabulary exercises for 2.1.

D **PAIR WORK** Use the expressions in exercise 2A to describe things you own. Say why they're important or not important to you.

3 GRAMMAR: Present perfect with *ever*, *never*, *for*, and *since*

A Circle the correct answers. Use the sentences in the grammar box to help you.
1 Use the present perfect with *for* / *since* and a point of time in the past. It shows when an action or event started.
2 Use the present perfect with *for* / *since* and a period of time. It shows the length of time of an action or event.

Present perfect with *ever* and *never*	Present perfect with *for* and *since*
Have you **ever felt** that way? I'**ve never played** computer games.	Our car **has been** outside **for** two years. We **haven't ridden** these bikes **for** years. I'**ve had** my comic books **since** I was 12.

B ▶ Now go to page 130. Look at the grammar chart and do the grammar exercise for 2.1.

C Complete the sentences with your own information.
1 I've lived _____ for _____ .
2 I've never owned _____ .
3 I've had _____ since _____ .
4 I haven't seen _____ for _____ .
5 I've known _____ since _____ .
6 I've never had a brand new _____ .
7 I've had my _____ since _____ , and it's still in good condition.
8 I haven't seen _____ for _____ .

D GROUP WORK Share your sentences from exercise 3C. Which answers surprised you?

4 SPEAKING

A Think of five things you own that you've had for a long time. Use the ideas below or your own ideas to make a list.

| a car | a pet | books | clothes | furniture |
| home | jewelry | things you collect | | |

B PAIR WORK Talk about the things on your list. How long have you had them? How did you get them? What's important to you about them?

> We have a black-and-white cat named Mr. Penny. He's been a part of our family since I was 13.

> How old is he?

> We've had him for about five years, but I think he's seven years old.

2.2 SO MANY FEATURES

LESSON OBJECTIVE
- talk about things you own

1 LANGUAGE IN CONTEXT

A 🔊 **1.12** Look at the picture. What do you think the people are talking about? Then read and listen to the conversation. Who knows more about her phone, Jen or Maya?

🔊 **1.12 Audio script**

Jen	Do you like my new phone? I bought the same model you have.
Maya	Oh, wow! You're going to love it. It has so many cool features.
Jen	I haven't tried many of them yet. I've already downloaded a lot of apps, though. I have so many now. It's hard to find one when I need it.
Maya	I can help with that. Have you already made folders?
Jen	No, I haven't. How does that work?
Maya	You create folders on the home screen, and then you can put your apps in them. Look, I have a folder for music apps, one for weather apps …
Jen	That's pretty cool. Can you help me set them up?
Maya	Sure. But first, I have to ask, have you tried the camera yet? With the "funny faces" feature?
Jen	Yes, I have. I love it! In fact, let me try it on you …
Maya	Hey!
Jen	Look … you look great with elephant ears!
Maya	Yeah, right! Now let me show you this feature … delete!

B 🔊 **1.12** Read and listen again. Are the statements true (T) or false (F)?

1 ___ Jen has a new phone.
2 ___ Jen doesn't have any apps on her phone.
3 ___ Maya needs help with her phone.
4 ___ Maya took a picture of Jen.

2 VOCABULARY: Tech features

FIND IT

A 🔊 **1.13** Listen and repeat the words. Which words are nouns and which are verbs? You can use a dictionary or your phone to help you. Then find and <u>underline</u> seven of these words in the conversation in exercise 1A.

delete	device	folder	home screen	model
set up	storage	sync	try	work

B ▶ Now go to page 142. Do the vocabulary exercises for 2.2.

C **PAIR WORK** Do you agree with these statements? Discuss with your partner.
1 It's not fair that phones with a lot of storage are more expensive.
2 Phone service doesn't work very well in our city.
3 No one needs more than one tech device. Just a phone is enough.
4 It's important to sync your phone with your computer frequently.

D **PAIR WORK** Talk about the features of a phone you have or want. Which features are the best? Why? For ideas, watch Celeste's video.

 **REAL STUDENT** *What feature of her phone does Celeste talk about?*

3 GRAMMAR: Present perfect with *already* and *yet*

A Circle the correct answers. Use the sentences in the grammar box to help you.
1 Use **already** / **yet** with things that haven't happened. It often means you expected something to happen or expect something to happen soon.
2 Use **already** / **yet** when something happened sooner than expected.

Present perfect with *already* and *yet*	
I've **already downloaded** a lot of apps.	Have you **tried** the camera **yet**?
I **haven't tried** many of them **yet**.	Yes, I **have**.

B ▶ Now go to page 130. Look at the grammar chart and do the grammar exercise for 2.2.

✓ **ACCURACY** CHECK

Already usually comes before the past participle. *Yet* usually comes at the end of a sentence.

~~I already have~~ downloaded the app. ✗
I've already downloaded the app. ✓
I haven't synced ~~yet~~ my phone. ✗
I haven't synced my phone yet. ✓

C Write sentences with the verbs so they're true for you. Use the present perfect and *already* or *yet*. Check your accuracy. Then compare with a partner.
1 not try to download   I haven't tried to download an emoji app yet.
2 not use _____
3 sync _____
4 try to set up _____
5 not delete _____

4 SPEAKING

A Choose one of the things below or your own idea. Think about how long you've had it. What have you done with it or to it already? What haven't you done yet?

a laptop   a microwave   a power tool   a refrigerator   a tablet   a video game

B **PAIR WORK** Take turns telling your partner about the item you chose in exercise 4A. Don't name it. Can your partner guess what it is?

> I've had it for a month. I bought the newest model, and it works really well. I've already used it several times. I used it to set up my new bookcase last weekend. I haven't let anyone borrow it yet.

> Hmm. It sounds like a tool. Is it an electric screwdriver?

2.3 GUESS WHAT!

LESSON OBJECTIVE
- switch from one topic to another

1 FUNCTIONAL LANGUAGE

A Look at the picture of the toy robots. Why do you think some people own these things?

B 🔊 1.14 Read and listen to a conversation between two friends. What do the friends plan to do?

🔊 1.14 Audio script

A So, **you know** I'm interested in old toys, right?
B Yeah, I guessed that! Look at this room. How many robots do you have now?
A Twenty-six! And **guess what**! I just bought two more online.
B Cool! Are they in good condition?
A I don't know. I haven't gotten them yet. I'm expecting them on Saturday. **Anyway,** they looked good in the photos. **By the way,** have you heard that Tori is in town?
B No. I haven't seen her since she moved.
A She's been here since Tuesday. So, why don't we have dinner together, the three of us – at my place?
B Sounds great.
A On Saturday?
B Sure. And that's the day you're expecting your robots.
A Yeah. So it'll be a big party: the three of us, and … 28 of my friends!

C Complete the chart with the expressions in bold from the conversations above.

Introducing new topics	Changing the subject	Staying on track
¹_____ I'm interested in old toys. And ²_____! I just bought two more online.	³_____, have you heard that Tori is in town? Oh, before I forget, …	⁴_____, they looked good in the photos.

D 🔊 1.15 Put the conversation in the correct order (1–6). Then listen and check.

___ I have no idea. Anyway, at least I have my phone now.
___ Well, guess what! I just found it – under the refrigerator.
___ Great. So I can text you again. Oh, before I forget, I want to show you this funny video.
___ Hey, Emma! So, you know I lost my phone.
___ That's funny! How did it get there?
___ That's right – you said you couldn't find it.

2 REAL-WORLD STRATEGY

A 🔊 **1.16** Listen to a conversation between two friends. Why is Yadira going to give her watch to Luke?

B 🔊 **1.16** Read the information in the box about using short questions to show interest. Then listen again. What three short questions do Yadira and Luke use to show interest?

> **USING SHORT QUESTIONS TO SHOW INTEREST**
> You can use short questions to show you're interested in what someone has said. Use *be* or an auxiliary verb in the same tense that the first speaker used.
>
> I just <u>bought</u> two more online.   Tori <u>is</u> in town.
> You <u>did</u>? Cool!   She <u>is</u>? I haven't seen her since she moved.

C 🔊 **1.17** Complete another conversation with short questions. Listen and check.

    A I found a gold watch on the street yesterday.
    B ¹ _____? What did you do with it?
    A Nothing. It's here in my bag.
    B ² _____? Can I see it?

D ▶ PAIR WORK Student A: Go to page 157. Student B: Go to page 159. Follow the instructions.

3 PRONUNCIATION: Saying /t/ at the start of words

A 🔊 **1.18** Listen and repeat. Focus on the /t/ sound at the start of the word in bold.
    1 **Tuesday**   She's been here since **Tuesday**.
    2 **text**   I can **text** you again.

B 🔊 **1.19** Listen. Which speaker (A or B) says the first /t/ sound most clearly? Write A or B.
    1 ___ Tuesday   3 ___ two   5 ___ tablet
    2 ___ text   4 ___ Tori   6 ___ time

C Practice the conversation with a partner. Does your partner say the /t/ sounds clearly?
    A So you know **Todd** just bought a new car.
    B Wait. You mean he sold his **truck**? He loved that **truck**. He's had it for like **ten** years.
    A Yeah, well, he sold it. He said he was **tired** of fixing it all the **time**.

4 SPEAKING

A Prepare to have a conversation with a partner. Choose three of the topics below or your own ideas.

> an interesting item you own   your favorite piece of clothing   a hobby or sport you like
> a friend with an interesting job   something you collect   weekend plans

B PAIR WORK Talk about one of the topics above. Use short questions to show you're interested in what your partner says. Use phrases to introduce new topics and to change the subject.

    You know, I play soccer every weekend.
    You do? Are you on a team?

2.4 IT'S USELESS, RIGHT?

LESSON OBJECTIVE
- write an ad for something you want

1 LISTENING

A   Look at the picture. Do you listen to any podcasts? Which ones?

B   🔊 1.20 **LISTEN FOR EXAMPLES** Listen to Hana Sanday, a podcaster, interview Felix Moss, a collector. What item does Felix talk about? Where is it now?

C   🔊 1.20 **LISTEN FOR REASONS** Listen again. Answer the questions.
   1 Why has Hana invited a collector to be on her podcast?
   2 Why does Felix collect things from race cars?

D   **PAIR WORK** **THINK CRITICALLY** Does Felix agree with Hana that his item is useless? Explain the reason he gives.

> **INSIDER ENGLISH**
>
> *Now* doesn't always mean *at the moment*. We can use it to introduce a topic or focus attention on what we're going to say next.

2 PRONUNCIATION: Listening for /w/ sounds between words

A   🔊 1.21 Listen to the extracts from the podcast below. Listen for the /w/ sound between the underlined words.
   1 Why do some people collect things? Have <u>you ever</u> wondered?
   2 Felix, most people want to *get rid of* old tires! Why do you want <u>to own</u> something like that?

B   🔊 1.22 Listen. <u>Underline</u> any words you hear a /w/ sound between.
   A Do you and your brother like to collect things?
   B He does. But I do everything I can to avoid collecting useless stuff.
   A So do you ever keep things just to keep them?
   B I guess I might keep a few if they're things I really like.

C   (Circle) the correct words to complete the statement.
   A /w/ sound is often used to connect two words when the first word *starts / ends* in an /uː/ sound and the second word starts with a *consonant / vowel*.

3 WRITING

A Read the online ad. What items does Emilia want? Why does she want them? What kind of personality do you think she has?

Account Ads Messages 📌 Post an ad

I'm looking for …   Search

WANTED:
TRAFFIC LIGHT, 2 STOP SIGNS

I'm interested in buying a Canadian traffic light (see picture for an example). Do you have one like this? Or do you know where I can get one? Yes, I know they're on every street corner – but please don't steal one! 😊 But seriously, I want one that's legal and that works. I've checked online every day for weeks, but I haven't seen any for sale yet.

I'm also looking for two red stop signs (see picture). They can be old, but they have to be in good condition. I've seen some for sale online, but they were fake, not real ones. I want "the real thing."

You're probably wondering why I want these things. They're for a party, and after that, I'll give them to my niece. She loves stuff like this.

I'll pay a reasonable price for items in good condition. Send an email with photos, and hopefully I can give you a "green light" for a sale. 😊 Contact Emilia at:

show contact info

GLOSSARY
legal (*adj*) allowed by the law

B **WRITING SKILLS** Read the explanation about using *one* and *ones*. Then find and underline more examples in the ad. What do they refer to?

We use *one* (singular) and *ones* (plural) to avoid repeating a subject we've already mentioned. We use *one* and *ones* when it's clear what they refer to. In the question below, *one* = a Canadian traffic light:

I'm interested in buying **a Canadian traffic light** (see picture for an example). Do you have **one** like this?

REGISTER CHECK

In an ad title, you can leave out unimportant words.
WANTED: TRAFFIC LIGHT, 2 STOP SIGNS =
I want a traffic light and two stop signs.

C Write an ad like Emilia's for something you want that is hard to find. Write a short title. Describe the item (condition, age, size, color, etc.). Give a reason why you want it. You can include pictures. You can go online to find ideas for an interesting item.

2.5 TIME TO SPEAK
Things to bring

LESSON OBJECTIVE
- discuss items to take when you move

A **DISCUSS** Look at the picture. What items are in the suitcase? What type of trip do you think the person traveling is planning? Which things do you think are essential items for a trip? Which things do you think are extra or non-essential items? Why do you think the person is bringing extra items?

B **RESEARCH** In groups, think of a country you would like to live in for one year. You can go online to learn more about countries you would like to live in. What would you need to take with you to live in this country?

C **DECIDE** What essential items are you going to take to your country? Make a list of 10 items that you agree you will all take with you. Then, for each person, add one extra item to bring that is special to you.

D **PRESENT** Tell the class your list of essential items. Were any items on your lists similar? Did any of you choose similar "special" items to bring?

E **AGREE** As a class, make a list of five items that you think are essential to live in any country the class discussed. What were the reasons for choosing these items?

>> To check your progress, go to page 153.

USEFUL PHRASES

DISCUSS
I think … is/are essential because …
I think … isn't essential because …
I think they are bringing this because …

DECIDE
I think we should bring … because …
How long have you had your special item?
I've had it for/since …

PRESENT
We chose … because …
We also chose …

UNIT OBJECTIVES
- ask and answer questions about your city
- talk about how to get from one place to another
- ask for and give directions in a building
- write a personal statement for a job application
- give a presentation about a secret spot in your city

SMART MOVES

3

START SPEAKING

A   Where is this man? Compare this place with your city: What's similar? What's different?

B   Where do you think he's going? Why do you think he's on a skateboard? Do you think this is a good way to get around? Why or why not?

C   How do you get around in your city? For ideas, watch Andrea's video.

REAL STUDENT

How does Andrea get around?

21

3.1 INS AND OUTS

LESSON OBJECTIVE
- ask and answer questions about your city

1 VOCABULARY: City features

A 🔊 1.23 **PAIR WORK** Listen and repeat the words. Are the words for buildings, art, or transportation? Make three lists with your partner. Add one more word to each list. You can go online to find new words.

bridge	clinic	embassy
ferry	fire station	highway
hostel	monument	parking lot
sculpture	sidewalk	tunnel

B **PAIR WORK** How often do you use or see these city features? Talk about ones you know.

C ▶ Now go to page 143. Do the vocabulary exercises for 3.1.

2 LANGUAGE IN CONTEXT

A Read the magazine quiz. Find and <u>underline</u> eight of the city features from exercise 1A.

Are you city smart?

You think you know all about your city, but how well do you really know it? If you can answer these difficult questions about your city, you're definitely city smart!

- ☐ I'm from Russia, and I wonder if there's a Russian embassy in the city. If so, where is it?
- ☐ I need a safe place to stay that's not expensive. Hostels are usually cheap. Do you know where I can find a good one? Or a nice, cheap hotel?
- ☐ I'd like to draw some monuments or sculptures that aren't very well known. Where can I find the most unusual ones?
- ☐ I'm studying to be an engineer and want to take pictures of bridges in this city. Where are they, and what are their names?
- ☐ Is there a ferry in this city? How often does it run? What time does the first ferry leave?
- ☐ I'm not feeling well. Do you know where I can find a walk-in clinic?
- ☐ I'm a street musician. Where are the best places I can play music on the sidewalk?

B Read the quiz again. Why does the person want to find unusual monuments? ask about bridges? ask about a clinic?

C Take the quiz. Check (✓) the questions you can answer. You can go online to find any answers you didn't know.

D **GROUP WORK** Compare your answers to the quiz. Do you think you're "city smart"? or why not? For ideas, watch Angie's video.

REAL STUDENT

What city features does Angie talk about? Is she city smart?

22

3 GRAMMAR: Articles

A Circle the correct answers. Use the sentences in the grammar box to help you.
1 Use *a* or *an* with **singular** / **plural** nouns.
2 Use **an article** / **no article** when you talk about things in general.
3 Use *a* / *the* when you mention something for the first time. Then use *a* / *the* when you mention it again.

> **Articles**
>
> Is there **a** ferry in this city?
> What time does **the** first ferry leave?
> I'm studying to be **an** engineer.
>
> Where can I find **the** most unusual sculptures?
> Hostels are usually cheap.
> Where can I play music?

B ▶ Now go to page 131. Look at the grammar chart and do the grammar exercise for 3.1.

C Complete the sentences with *a*, *an*, *the*, or – (no article). Then ask and answer the questions with a partner. Change the answers so they're true for you.
1 A Where is _____the_____ biggest fire station in town?
   B It's on _____–_____ Clark Street.
2 A Is there _____ embassy near the school?
   B Yes, _____ Canadian embassy is across _____ street.
3 A Do you stay in _____ hostels when you travel?
   B No, I don't. I usually stay with _____ friends.
4 A Do you have _____ good view of _____ city from your home?
   B Yes, I do. _____ view is excellent.
5 A Where's _____ best place to go shopping near here?
   B There's _____ mall on _____ Sixth Avenue.

D Complete the questions about city features. Then ask and answer the questions with a partner.
1 Where can I find _____?
2 Do you know where _____ is?
3 Is there _____ in the city?

4 SPEAKING

FIND IT

A PAIR WORK Think of four difficult questions about your city that you and your partner know the answers to. Use the ideas below or your own ideas. You can go online to learn more about your city.
- Where is/are …?
- Where can you find …?
- What time does … open?
- Is there a … near school?

B GROUP WORK Ask another pair your questions. How many can they answer?

> Where are the sculptures of birds by Fernando Botero?

> They're in San Antonio Park.

3.2 A MAP LIKE SPAGHETTI

LESSON OBJECTIVE
- talk about how to get from one place to another

1 LANGUAGE IN CONTEXT

A 🔊 1.24 **PAIR WORK** What's good about using public transportation, like subways, buses, and trains? What's bad about it? Then read and listen to the video chat between two coworkers in different offices. Where is Aida going? How is she going to get there?

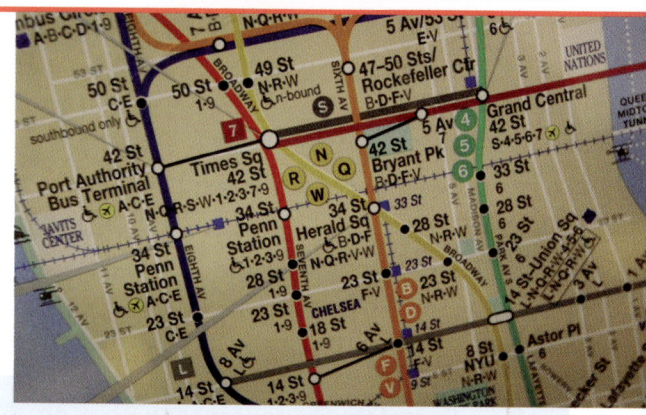

🔊 1.24 Audio script

Aida	So, I've already **booked** my flight for the meeting in the New York office. I have the **schedule** right here. **Departure** from Mexico City: 1:55 p.m. **Arrival** at JFK: 7:50 p.m.
Dean	You're all set to go!
Aida	Well, I haven't figured out my **route** from the airport **terminal** to the hotel yet. I found some maps of train and subway **lines**, and buses. But they look complicated – like spaghetti!
Dean	You shouldn't look at those maps. You should ask a New Yorker!
Aida	OK, Mr. New Yorker, which subway line should I take? Or should I take a bus?
Dean	Well, you could get the AirTrain from the airport to the subway. You'll have to change lines on the subway and then walk from the subway station to the hotel.
Aida	I don't know. My suitcase is pretty big.
Dean	Then I wouldn't take the subway. I'd get a taxi. The company will pay for the **fare**.
Aida	OK. Then no spaghetti … or, at least, not until I get to the hotel restaurant!

B 🔊 1.24 Read and listen again. How does Dean first suggest that Aida get from the airport to the hotel? Why do they decide it's <u>not</u> a good idea?

2 VOCABULARY: Public transportation

A 🔊 1.25 Complete the sentences with words from the box. Then listen and check.

arrival	book	departure	direct	fare
lines	reservation	route	schedule	terminal

1 I need to _____ my flight. First, I want to compare airlines, so I can find the cheapest _____ . And then I can make a _____ .
2 I'm just checking my _____ , and these are my flight details: It says my _____ is from _____ B at 8:10 a.m., and my _____ is at 12:55 p.m.
3 If you go there on the subway, you need to take two different _____ . Take the 4 and transfer to the 6 because it's not _____ . It's not an easy _____ .

B ▶ Now go to page 143. Do the vocabulary exercises for 3.2.

C **PAIR WORK** When did you last take public transportation? Did you ride the bus? take the subway? How was your experience?

24

3 GRAMMAR: Modals for advice

A Circle the correct answers. Use the sentences in the grammar box to help you.
1. Use *you could / you shouldn't* to say something is a bad idea.
2. Use *you should / I wouldn't* to say something is a good idea.
3. Use *you should / you could* to say something is possible.
4. You can use *I would / you would* to give advice.

> **Modals for advice**
>
> What **should** I **do**?
> You **should ask** a New Yorker. You **shouldn't look** at those maps.
> You **could get** the AirTrain.
> I **wouldn't take** the subway. I**'d get** a taxi.
> **Could** I **take** a train?
> Yes, you **could**. / No, you **couldn't**.

B Now go to page 131. Look at the grammar chart and do the grammar exercise for 3.2.

C Complete the sentences so they're true for your city. Check your accuracy. Then compare with a partner.
1. To travel around in this city, you could take … Or you could …
2. To get to from here to the airport, I would take … I wouldn't …
3. At some times of day, the traffic is really bad here. You shouldn't … You should …

> ✓ **ACCURACY CHECK**
>
> For statements giving advice, we only use *would* with the subject *I*.
> ~~You~~ would take the subway. ✗
> ~~She~~ would take the subway. ✗
> I would take the subway. ✓

4 SPEAKING

A Choose a few places in your city that you'd like to go to. Use the ideas below or your own ideas. Make notes.

> cafes   movie theaters   museums   restaurants   sports stadiums

B **PAIR WORK** Take turns asking for advice about how to get to your places. You can go online to get more information or to check the routes.

FIND IT

> I want to get from here to the baseball stadium. Should I take the subway? Or the bus?

> I wouldn't take the bus. I'd take the subway. But you'll have to transfer – it's not a direct route.

3.3 UP AND DOWN

LESSON OBJECTIVE
- ask for and give directions in a building

1 FUNCTIONAL LANGUAGE

A Look at the picture. What do you think the people are talking about?

B 🔊 **1.26** Read and listen to a conversation between two people at an international conference. Which two places does the woman want to go to?

🔊 **1.26 Audio script**

A Excuse me, **can you tell me how to get to meeting room C?**
B Uh, **it's upstairs on the fifth floor.**
A OK, thanks. And **how do I get to the stairs?**
B **Go down that hallway, and they're on your right.** But I would take the elevator!
A Good idea. Um, **which way is the elevator?**
B **Go through the lobby, and it's on the left.**

A OK. Sorry, one more question. **Do you know which floor the cafeteria is on?** I want to get a coffee.
B **It's downstairs in the basement.**
A OK. Thanks.
B Hey, I'm going that way. Can I join you for coffee?

INSIDER ENGLISH

We often say *Sorry, one more question* to be polite when we're asking a lot of questions.

C Complete the chart with expressions in bold from the conversation in exercise 1B.

Asking for directions	Giving directions
1 _____ meeting room C?	5 _____ on the fifth floor.
2 _____ the stairs?	6 _____ that hallway, and they're 7 _____.
3 _____ is the elevator?	8 _____ the lobby, and it's 9 _____.
4 _____ the cafeteria is on?	10 _____ in the basement.
Which floor are the restrooms on?	Take the elevator to the third floor.

D **PAIR WORK** Write the words in the correct order. Then practice the conversations with a partner.

1 A you / get / how / me / to / the front desk / tell / Can / to / ?
   _____

   B on / the lobby, / right / and / through / it's / the / Go / .
   _____

2 A floor / on / are / Which / meeting rooms / the / ?
   _____

   B the / floor / downstairs / on / first / They're / .
   _____

26

2 REAL-WORLD STRATEGY

A 🔊 **1.27** Listen to a conversation in a hotel. Where does the man want to go?

B 🔊 **1.27** Read the information in the box about repeating details to show you understand. Then listen to the conversation again. Which details does the woman repeat?

> **REPEATING DETAILS TO SHOW YOU UNDERSTAND**
> We often repeat key details when people ask questions so they know we've understood them.
> *Can you tell me how to get to <u>meeting room C</u>?*
> **Meeting room C** … *Uh, it's upstairs on the fifth floor.*
>
> *How do I get to <u>the stairs</u>?*
> **The stairs?** *Go down that hallway, and they're on your right.*

C Complete the conversation with repeated details. Then practice with a partner.

A Excuse me? Where does the bus stop?
B The ¹_____ ? It stops across the street.
A OK. Thank you. Does it come by often?
B ²_____ ? Yes, about every 20 minutes.

3 PRONUNCIATION: Saying consonant clusters at the start of a word

A 🔊 **1.28** Listen and repeat. Focus on the sound of the consonants in **bold** at the beginning of the word.

1 **fl**oor / **fr**ont   2 **st**airs / **str**eet   3 **thr**ough / **shr**ed

B 🔊 **1.29** Which speaker (A or B) says the consonant clusters in **bold** most clearly? Write A or B.

1 ___ **fl**ight   2 ___ **str**aight   3 ___ **thr**ee

C Practice the conversation with a partner. Does your partner say the consonant clusters clearly?

A Excuse me. Can you tell me how to get to gate B37? I'm late for a **fl**ight.
B B37? Just go **str**aight down this hallway. I think it's **thr**ee or four gates down.
A Just **thr**ee or four gates? Fantastic. If I hurry, I can still make my **fl**ight.

4 SPEAKING

A **PAIR WORK** How many of these places are in your school or workplace? Can you think of any more places?

reception desk

computer lab

restrooms

cafeteria

meeting room

library

B **PAIR WORK** Imagine you and your partner are standing outside of your classroom. Ask for and give directions to places in your building.

> *Excuse me, which way is the reception desk?*
>
> *The reception desk? Go down that hallway, and it's on your left.*

3.4 MAYBE YOU CAN HELP!

LESSON OBJECTIVE
- write a personal statement for a job application

1 READING

A Look at the picture. Do you ever do volunteer work? What kind of volunteer work interests you?

B **READ FOR GIST** Read the ad. What are the two kinds of volunteer jobs? Why are these jobs useful for a student?

volunteer

Volunteer at the Street Beats Festival!

Are you good with people? Do you know the city well? Then maybe you can help …

We're looking for volunteers to help at the **Street Beats Festival**. Next year, this amazing festival will bring together a cast of more than 1,000 street performers, including dancers and musicians, from more than 20 countries. And it will happen right here, on the streets of our city, from July 25–27.

We're looking for:

Cast Helpers: You'll meet cast members at the airport on arrival and help them get to their hotels. At the hotel, you'll tell them where they should go for festival events and how to get there. You'll also help them with the schedule and organization of the festival.

City Guides: You'll stand on sidewalks around the city and help visitors find their way around. You'll also give advice on things to see and do during the festival.

If you're a student, volunteering is a smart career move. This position is unpaid, but we'll give you a certificate to show you helped at the event – a useful experience that you can put on your résumé.

If you are interested, complete the **application** in English.

GLOSSARY
cast (*n*) all the actors in a movie, play, or show

C **READ FOR DETAILS** Read the ad again. Answer the questions.
  1 What two skills does the company want the volunteers to have?
  2 Who will the cast be?
  3 What four things will the volunteers do?

D **PAIR WORK** What do you think it would be like to be a Street Beats Festival volunteer? Which parts of the job would you like? Which parts wouldn't you like?

2 WRITING

A Manuela is applying to be a volunteer for the Street Beats Festival. Read her personal statement in the application below. Answer the questions.

1 What language skills does Manuela have?
2 What experience does she have with events? What volunteer experiences does she have?
3 How well does she know the city?

Street Beats Festival!
Volunteer Application

Last name: Gomez
First name: Manuela
Position: City Guide

Personal Statement
Explain in 100–150 words why you're the right person to be a Street Beats Festival volunteer.

The volunteer job of City Guide is perfect for me. I am fluent in Spanish and English, and I'm learning French and Portuguese in college. Fortunately, your festival happens during our summer break, so I am free to help all day from July 25th to the 27th. I am very interested in world cultures and have organized two cultural events at my school. I've never worked at a big festival or volunteered before, but I'm excited to try. I was born and raised in this city and have lived here all my life, so I know the transportation system well. I am also familiar with different neighborhoods because I have studied, worked, and lived in a few parts of the city. For these reasons, I think I would be an excellent City Guide.

B THINK CRITICALLY Do you think Manuela will be a good City Guide? Why or why not?

C WRITING SKILLS Accuracy is important, especially in a volunteer or job application. Read about how to check your own writing. Find examples in Manuela's personal statement.

Punctuation: Use capital letters at the beginnings of sentences and for job titles, names, places, months, languages, and nationalities.

Put a period (.), exclamation mark (!), or question mark (?) at the end of each sentence.

Use a comma before *but* and *so*. There's <u>no</u> comma before *because*.

Grammar: Use the present perfect for experiences in your life up to now.

 **WRITE IT**

D Imagine you're applying to be a City Guide or Cast Helper. Write a personal statement for the volunteer application. You can use your own information or make it up. Check your writing after you are finished.

E PAIR WORK Exchange personal statements with a partner. What was the best reason your partner gave for wanting the job?

REGISTER CHECK

It's important to be clear in formal writing, like an application. We often repeat information, like job titles, to make sure we are clear.

The volunteer job of <u>City Guide</u> is perfect for me.
(NOT: *The volunteer job is perfect for me.*)

I think I would be an excellent <u>City Guide</u>.
(NOT: *I think I would be excellent at this job.*)

29

3.5 TIME TO SPEAK
Secret spots

LESSON OBJECTIVE
- give a presentation about a secret spot in your city

An artist in Insadong, Seoul, South Korea

Feira Kantuta, a Bolivian market in São Paulo, Brazil

A   **DISCUSS**   Look at the pictures and talk in groups. Do you think these places are popular with tourists? Which one would you like to visit the most? Why?

B   **RESEARCH**   In pairs, think of interesting places in your city that tourists might not know about. Make a list of these "secret spots." You can go online for ideas.

C   **DECIDE**   Choose a secret spot from your list. Answer the questions together.

1. How do you get there?
2. Do you need to make a reservation before you go?
3. Should you take anything with you?
4. What's the best way to get there? How long should you plan to stay?
5. What should you do when you get there?

D   **PREPARE**   With a partner, prepare a presentation about your secret spot. Use the information from part C and any other information you know or find online.

E   **PRESENT**   In pairs, give your presentation about the secret spot to the class. Which secret spots are new to you? Which ones would you like to visit the most?

> To check your progress, go to page 153.

USEFUL PHRASES

DISCUSS
I think … / I don't think …
In my opinion …

RESEARCH
… isn't very well known.
… is a good choice because …
I think we should include …

PREPARE
Let's say … first.
Then we can talk about …
Next, we should …
Finally, we can tell the class about …

REVIEW 1 (UNITS 1–3)

1 VOCABULARY

A Find five words or phrases for each category below.

arrival	be born	be raised	brand new	celebrate
cheerful	clinic	damaged	departure	easygoing
embassy	fancy	fare	fire station	hostel
live alone	nervous	outdated	parking lot	reservation
retire	route	selfish	sociable	useless

1 Describing personalities: _____
2 Personal information: _____
3 Describing possessions: _____
4 City features: _____
5 Public transportation: _____

B Add three more words or phrases that you know to each category.

2 GRAMMAR

A Circle the correct words to complete the conversation.

A Hi, I'm Laura. Are you a new student?
B Yeah, this is my first day. I'm Sofia.
A So, ¹ *who / whose* class are you in?
B Ms. Power's. And you?
A Me, too.
B Do you know where ² *is our room / our room is*?
A We're in ³ *Room / the Room* 203. It's on ⁴ *second / the second* floor.
B How long ⁵ *did you study / have you studied* in this school?

A ⁶ *For / Since* a year.
B So you know lots of other students … I haven't met anybody ⁷ *yet / already*.
A Well, you ⁸ *would / could* join the English conversation club.
B That sounds interesting. Do you have any idea when ⁹ *the group meets / does the group meet*?
A No, I don't. I ¹⁰ *would / should* ask somebody at the information desk.
B Thanks for the tip.

B PAIR WORK Have you ever joined a conversation club? What have you done to practice your English outside the classroom?

3 SPEAKING

A PAIR WORK How much do you and your partner know about your teacher? Ask and answer questions to find out.

A Do you know where our teacher was born?
B I think he was born in California.
A Do you have any idea how long he has worked here?

B GROUP WORK What have you learned about your teacher? Check with your teacher to confirm.

> Our teacher was born in California, but we don't know where he was raised …

4 FUNCTIONAL LANGUAGE

A Read the conversations at a birthday party. Use the words and phrases below to complete them.

by the way	do you know	go down	good things	guess what
how do you know	in the basement	I've heard	meet	on the right
talking	you did	you know	with her	

A Hi. I'm Pat. Nice to meet you.
B I'm Mike, Ann's brother. [1]_____ Ann?
A I run [2]_____ a lot. We're on the track team together.
B [3]_____, I'm into sports, too. I'm on the university basketball team.
A I know. [4]_____ a lot about you.
B [5]_____, I hope.
A Of course.
B [6]_____, would you like to come to one of our games?
A Sure. [7]_____! I played basketball on my high school team.
B [8]_____? Then we should play together one of these days.
A I'd love to! Oh, sorry, my grandparents just got here. I have to go talk to them. It was really nice to [9]_____ you.
B It was nice [10]_____ to you.

A few moments later.

A Excuse me. [11]_____ where the bathroom is?
C Sure. [12]_____ the hall, and it's [13]_____. And there's another one downstairs [14]_____.
A Thank you.

5 SPEAKING

A **PAIR WORK** Choose one of the situations. Act it out in pairs.

- You and your partner are meeting for the first time. Introduce yourself, ask questions to get to know each other, and end the conversation. Talk about your job, where you live, your interests, and your own ideas. Go to page 6 for useful language.

  > Hello. I'm (your name).
  > Nice to meet you. I'm …

- You and your partner meet by accident at an event. It can be a sports event, a concert, an art exhibit, or any other event you choose. Talk to your partner about this interest you both have in common. Go to page 16 for useful language.

  > Do you come here often?
  > Yeah. You know I'm really into pop music. What about you?

- You are a new student at your school. You want to get a bottle of water, go to the restroom, and get a book from the library. Get directions to those places. Go to page 26 for useful language.

  > Excuse me. Can you tell me where the cafeteria is? I want to get a bottle of water.
  > The cafeteria? It's on the third floor. But you could get water from the vending machine …

B Change roles and repeat the role play.

UNIT OBJECTIVES
- describe opinions and reactions
- make plans for a trip
- offer and respond to reassurance
- write an email describing plans for an event
- choose activities for different groups of people

THINK FIRST

4

START SPEAKING

A How do you think the customer is feeling? Why do you think she's feeling this way?

B Have you ever been worried about a new hairstyle or haircut? Did it turn out differently than you thought?

C Can you usually guess how you'll feel about something? Have you ever been wrong about your guesses? For ideas, watch Celeste's video.

How did Celeste think she was going to feel? Was she right?

4.1 HERO OR ZERO?

LESSON OBJECTIVE
- describe opinions and reactions

1 VOCABULARY: Describing opinions and reactions

A 🔊 **1.30** **PAIR WORK** Listen and repeat the adjectives. Circle the correct answers. Explain your answers. Use the words you didn't circle in sentences with your partner.

1. Is Brad early? I'm really **(surprised)** / *surprising*. He's usually late.
2. I feel a little angry with my boss. I'm *annoyed* / *annoying*.
3. The restaurant looked good, but it wasn't. Our meal was really *disappointed* / *disappointing*.
4. Everyone looked at me. My face was red. I was so *embarrassed* / *embarrassing*!
5. I'm really interested in history. I think it's *fascinated* / *fascinating*.
6. My son said the movie was too *frightened* / *frightening*. We had to leave early.
7. When I heard the news, I was *shocked* / *shocking*. What an awful surprise!
8. Daniela is so *amused* / *amusing*. She always makes me laugh.

B ▶ Now go to page 144. Do the vocabulary exercises for 4.1.

2 LANGUAGE IN CONTEXT

A 🔊 **1.31** Look at the picture. Why do people wear costumes like this? Then read and listen to the conversation. Why does Pedro plan to wear a costume? What do Grant and Tony think of the plan?

🔊 **1.31 Audio script**

Pedro So, listen to this. I'm planning to buy two tickets for the zoo – for Isabel and me.
Grant Isabel, your new girlfriend?
Pedro Yeah. And I'll rent a bear costume. Here's a picture of it. I can see you're **fascinated**, Tony.
Tony Yeah … and **frightened**! Please don't say you want *me* to wear it.
Pedro No. It's for me. I'm planning to wear it outside Isabel's office. So after work, she'll find a bear waiting for her, with an invitation to the zoo. Well? What do you think?
Tony She won't like it. Her coworkers will be there, so it's going to be really **embarrassing** for her. I don't think she'll be **amused** at all. And this costume is awful! It's going to scare her.
Pedro But I …
Tony And why did you choose the zoo? I mean, she's not a kid. It'll be a **disappointing** date.
Grant You're so **annoying**, Tony. Where's your sense of fun? OK, so maybe she'll be a little **shocked** at first, but I think she'll laugh. You should do it, Pedro! You'll be a hero!

B 🔊 **1.31** Read and listen again. Answer the questions.
1. Who will see Pedro in his costume?
2. What does Tony think about the costume?
3. Why does Tony think the zoo is not good for a date?

C **PAIR WORK** Do you think Pedro's plan is good? Why or why not?

3 GRAMMAR: *be going to* and *will* for predictions

A Complete the sentences with the correct answers. Use the sentences in the grammar box to help you.
1 Use *be going to* or _____ to make predictions about the future.
2 You can use _____ and *I don't think* before a prediction to express an opinion.

> **be going to and will for predictions**
>
> It's **going to** be embarrassing for her.
> This costume is awful! It's **going to** scare her.
> She**'ll** be shocked.
> She **won't** like it.
> **I think** she**'ll** laugh.

> ⚠ Don't use *will* when you see something right now that makes you think something will happen. Use *be going to* instead.
> *The sky is getting dark. It's **going to** rain.*
> NOT ~~It'll rain~~.

> ✓ **ACCURACY CHECK**
> Be sure to use *will* instead of the simple present in predictions with *I think*.
> I think ~~you~~ love the zoo. ✗
> I think you'll love the zoo. ✓

B Read the sentences and complete the predictions. Use the correct forms of the words in parentheses ( ). Check your accuracy. Then compare with a partner.
1 I'm planning a party for Saturday. I 'm going to have (be going to / have) a lot of fun.
2 The forecast calls for bad weather tomorrow. It _____ (be going to / rain) all day.
3 I studied hard for my test. I _____ (not think / I / will / be) disappointed with my grade.
4 My roommate has concert tickets, so I _____ (think / he / will / come) home late tonight.
5 I just got a new client at my job. Tomorrow there _____ (be going to / be) a lot of work to do!
6 I have unusual music tastes. I _____ (not think / you / will / like) my favorite song.

C ▶ Now go to page 132. Look at the grammar chart and do the grammar exercise for 4.1.

D PAIR WORK Make four predictions about tomorrow. Think about the weather, your activities, and other events.

4 SPEAKING

A Think about things you usually do during the week and on the weekend. Use the topics below or think of your own. Take notes.

> classes   events   family time   going out with friends   hobbies   parties   work

B PAIR WORK Talk about your plans for this week and weekend. How do you think you will feel during those plans? Which of your plans might amuse, disappoint, embarrass, or fascinate your friends and family?

> Molly invited me to a party on Saturday, but I can't go. I'm really disappointed, and I think Molly will be disappointed, too.

35

4.2 A PERUVIAN ADVENTURE

LESSON OBJECTIVE
- make plans for a trip

1 LANGUAGE IN CONTEXT

A Look at the picture. What kind of vacation is this? Then read the messages between Leo and his friends. Who is happy? Who seems worried? Who isn't getting the messages?

◀ back   Sandra, Pavel, Leo

Leo Time to chat about our trip! I am so excited to hike the Santa Cruz Trek. 😊

Sandra Me, too! But there are still a few things to arrange. Leo, are we staying with your cousin when we meet up in Huaraz?

Leo Sorry, I forgot to ask him. I'll get in touch with him tonight.

Pavel So, we're getting a guide, right?

Leo No way! I'll be the guide. Remember, I've done this hike before. That reminds me … I'll check the bookstore for the latest guidebook. There's no Wi-Fi where we're going!

Pavel OK, and I'll check places to stay.

Sandra Pavel, remember: We're camping on this trip! ⛺ I'll deal with renting tents, OK? And I'll let you know ASAP. You can look into the fees for the park where we're camping. 💲

Pavel Hmm … I'll have to think about this. Ariana, did you know we're camping?

Leo Oh, no! I forgot to include Ariana in the group. 😫 I'll add her now.

B Read again. Check (✓) the things the group plans to do.

☐ stay with Leo's cousin   ☐ stay in hostels
☐ get a guide   ☐ rent tents
☐ use a guidebook

INSIDER ENGLISH

ASAP means *as soon as possible*. We pronounce it "A-S-A-P" or "asap."

2 VOCABULARY: Making decisions and plans

A 🔊 1.32 **PAIR WORK** Listen and repeat the expressions. Find and underline these expressions in exercise 1A. Then discuss the meaning of the words.

arrange	check	deal with	forget	get in touch with
let (someone) know	look into	meet up	remind	think about

B ▶ Now go to page 144. Do the vocabulary exercises for 4.2.

C Complete the questions with some of the words in exercise 2A. Then ask and answer the questions with a partner.

1 Where do you usually _____ with friends?
2 How do you _____ friends when you make plans?
3 Do you _____ your friends _____ when you'll be late?
4 How do you _____ yourself about all your plans and arrangements?

3 GRAMMAR: *will* for sudden decisions; present continuous for future plans

A Circle the correct answers. Use the sentences in the grammar box to help you.
1 Use *will* / **the present continuous** for sudden decisions you make at the moment of speaking.
2 Use *will* / **the present continuous** for plans that are already made or agreed on.

will for sudden decisions and present continuous for future plans
I'**ll deal** with renting tents, OK?   **Are** we **staying** with your cousin?
OK, and I'**ll check** places to stay.   They'**re staying** with Leo's cousin.
They'**re not hiring** a guide.

! The present continuous is also used for ongoing actions:
I'**m working** as a guide in a national park. It's a great job.

B Complete the conversation with *will* or the present continuous and the words in parentheses ( ). Then practice with a partner.
A I just missed a call from Bryn. It's probably about lunch. ¹_____ her now. (I / call)
B Oh, ²_____ her for lunch today? (you / meet)
A Yes. ³_____ to her office in an hour. (I / drive) Do you want to come?
B I'd love to! ⁴_____ and cancel my doctor's appointment. (I / call)
A No, don't do that. Remember, ⁵_____ in a week, anyway. (we all / meet up)

C ▶ Now go to page 132. Look at the grammar chart and do the grammar exercise for 4.2.

D Complete the sentences with your own ideas.
1 Look! Reggie left his phone here. I'll _____ .
2 Can everyone bring something for the party? I'll _____ .
3 We're meeting up on Saturday night. We're going _____ .

4 SPEAKING

A [GROUP WORK] Where would you like to go on a weekend trip? Use a place below or think of your own ideas. Decide on a place you all want to go together. For more ideas, watch Andres's video.

| beach | city | desert |
| lake | mountains | rain forest |

REAL STUDENT

Where does Andres want to go?

FIND IT

B [GROUP WORK] Make plans to go on your trip. As you talk, decide what each of you will do to prepare for the trip. You can go online to find things to do and places to stay.

> I'm really looking forward to a weekend at the beach.

> Me, too. But we have a lot to do. We're staying in a hostel, right?

> Yes, definitely. I'll look into hostels in the area and make a reservation.

4.3 A DRIVING TEST

LESSON OBJECTIVE
- offer and respond to reassurance

1 FUNCTIONAL LANGUAGE

A Look at the picture. The woman is taking her driving test. How do you think she's feeling? Have you ever taken a driving test? How did you feel?

B 🔊 **1.33** Read and listen to two conversations between a woman and her teacher. What is the woman worried about? What does her teacher tell her? What happens next?

🔊 1.33 Audio script

A I'm taking my driving test tomorrow, and I really hope I don't fail.
B **There's no need to worry.** You can take the test again, I think.
A Yes, but this is really important. My friends and I are driving from Salinas to Esmeraldas next month, and I'll be one of the drivers. I have to pass!
B You sound really stressed, Andrea. Try to relax. **You'll be fine.** I know it.
A Thanks. **I really appreciate it.** And you're right – I should relax.

A few days later

B Hello, Andrea. Are you coming to my English conversation hour tonight?
A Oh, no! I forgot! My parents are taking me out for dinner tonight – you know, because I passed my driving test. I'm sorry, Ms. Ellis. I'm embarrassed!
B **Don't worry about it**, Andrea.
A **Thanks, but I feel so bad.** Maybe I'll text my parents and cancel …
B No, don't do that. **It's no problem.** And congratulations on passing the test!
A Thank you.

C Complete the chart with the expressions in bold from the conversations.

Offering reassurance	Responding to reassurance
It'll be fine.	I hope so.
These things happen sometimes.	5 _____
1 _____	6 _____
2 _____	
3 _____	
4 _____	

D 🔊 **1.34** Put the conversation in the correct order (1–4). Then listen and check.

___ Thanks, but I feel so bad!
___ Don't worry about it.
___ You don't need to. These things happen.
___ I'm sorry I forgot your birthday.

2 REAL-WORLD STRATEGY

A 🔊 1.35 Listen to a conversation between Liam and Ava. Why is Liam worried about moving to Buenos Aires?

B 🔊 1.35 Read the information in the box about using *at least* to point out the good side of a situation. Then listen to the conversation again. What's the good side of Liam's situation?

> **USING *AT LEAST* TO POINT OUT THE GOOD SIDE OF A SITUATION**
> You can use *at least* to point out the good side of a difficult or worrying situation.
> Maybe I'll text my parents and cancel …
> No, don't do that. It's no problem. **At least** you're not missing your main class today.

C ▶ PAIR WORK Student A: Go to page 157. Student B: Go to page 159. Follow the instructions.

3 PRONUNCIATION: Saying /p/ at the start of a word

A 🔊 1.36 Listen and repeat. Focus on the /p/ sounds.
1 I have to pass!
2 It's no problem.

B 🔊 1.37 Listen. Which speaker (A or B) says the /p/ sound? Write A or B.
1 ___ pass
2 ___ problem
3 ___ parents
4 ___ plans
5 ___ probably
6 ___ paint

C PAIR WORK Work with a partner. Say the words in exercise 3B. Does your partner say the English /p/ sound?

4 SPEAKING

A Imagine that you are in one of these difficult situations. What worries do you think you would have about it? Take notes.

> giving a speech   going on a date with someone new
> moving to another city   starting a new job

B PAIR WORK Take turns describing your situations. Offer and respond to reassurance. Try to point out a good side of each situation.

> I'm going to go on a date tomorrow with someone new. I'm nervous that I will say something silly.

> You'll be fine. Everyone gets nervous about dates.

> I guess so … And we're going to go to my favorite restaurant. Maybe my date won't like it.

> Well, *at least* you can have some good food!

4.4 BUSINESS AND PLEASURE

LESSON OBJECTIVE
- write an email describing plans for an event

1 LISTENING

A [PAIR WORK] Imagine you're planning a fun afternoon for a group of exchange students from different countries. Suggest some good ideas for the event.

B 🔊 1.38 [LISTEN FOR EXAMPLES] Listen to a conversation between two teachers, Cindy and Min-soo. They're planning the event. Do they suggest any of the ideas you had in exercise 1A?

C 🔊 1.38 [LISTEN FOR DETAILS] Listen again. Find the reasons that …
1. Min-soo says "no" to the barbecue.
2. Min-soo says "no" to the quiz show.
3. Cindy says "no" to the baseball game.
4. Cindy says "yes" to the video.

D [THINK CRITICALLY] What do you think of Cindy's and Min-soo's ideas? Which one would you choose? Are these activities good for all age groups? Why or why not?

2 PRONUNCIATION: Listening for linked sounds – final /n/

A 🔊 1.39 Listen to the extracts from the conversation. Focus on the sound of the letters in bold. How is the spoken sound different from the written words?
1. There are lots of games at Gree**n** Park stadium.
2. And we ca**n** post the video online.

B 🔊 1.40 Listen. Focus on the words in bold. Do you hear a /n/ sound or a /m/ sound at the end? Write *N* or *M*.
1. ___ We **can** take pictures and post them online.
2. ___ We could make a **fan** page for the best videos.
3. ___ Can you **turn** down the volume?
4. ___ Do you know where I **can buy** a new phone around here?

C Circle the correct option to complete the statement.

When a word ending in a /n/ sound is followed by a word beginning in a */p/ / /t/* sound, the /n/ sounds more like a /m/.

3 WRITING

A Read the email. What three locations will the students use for the event?

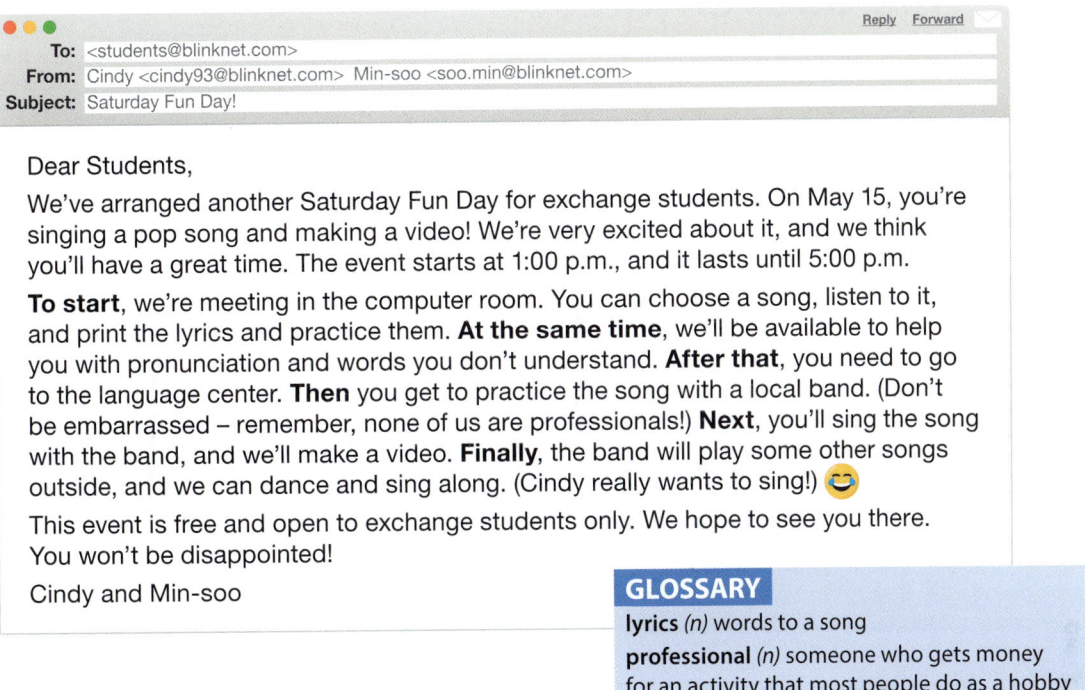

To: <students@blinknet.com>
From: Cindy <cindy93@blinknet.com> Min-soo <soo.min@blinknet.com>
Subject: Saturday Fun Day!

Dear Students,

We've arranged another Saturday Fun Day for exchange students. On May 15, you're singing a pop song and making a video! We're very excited about it, and we think you'll have a great time. The event starts at 1:00 p.m., and it lasts until 5:00 p.m.

To start, we're meeting in the computer room. You can choose a song, listen to it, and print the lyrics and practice them. **At the same time**, we'll be available to help you with pronunciation and words you don't understand. **After that**, you need to go to the language center. **Then** you get to practice the song with a local band. (Don't be embarrassed – remember, none of us are professionals!) **Next**, you'll sing the song with the band, and we'll make a video. **Finally**, the band will play some other songs outside, and we can dance and sing along. (Cindy really wants to sing!) 😊

This event is free and open to exchange students only. We hope to see you there. You won't be disappointed!

Cindy and Min-soo

GLOSSARY
lyrics *(n)* words to a song
professional *(n)* someone who gets money for an activity that most people do as a hobby

B **WRITING SKILLS** Look at the linking words in bold in the email. When do you use them? Complete the sentences.

1. Use _____ for the first thing that happens.
2. Use _____ for two things that happen together. This phrase goes at the beginning of the second thing.
3. Use _____, _____, and _____ for something that happens after something else.
4. Use _____ for something that happens last.

REGISTER CHECK

We sometimes put information in parentheses ( ) when we write. In emails, this information is usually extra – not essential or necessary.

WRITE IT

C Imagine you are organizing an event for exchange students. Use one of the events below or your own idea. Write an email to the students describing the plans. Use linking words to show the order of events.

a barbecue   a baseball or soccer game   a quiz show

D **PAIR WORK** Exchange emails with a partner. Would you like to go to each other's events? Why or why not?

41

4.5 TIME TO SPEAK
Microadventures

LESSON OBJECTIVE
- choose activities for different groups of people

A **DISCUSS** Read the text. What's a *microadventure*? Have you ever had one? Talk about it.

In his book *Microadventures*, Alastair Humphreys explains how adventures can be short, cheap, and close to home – but also exciting. Examples of *microadventures* are sleeping in your yard with friends, swimming in a river, going "urban hiking" in a nice part of your city, going to a wild place near your city, and cooking food on a fire.

B **RESEARCH** In pairs, think of three ideas for microadventures in or near your city. Think about what to take, what clothes to wear, and how to get there. You can go online for ideas.

FIND IT

C **PREPARE** When you have your ideas, think about what kind of people will like each microadventure, for example: young adults, older adults, families with children.

D **PRESENT** Work in groups. Present your ideas to the group. Say what kind of people the adventures are good for and describe the adventures they're going to have. Exchange feedback and suggestions for improvements.

E **DECIDE** Use the feedback to help you choose and improve your best idea.

F **AGREE** Tell the class your best idea. The class agrees on the best microadventure for each of these groups: young adults, older adults, and families with children.

>> To check your progress, go to page 154.

USEFUL PHRASES

RESEARCH
We can …
Here's a good idea.
We need …
I think / don't think … will like …

PRESENT
They're going to … They'll also …
We/I think they'll be …
We/I don't think they'll …

DECIDE
This is our best idea.
We think it's perfect for …

AND THEN ...

5

UNIT OBJECTIVES
- talk about lost and found things
- talk about needing and giving help
- talk about surprising situations
- write a short story
- tell and compare stories

START SPEAKING

A Look at the picture. What's surprising about this picture? How could you explain what's happening?

B Look at the picture again. What do you think happened next?

C What extreme weather do you have where you live? Have you ever had a surprising experience with weather? For ideas, watch Angie's video.

What extreme weather does Angie talk about?

5.1 LOST ... AND THEN FOUND

LESSON OBJECTIVE
- talk about lost and found things

1 LANGUAGE IN CONTEXT

A Read the title of the article and look at the pictures. How do you think the rings were lost? How long were they lost? Then read the stories and check your ideas.

RINGS THAT RETURNED ...

... FROM THE SEA

In 1979, soon after he got married, Agustín Aliaga lost his wedding ring. As he swam in the Mediterranean Sea near Benidorm, Spain, the ring fell off his finger and disappeared. He searched for it in the water but didn't find it, of course. So he left it behind. In 2016, a diver, Jessica Cuesta, discovered the ring at the bottom of the sea. She posted a message online and asked people to help her find the owner. The post was shared 80,000 times. Finally, Agustín saw it and contacted Jessica, who returned the ring to him ... 37 years after he lost it.

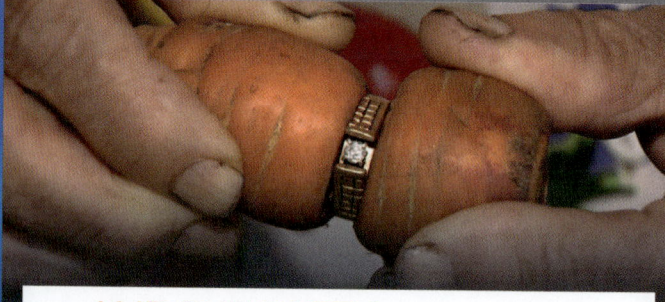

... AND THE EARTH.

Canadian Mary Grams was 71 when she dropped her engagement ring in her vegetable garden. She looked everywhere, but she couldn't locate it. She didn't want to tell her husband the ring was lost, so she bought a new one that looked almost the same. Thirteen years later, the old ring suddenly appeared. Amazingly, it was wrapped around a carrot in her garden! So at age 84, Mary got her ring back. It was in perfect condition and still fit her finger – but it was clearly too small for the carrot!

B Read the stories again. How did social media help Agustín get his ring back? How did Mary get her ring back?

2 VOCABULARY: Losing and finding things

A 🔊 **1.41** Listen and repeat the words. <u>Underline</u> these words in the stories in exercise 1A. Which words are about losing something? looking for something? finding something? Make three lists.

appear	disappear	discover	drop	get (something) back
locate	return	search (for)	fall off	leave (something) behind

FIND IT

B **PAIR WORK** What's the difference between *drop*, *fall off*, and *leave behind*? You can use a dictionary or your phone to check.

C ▶ Now go to page 145. Do the vocabulary exercises for 5.1.

D **PAIR WORK** Think about a time you lost something small. Was it valuable? Where did you lose it? Did you get it back? For ideas, watch Andres's video.

REAL STUDENT

What does Andres think happened to his lost item?

3 GRAMMAR: Simple past

A (Circle) the correct answer. Use the sentences in the grammar box to help you.
Use the simple past to talk about events in the past that are **completed** / **in progress**.

> **Simple past**
>
> Agustín Aliaga **lost** his wedding ring. She **looked** everywhere.
> He **didn't find** it in the water. She **couldn't locate** it.

B Complete the conversation with the simple past form of the verbs in parentheses ( ).
Then practice the conversation with a partner.

A What ¹_____ (happen)? You look really unhappy.
B I am. I ²_____ (leave behind) my bag at the gym yesterday.
A Don't tell me! It ³_____ (disappear). ⁴_____ someone _____ (take) it?
B Yes. I ⁵_____ (look) everywhere, but I ⁶_____ (not find) it.
A ⁷_____ you _____ (ask) the staff at the main desk?
B Of course, but they ⁸_____ (not know) anything about it.

C ▶ Now go to page 133. Look at the grammar chart and do the grammar exercise for 5.1.

D [PAIR WORK] Complete the sentences. You can talk about real events or make up stories.
Then tell a partner. Ask questions to find out more.

1 A few _____ ago, my _____ disappeared. I was really upset!
2 I once dropped _____ in _____ . I never got it back.
3 My friend lost _____ . She searched for a long time but _____ .

4 SPEAKING

A Think about things you've lost or found in your life. They could be your own things or other people's things. Think about:

> when it happened   what the things were
> what you did next   where you lost or found them

B [GROUP WORK] Talk about the things you lost or found. Ask and answer questions. Then decide which was the most interesting or unusual story you heard.

> So, what did you lose or find?

>> I lost my wallet in a park a few months ago. It had some money and all my credit cards in it. Unfortunately, I didn't get it back!

5.2 HELP FROM A STRANGER

LESSON OBJECTIVE
- talk about needing and giving help

1 VOCABULARY: Needing and giving help

A 🔊 **1.42** Read the sentences. Who says them: someone who needs help (N) or someone who gives help (G)? Write *N* or *G*. You can use a dictionary or your phone to help with words you don't know. Then listen and check.

1 My friend doesn't have a car, so sometimes I **give** her **a ride** to the airport. ___
2 I really **was in trouble**. My car **broke down**, and I couldn't **figure out** what to do. ___
3 I **was grateful** to a stranger. I **got lost**, and he **showed** me where to go. ___
4 I **warned** my neighbors that a storm was coming and told them to stay inside. ___
5 My mother **takes care of** me when I get sick. ___
6 My little cousin dropped his ice-cream cone. I **felt sorry for** him, so I bought him another one. ___

B **PAIR WORK** Are any of the sentences in exercise 1A true for you? Tell a partner.

C ▶ Now go to page 145. Do the vocabulary exercises for 5.2.

2 LANGUAGE IN CONTEXT

A 🔊 **1.43** Look at the picture. What problems could happen on a subway? Then read and listen to the conversation. What was Shawn's problem? Who helped him? How?

B 🔊 **1.43** Read and listen again. What good thing happened to Shawn at the end?

🔊 **1.43 Audio script**

Alexa So, I haven't seen any pictures from your visit to São Paulo.

Shawn I know – I'm sorry! I was trying to post some pics when my phone battery died. It was at the worst time, too. My friends and I were on our way to a restaurant, and we were waiting for a train. While I was looking at some art on the wall, the train came. When I looked up, the doors were closing, and all of my friends were on it!

Alexa Oh, no! What did you do?

Shawn Well, I got on the next train and got off at the next station to see if my friends were waiting for me there, but they weren't. So I tried to text them, and that's when I **figured out** my phone wasn't working. I didn't know what to do. Then a woman saw that I **was in trouble** and **felt sorry for** me. Luckily, she knew where the restaurant was, and she **showed** me which lines to take. I **was** really **grateful**.

Alexa So, you didn't **get lost**?

Shawn No, her directions were perfect. And she told me about a great dish at the restaurant, too. It was delicious!

C **PAIR WORK** Talk about a time you got lost. What happened? Did anyone help you? Who?

INSIDER ENGLISH

A <u>subway</u> is the system of underground <u>trains</u> in a city. You get on a **train** when you take the **subway**.

3 GRAMMAR: Past continuous and simple past

A Circle the correct answers. Use the sentences in the grammar box to help you.
1. Use the **simple past** / **past continuous** to show an event in progress.
2. Use the **simple past** / **past continuous** to show a completed action that interrupts the event in progress.

> **Past continuous and simple past**
>
> While I **was looking** at some art, the train **came**.
> When I **looked up**, the doors **were closing**.

 The order can change.
The train came while I was looking at some art.
When the train came, I was looking at some art.

B Complete the sentences with the past continuous or simple past of the verbs in parentheses ( ). Check your accuracy. Then check (✓) the sentences that have happened to you and tell a partner.

☐ 1 When my friends and I _____ (walk) downtown, we _____ (get) lost.
☐ 2 I _____ (show) my guests how to get around while they _____ (visit) this city.
☐ 3 I _____ (warn) my friend to be careful when she _____ (travel).
☐ 4 I _____ (wait) for the bus without an umbrella when it _____ (start) to rain.
☐ 5 While I _____ (look) at my phone, I _____ (miss) the train.

ACCURACY CHECK

Use *when*, not *while*, to introduce an action in the simple past that interrupts.

We were driving to Dallas ~~while~~ the car broke down. ✗
We were driving to Dallas when the car broke down. ✓

C ▶ Now go to page 133. Look at the grammar chart and do the grammar exercise for 5.2.

D PAIR WORK Complete the sentences with your own information. Then share your sentences.
1. While I was searching for _____, I _____.
2. When some strangers asked for directions, I _____.
3. When I _____, I got lost.
4. I lost my _____ while I _____.

4 SPEAKING

A Think about a time when you helped a stranger or a friend. Make notes about your answers to these questions.

> What were you doing?   What was the other person doing?   Where were you?
> Who did you help?   How did you help the person?   How did it end?

B PAIR WORK Take turns talking about your experience and asking questions.

> What were you doing when you helped someone?

> I was waiting for the bus when an older man asked me for help. He couldn't find his bus pass. I guess he dropped it while he was walking to the bus stop.

> That's too bad! How did you help him?

> Well, we looked for it together, and we found it just before the bus came!

47

5.3 YOU'RE KIDDING!

LESSON OBJECTIVE
- talk about surprising situations

1 FUNCTIONAL LANGUAGE

A 🔊 1.44 Look at the picture. What do you think these two friends are talking about? Then read and listen to their conversation. Answer the questions.

1 Where did the woman live before?
2 Where is she living now? Why?
3 Why was she surprised?

🔊 1.44 Audio script

A **I had a real surprise** this morning. I was getting on the bus, and someone shouted my name. So I turned around. And **you'll never guess** who was standing behind me.
B Who?
A An old school friend from Seoul.
B **Are you serious?**
A Yeah. I haven't seen her for a long time. She didn't even know I was studying here.
B **You're kidding!** What's she doing in Seattle?
A Well, **you're not going to believe this**. She's studying here, too.
B That's incredible!
A I know. **I can't believe it**.
B So, who was more surprised? You or her?
A I'm not sure. We were both pretty shocked. And so was the bus driver! He couldn't understand why we were so excited!

B Complete the chart with the expressions in bold from the conversation.

Giving surprising news	Reacting with surprise
I had ¹_____ this morning. You'll ²_____ who was standing behind me. You're not going to ³_____. I ⁴_____ believe it.	Are you ⁵_____? Is that true? You're ⁶_____! Seriously?

C PAIR WORK Put the conversation in the correct order (1–4). Then practice with your partner.

___ You're kidding! I helped you search for it for ages. Where was it?
___ Are you serious? I wonder how it got there.
___ You'll never guess what I found yesterday. My car key. Remember? I lost it last year.
___ You're not going to believe this. It was in that big flower pot in my living room.

48

2 REAL-WORLD STRATEGY

A 🔊 **1.45** Listen to the conversation between Jenny and Eric. What surprising thing happened? How did it happen?

B 🔊 **1.45** Read the information in the box about repeating words to express surprise. Then listen again. What does Eric repeat?

> **REPEATING WORDS TO EXPRESS SURPRISE**
> When people tell us surprising things, we often repeat the words or phrases that surprised us.
> *You'll never guess who was standing behind me.*
> **Who?**
> *An old school friend <u>from Seoul</u>.*
> **From Seoul?** *Are you serious?*

C 🔊 **1.46** Complete the conversation with repeated words to express surprise. Listen and check.

A Hi, it's me. Sorry about the noise – I'm calling from the top of a mountain, and it's really windy.

B _____ ?

D ▶ PAIR WORK **Student A:** Go to page 157. **Student B:** Go to page 159. Follow the instructions.

3 PRONUNCIATION: Showing surprise

A 🔊 **1.47** Listen and repeat. Focus on how the speaker uses stress and intonation to show surprise.
1 Are you serious?   2 That's incredible!

B 🔊 **1.48** Listen to each conversation. Does speaker B show surprise? Write *Y (Yes)* or *N (No)*.

1 ___ A My brother speaks six languages.   B No way!
2 ___ A Did you hear? Julie's moving to California. B She's moving to California?
3 ___ A So guess what. I got the job!   B I don't believe it!
4 ___ A Jose and Mariel are having another baby.   B You're kidding me.

C PAIR WORK Work with a partner. Practice the conversations in 3B. Does your partner show surprise?

4 SPEAKING

A Think of something surprising that happened to you. Use the ideas below or your own ideas. Prepare to tell someone about this experience.

- someone you saw
- someone that called you with surprising news
- someone that asked you to do something you weren't expecting
- something strange you saw in your neighborhood

B PAIR WORK Tell your partner what happened. Take turns.

> You'll never guess who I saw when I was on vacation.
> Who?
> My boss.
> Your boss? You're kidding!

5.4 STORYTELLING

LESSON OBJECTIVE
- write a short story

1 READING

Cave painting

A   Look at the picture of the cave painting. What story do you think it tells?

B   **SCAN** Scan the article. What are the four "S"s?

Author Q & A: The Art of Storytelling

Everyone loves a good story. Why? And what makes a story good? I discussed the topic with author Rhonda Howard.

Author Rhonda Howard

Q: Why do people like stories?
A: A story makes you feel like you're experiencing something, and people enjoy this. Storytelling is very old. Think of cave paintings. Those are examples of people sharing stories – in a very simple way.
Q: But our stories are more complicated today, right?
A: Well, not always. And sometimes the best stories are simple ones.
Q: Speaking of the best stories, what makes a story good?
A: I narrowed it down to the four "S"s of storytelling. We already talked about the first S: *Simple*. People often like stories with ideas and language that are easy to understand. We discussed the second S, too: *Shared experiences*. People don't need to actually experience the events in the story, but they want to feel like they did. And this leads us to a famous storytelling S: *Show, don't tell*.
Q: I've heard that. What does it mean?
A: Here's a quick example: "Jorge was walking into his house when he saw an animal." That's telling. "Jorge was nervously walking into his dark living room when two large, yellow eyes appeared in front of him." That's showing!
Q: I get it – I felt like I was walking with Jorge in the second example.
A: Exactly!
Q: So, what's the fourth S?
A: Surprise! People love surprises – especially at the end of the story.

GLOSSARY
narrow down (v) make the number of choices smaller

C   **PAIR WORK** **SUMMARIZE A TEXT** Read the article. Then summarize the answers for these two questions: Why do people like stories? What makes a story good?

2 WRITING

A Read the story. How did the different characters in the story feel? What was the monster in the woods?

The MONSTER in the WOODS
by Hannah Miller

When I was 15, I loved reading scary stories about monsters. It was summer, and my family and I were on vacation near a lake. One evening, they went down to the beach to meet friends for a barbecue. I was reading a monster story and wanted to finish it before the barbecue, so they left me behind. An hour later, my brother David came to get me, and we started walking to the beach. It was totally dark, and I was telling David about the awful monster in the story – a huge, black, animal-like monster. We were both frightened by the story and the dark night. Then suddenly – out of the trees right beside us – a huge, black, animal-like monster appeared! We screamed and screamed! While we were screaming, my father ran to us. Then we told him our horrible story. And what did he do? He laughed – because standing in the distance was King, our neighbor's dog. He was black and pretty big – but definitely not a monster!

GLOSSARY
monster (n) a frightening creature that isn't real

B PAIR WORK THINK CRITICALLY Do you think the story in exercise 2A has the four "S"s that Rhonda Howard describes? Why or why not?

C WRITING SKILLS Read about different kinds of storytelling expressions. Then find and <u>underline</u> them in the story. Think of more expressions for each group.

We can use different kinds of expressions to …

1. describe when the story happened in general: *When I was 15, …* *It was summer.*
2. say when particular events happened: *One evening, …* *An hour later, …* *Then …*
3. describe a scene: *It was totally dark.*

WRITE IT

D Write a short story like the one in exercise 2A. It can be true, or you can make it up. Remember the four "S"s. Use storytelling expressions from exercise 2C. You can repeat a verb to make a strong impact if you wish.

> **REGISTER CHECK**
>
> In stories, we sometimes repeat a verb to make a strong impact. The verb usually shows an action or a feeling that lasts for longer than usual. In formal writing, like an essay or news story, we don't repeat verbs.
>
> **Informal story**
> *We screamed and screamed!*
> *They ate and ate until they were full.*
>
> **Formal writing**
> *We screamed.*
> *They ate until they were full.*

E PAIR WORK Exchange stories with a partner. Did they use the 4 "S"s? How did their story make you feel?

5.5 TIME TO SPEAK
Believe it or not …

LESSON OBJECTIVE
- tell and compare stories

A **PREPARE** Think of something surprising or amusing that happened to you recently or a long time ago. Use the ideas below to help you, or think of your own idea.

breaking things / making a mess	kids doing funny things
making mistakes	seeing animals and insects
travel experiences	incredible weather
losing/forgetting things	meeting/seeing people

B **DISCUSS** Share your stories in small groups. Use some of the four "S"s and storytelling expressions from Lesson 5.4 to make your story more interesting. Which story is the most amazing?

C **DECIDE** Your group is going to enter an amazing-but-true story competition. Choose one of these options and decide what story you will tell.
- Choose a true story from your group – if you think it's amazing enough to win the competition.
- Exaggerate a true story from your group to make it more amazing – but it should still sound true.
- Make up an amazing story that sounds true but isn't.

D **PREPARE** Practice, exaggerate, or make up your group's story. Get ready to tell it in an entertaining way.

E **PRESENT** Tell your group's story to the class. At the end of each story, others in the class ask questions to try to discover if the story is totally true, exaggerated, or totally made-up.

F **AGREE** The class chooses the best story that seems to be totally true. Then the winning group says whether their story is totally true, exaggerated, or totally made-up.

 To check your progress, go to page 154.

USEFUL PHRASES

DISCUSS
A few weeks/months/years ago …
When/While I was …
Then suddenly …
Later …

DECIDE
Seriously?
You're kidding!
That's a great story!
They won't believe that.
Let's say that …

AGREE
I think it's true.
It's not true.
No way!
I (can't) believe that …

UNIT OBJECTIVES
- talk about urban problems
- talk about problems and solutions
- express concern and relief in different situations
- write a post giving your point of view
- decide if a "green" plan will work

IMPACT

6

START SPEAKING

A What's happening in the picture? How do you feel about projects like this?

B Talk about different ways this project is having an effect on the city and its people. Do you think this impact is mostly positive or negative?

C What change is having an impact on your city at the moment? Is it positive or negative? For ideas, watch Brenda's video.

What is happening in Brenda's city?

6.1 MOVING TO A MEGACITY

LESSON OBJECTIVE
- talk about urban problems

1 LANGUAGE IN CONTEXT

A Look at the pictures. How do you think life is different in these two places?

B Read the blog. What is interesting about Dan's situation? Who is he writing his blog for?

C Read the blog again. What things in Los Angeles does Dan like? What doesn't he like?

I'm Dan. I just moved from Barrow, Alaska, to Los Angeles, California for college. I'm a small-town boy writing about big-city life for students like me!

L.A. Update!

I've been in my new city for two weeks now. Living in Los Angeles has been a really big change. Here are some things I never had to worry about in Alaska:

Pollution: There's so much traffic, and it makes the air so dirty. Plus, there's smoke in the air from factories. And since I arrived, there's been almost no wind, so the air is never really clean.

Concrete: Sometimes I see a few trees and a little grass here and there, but almost all of the land between buildings is concrete. Sometimes there is graffiti on the buildings, too, which I don't like.

Noise: I expected a lot of noise during the day, but I'm really surprised how much noise there is at night. In Alaska, there's almost none. Here, I wake up several times a night.

Crowds: L.A. is a megacity (more than 10 million people). Because it's so crowded, there's very little space. But I love living close to so many people. There's stuff happening all the time.

Heat: It's a lot hotter here than in Alaska. I actually like that – but I need to buy some cooler clothes!

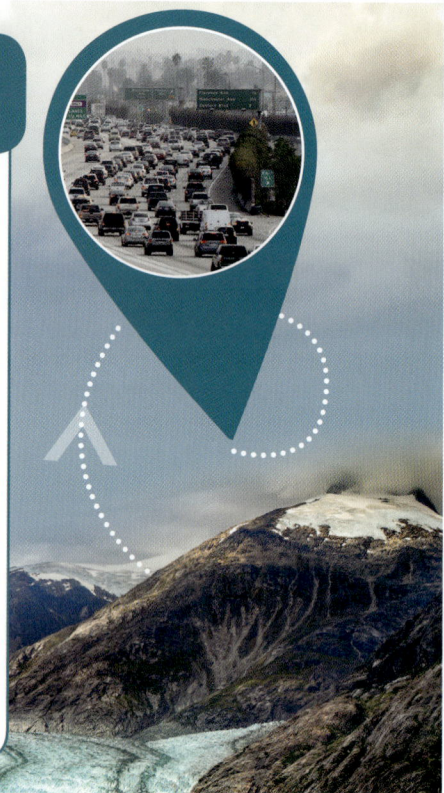

2 VOCABULARY: Urban problems

A 🔊 **1.49** Listen and repeat the words. Find and <u>underline</u> nine of these words in the blog post in exercise 1C. Then use all of the words to complete the paragraphs below.

| air | concrete | graffiti | land | noise | pollution |
| smoke | space | traffic | traffic jam | trash | |

Cities are full of cars, so there's often ¹_____ on the roads. This often leads to a ²_____, which means delays. The cars cause ³_____, along with the ⁴_____ from factories, and dirty ⁵_____ is bad for our health. You can also hear the ⁶_____ of the traffic all over the city.

Cities can be ugly, too. Most of the ⁷_____ has high-rise buildings and ⁸_____ sidewalks on it. And when people share the same ⁹_____, they produce tons of garbage. Some people leave their ¹⁰_____ on the street. There's ¹¹_____ on some buildings, and even if it looks nice, business owners usually don't like it.

B ▶ Now go to page 146. Do the vocabulary exercises for 6.1.

C **PAIR WORK** Which urban problems does your city or town have? For ideas, watch Angie's video.

 **REAL STUDENT** What problem does Angie talk about?

3 GRAMMAR: Quantifiers

A Circle the correct answers. Use the sentences in the grammar box to help you.
1 With quantifiers like *a few*, *several*, and *so many*, use **count nouns** / **non-count nouns**.
2 With quantifiers like *a little*, *very little*, and *so much*, use **count nouns** / **non-count nouns**.
3 Some quantifiers, like **a lot of** / **a few**, can be used with both count and non-count nouns.

Quantifiers	
Almost all of the land is concrete.	I see **a little** grass here and there.
There's **so much** traffic.	I see **a few** trees.
I love living close to **so many** people.	There's **very little** space.
I expected **a lot of** noise.	There's been **almost no** wind.
I wake up **several** times a night.	In Alaska, there's **almost none**.

B ▶ Now go to page 134. Look at the grammar chart and do the grammar exercise for 6.1.

C Circle the correct answers. Sometimes both are possible. Then check (✓) the ones that are true for you and share your answers with a partner.
☐ 1 I had several good *meals* / *food* on my last vacation.
☐ 2 I saw almost no *cars* / *traffic* on my way home yesterday.
☐ 3 My home has several large *windows* / *glass*.
☐ 4 I've already finished almost all of my *exercises* / *work* for the week.
☐ 5 I'm really busy these days – I have so little *days* / *time* off.

D **PAIR WORK** Complete these sentences so they're true for your city. Check your accuracy. Then share them with a partner. Do you agree?
1 There are several …
2 There's so much …
3 There are very few …
4 There's / There are almost no …

> ✓ **ACCURACY CHECK**
>
> Remember, there is no plural form of non-count nouns. Some quantifiers cannot be used with them.
>
> The traffic report gave us ~~several informations.~~ ✗
> The traffic report gave us a lot of information. ✓

4 SPEAKING

A Look at the urban problems in exercise 2A. Which ones do you think will have an effect for a long time? You can go online to learn more. Make notes.

B **PAIR WORK** Do you agree about the problems that will last into the future? What effects will these problems cause? How many can you list?

> *Graffiti is a problem, but it's not going to hurt anybody.*

> *Yeah. I worry more about pollution. That will make the air hard to breathe for a long time.*

6.2 INTELLIGENT SOLUTIONS

LESSON OBJECTIVE
- talk about problems and solutions

1 LANGUAGE IN CONTEXT

A Look at the picture. Do you think the paintings make the area look better or worse? Why?

B 🔊 1.50 Read and listen to the radio show. What three problems do the people talk about?

C 🔊 1.50 Read and listen again. What are the solutions to the problems?

🔊 1.50 Audio script

Host Today we're talking trash, along with other community problems. These problems can take a lot of time and money to fix, but sometimes solutions are easier than you think. We asked community members for their ideas.

Margot Garbage is a big problem. And if there is a lot of garbage in the street, people often leave more trash there. They see garbage and think it's OK to add a little more. But if you keep the area clean, people will think twice before throwing trash on the street.

Josh Graffiti makes local business owners angry. But if you make a special area for graffiti, people won't paint on other buildings. Many graffiti artists paint beautifully and can really improve an area.

Frida Noise at night is a common problem. When you speak angrily to noisy neighbors, they just keep making noise. But if you talk to them calmly and politely, they'll probably listen. And if you explain your feelings clearly, they will understand.

Host So, some interesting ideas. They may not work in every community, but some of them just might in yours!

D GROUP WORK Do you think the community members' solutions from the radio show in exercise 1C will work? Why or why not?

> **INSIDER ENGLISH**
> We use *think twice* to mean think about something again, more carefully.

2 VOCABULARY: Adverbs of manner

A 🔊 1.51 Listen and repeat the words. Which words are positive? negative? neutral? Then find and underline five of the words in the conversation in exercise 1B.

angrily	beautifully	calmly	clearly	completely	correctly
dangerously	loudly	politely	quietly	safely	

B PAIR WORK Ask and answer the questions.
1. Do you play music loudly or quietly?
2. How should people explain things to children?
3. Who do you know that drives safely? Dangerously?
4. When is it important to do something correctly?

C ▶ Now go to page 146. Do the vocabulary exercises for 6.2.

3 GRAMMAR: Present and future real conditionals

A Circle the correct answers. Use the sentences in the grammar box to help you.
1. For present real conditionals, use the **simple present** / **simple past** for the condition and the result.
2. For future real conditionals, use **the simple present** / **will** for the condition and **the simple present** / **will** for the result.

> **Present and future real conditionals**
>
> **Present real conditionals**
> **If** there **is** a lot of garbage in the street, people often **leave** more trash there.
> **When** you **speak** angrily to noisy neighbors, they **just keep** making noise.
>
> **Future real conditionals**
> **If** you **explain** your feelings clearly, they **will understand**.
> **If** you **make** a special area for graffiti, people **won't paint** on other buildings.

B ▶ Now go to page 134. Look at the grammar chart and do the grammar exercise for 6.2.

C Complete the sentences with your opinion. Use the simple present or the future with *will*.

Present Situations:
1. If people throw trash in the street, _____ .
2. When people talk loudly, _____ .
3. I speak politely when _____ .

> ❗ The order can change. There is no comma when the *if* clause is second.
> They **will understand if** you **explain** your feelings clearly.

Future Situations:
4. If a store clerk speaks angrily, _____ .
5. I won't listen to you if _____ .
6. If I don't do the exercise correctly, _____ .

D **PAIR WORK** Share your answers from exercise 3C. Were any of your answers similar?

4 SPEAKING

A Read the three city problems and solutions. Add a problem you want to solve and an idea for a solution to the chart.

Problem	Solution
noise	People have to be quiet before 8:00 a.m. and after 10:00 p.m.
pollution	People have to use bikes or electric cars.
traffic	People have to drive with two or more people in a car.
_____	_____

B **PAIR WORK** Do you think the solutions in exercise 4A will work? Why or why not? Does your partner agree?

> I don't think a rule with times to be quiet will work. If people work in the morning or come home late, it's hard to be quiet.

> I disagree. People don't have to be quiet all the time. If they think of others, they'll speak quietly early in the morning and late at night.

6.3 BREAKDOWN

LESSON OBJECTIVE
- express concern and relief in different situations

1 FUNCTIONAL LANGUAGE

A 🔊 **1.52** Look at the picture. What can cause a traffic jam? Then read and listen. Who helped the people on the bus?

> 🔊 **1.52 Audio script**
>
> A I'm really happy you made it home. **Are you all right?**
> B Yeah, I'm fine.
> A **I'm so relieved.**
> B I can't believe my bus broke down in the middle of the longest tunnel in the city!
> A I know. I saw it on the local news before you texted me. At first, they said the bus was on fire. **I was really worried!** Then they said there was no fire, just a lot of smoke.
> B It's true there was a lot of smoke.
>
> A **Was everyone OK?**
> B Yes. No one was hurt.
> A **I'm glad to hear that.**
> B Yeah, and the bus driver was great. She helped everyone stay calm until the police came. Then we all walked out of the tunnel, and they put us on another bus.
> A **What a relief!** I'm glad it's over. And I'm glad I wasn't in the traffic jam behind your bus!

B Complete the chart with the expressions in bold from the conversation.

Expressing concern	Expressing relief
Are you ¹_____ ?	I'm so ⁴_____ .
I was ²_____ !	I'm glad ⁵_____ .
Is/Was ³_____ ?	What ⁶_____ !
Is anything wrong?	That's such a relief.

C 🔊 **1.53** Put the conversation in the correct order from 1 to 4. Then listen and check.

___ Where are you? You're late. Is anything wrong?
___ That's such a relief. I was really starting to worry.
___ No. Everything's fine. I just had to buy a few things at the market.
___ Hi, Mom. It's Kerry.

58

2 REAL-WORLD STRATEGY

A 🔊 **1.54** Listen to a conversation between Ruby and her friend Marina. What did Marina do this morning? Was she successful?

B 🔊 **1.54** Read the information in the box about using *though* to give a contrasting idea. Then listen again. What is Marina's contrasting idea? What did she say before that?

> **USING *THOUGH* TO GIVE A CONTRASTING IDEA**
>
> We can use *though* when we say something that contrasts an idea that was already said. It goes at the end of a sentence, after a comma.
>
> *Was everyone OK?*
>
> *Yes. No one was hurt. It was a dangerous situation, **though**.*

C 🔊 **1.55** Listen to another conversation and complete the contrasting idea. Then practice with a partner.
- A Did you go to the street festival last night? I heard there were some problems.
- B Yeah. It was really crowded, and some people fell down. Two people were hurt and had to go to the hospital. I was ¹_____, ²_____.
- A I'm so relieved! I was really worried.

D ▶ PAIR WORK Student A: Go to page 158. Student B: Go to page 160. Follow the instructions.

3 PRONUNCIATION: Saying unstressed vowels at the end of a word

A 🔊 **1.56** Listen. Focus on the sound of the letter *y* at the end of the words in **bold**.

1 **really**   I was **really** worried.   2 **worry**   I was starting to **worry**.

B 🔊 **1.57** Listen. Focus on the words in **bold**. Does the speaker say the final vowel sound clearly? Write *Y* (*Yes*) or *N* (*No*).

1 ___ Please walk **calmly** to the front of the train.   3 ___ Did you enter the password **correctly**?
2 ___ Please fill out the form **clearly**.   4 ___ Did everyone arrive **safely**?

C Practice the conversation with a partner. Does your partner say the final vowel sounds clearly?
- A Where have you been? I was starting to **worry**.
- B There was a huge accident. The road was **completely** blocked.
- A Well I'm just glad you got home **safely**.

4 SPEAKING

A PAIR WORK Choose one of the situations below. Student A: Ask about the situation and express concern and relief. Student B: Answer questions and explain everything is OK. Include a contrasting idea.

- There was a flood in your neighborhood.
- There was a problem at your soccer game.
- You had a very important exam today.
- Your pet disappeared a few days ago.

> I heard there was a flood in your neighborhood. Is everyone OK?
>
> Yes, we're all OK, thanks. It was pretty scary, though.

B GROUP WORK Work with another pair and listen to each other's conversations. What situation did they choose? What was the contrasting idea?

6.4 BEATING THE TRAFFIC

LESSON OBJECTIVE
- write a post giving your point of view

1 LISTENING

A Look at the picture of the drone delivering a package. What types of things do you think a drone can – and can't – deliver?

B 🔊 **1.58** **LISTEN FOR GIST** Listen to Doug's podcast. What is his interview with Elsa about?
a how quickly drones can deliver packages
b how drones can reduce traffic problems
c how drones can cause problems for cities

C 🔊 **1.58** **LISTEN FOR SPECIFIC INFORMATION** Listen again. How does Elsa think drones will fix these problems: traffic, pollution, and noise?

2 PRONUNCIATION: Listening for weak words

A 🔊 **1.59** Listen to the extracts from the podcast below. Circle the words that aren't fully pronounced.
1 Traffic! It can cause a lot of problems …
2 And who better to discuss the topic …
3 But they're a lot quieter than trucks.

B 🔊 **1.60** Listen. Write the missing words.
1 Won't there be _____ accidents?
2 Drones are more useful _____ I thought.
3 And drones usually use batteries, so they cause almost no pollution compared _____ delivery trucks.

C Complete the statement.
The words *than*, *of*, and *to* are often *stressed / reduced* in fluent speech.

3 WRITING

A Read the comment by SensibleGuy, responding to Doug's podcast. What problems does he write about that Doug and Elsa don't mention?

🎧 PODCAST

SensibleGuy wrote:

I think using drones for deliveries is a bad idea. One truck can deliver a lot of packages, but a drone can only carry one package at a time. In a large city, trucks deliver thousands of packages every day. I don't really want thousands of drones in the air!

According to Elsa, drones will help solve the problem of traffic noise. Have you ever heard a drone? They're really loud – so I don't think that solves anything. Also, I don't trust this "sense and avoid" technology. I'm sure there will be accidents with so many drones in the air. And if they crash, the drones – and their packages – will fall into the streets or onto people.

Also, what happens if a drone arrives and you're not at home? Will it just drop the package into your yard? Maybe. If it does, I'm sure someone will steal it. What about delivering packages to apartment buildings? They can't fly in through people's windows. And who wants drones outside of your window anyway? Not me. It's creepy!

Drones are definitely not the answer. We need to find another solution to the traffic problem.

GLOSSARY
steal *(v)* secretly take something that belongs to someone else
creepy *(adj)* strange and making you feel frightened

B **WRITING SKILLS** Read about using questions to make points. Then find and underline all the questions in the comment in exercise 3A. What are SensibleGuy's answers to the questions?

We often ask questions to introduce or make a strong point. Then we answer the questions. Questions can make the readers feel like you're speaking directly to them. Compare the two ideas below. The first one is stronger and more interesting.

1 Have you ever heard a drone? They're really loud.
2 Drones are really loud.

C  What do you think of SensibleGuy's ideas? What kind of person do you think he is?

REGISTER CHECK

In informal writing, people often give their opinions without supporting their ideas with facts.
Informal
Also, I don't trust this "sense and avoid" technology. I'm sure there will be accidents with so many drones in the air.
Formal
I don't trust the "sense and avoid" technology. One study has shown that 64% of drone accidents happened because of errors with technology.

⌚ WRITE IT

D Write your own comment responding to Doug's podcast and SensibleGuy's comment. Decide if you think drones are good or not. You can use some of the ideas below and your own ideas. Add details. Use questions to make some of your points stronger.

| Positive: | people don't have to wait at home | fast | less pollution |
| | fewer delivery trucks on roads | cheap | |

| Negative: | are dangerous | frightening for pets and wildlife |
| | use energy | take away jobs from delivery drivers |

E **PAIR WORK** Exchange posts with a partner. Do you agree? How many of your points are different?

6.5 TIME TO SPEAK
If everyone plants something …

LESSON OBJECTIVE
- decide if a "green" plan will work

A DISCUSS Look at the picture. What is unusual about the roofs of these city buildings? Do you think this is a good idea? Why or why not?

B RESEARCH Why is it good to have a lot of trees and plants in a city? In small groups, think of different benefits. Look at the ideas below to help you. You can go online for more ideas.

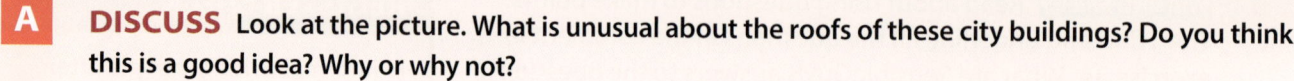

heat   noise   pollution   shade   the air   visual impact   wildlife

C ROLE PLAY Imagine you're city planners, and you're thinking about putting plants on every building in your city. In small groups, discuss the problems you'll have if you do this, and possible solutions to those problems.

> If the city buys all the plants, it'll be too expensive. So community members will have to buy them.

> But if they have to pay, they won't do it.

> If they want, they can buy smaller plants. That won't be too expensive.

D PRESENT Explain your group's ideas to the class.

E DECIDE Think about the benefits you researched in part B and the problems and solutions everyone presented in part D. As a class, decide whether your city should put plants on all rooftops.

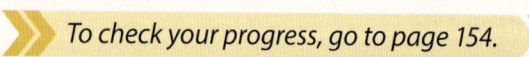
To check your progress, go to page 154.

USEFUL PHRASES

DISCUSS
It looks amazing.
It looks strange.
It looks real.
It's a great idea.
I'm not sure about it.

RESEARCH
That's true, but …
Well, it also …
So, you're saying …
But then …

ROLE PLAY
If we … , we'll have to …
People will/won't …
I (don't) think … will …

DECIDE
I (don't) think it will work.
I (don't) think we can …
We'll need to …
It will be too …

REVIEW 2 (UNITS 4–6)

1 VOCABULARY

A Which word or phrase doesn't belong in each set? Cross it out. Add it to the correct set.

1 Opinions and reactions:	annoying	disappointed	frightening	loudly	shocked
2 Decisions and plans:	arrange	be grateful	deal with	look into	think about
3 Losing and finding things:	disappear	drop	graffiti	return	search for
4 Needing and giving help:	amusing	be in trouble	feel sorry for	take care of	warn
5 Urban problems:	forget	noise	pollution	traffic	trash
6 Adverbs of manner:	clearly	dangerously	locate	politely	safely

B Add two more words or phrases that you know to each category.

2 GRAMMAR

A Circle the correct words to complete the conversation.

A What ¹*are you doing / will you do* this weekend?

B My cousin Jeff and I ²*are going camping / will go camping* in Hill Valley. Would you like to come?

A No, thanks. Once I ³*went camping / was camping* with my family when it ⁴*started / was starting* to rain really heavily. There was a flood at the campground, and all our belongings got ⁵*complete / completely* wet.

B What ⁶*did happen / happened* next?

A We had to come back home the next day. And I ⁷*got / was getting* a really bad cold. That trip was a disaster. Why don't we stay at a hotel?

B If ⁸*we stay / we'll stay* at a hotel, ⁹*we spend / we'll spend* a lot of money.

A Come on. There are ¹⁰*so much / so many* inexpensive hotels in Hill Valley. Look, this travel app shows ¹¹*a few / a little* hostels available. I'm sure ¹²*we find / we'll find* a good place.

B PAIR WORK Talk about your plans for the coming weekend. Tell your partner about the things you've planned and the things you haven't decided yet.

3 SPEAKING

A PAIR WORK Think of one item that you lost. Answer the questions below.

- What item was it? Where did you lose it? When?
- What were you doing when you lost it? How did you feel?
- Did you find it? Where? How?

> Once, I was hanging out with friends at the mall when I lost my phone. I think it fell out of my pocket. I was really annoyed …

B GROUP WORK Tell your partner's story to your classmates.

4 FUNCTIONAL LANGUAGE

A Use the words and phrases below to complete the conversation between two sisters.

| anything wrong | are you serious | at least | I hope so | it'll be fine |
| really worried | so relieved | though | you dropped | you're not going to |

A What happened? You're almost three hours late. Is ¹_____?
B There was a fire in the university neighborhood, and the streets were closed.
A Why didn't you call me? I was ²_____.
B ³_____ believe this, but my cell phone is broken.
A ⁴_____?
B Yeah, I was leaving the library when I dropped my phone on the sidewalk.
A ⁵_____ your phone?
B Yeah. My brand-new phone! I bought it just last month! What am I going to do without my cell phone?
A ⁶_____. You can use your old phone. And I'm sure they can fix your new one.
B ⁷_____. It'll probably cost a lot to repair, ⁸_____.
A ⁹_____ you're OK.
B Well, I'm ¹⁰_____ that I'm finally home.

5 SPEAKING

A **PAIR WORK** Choose one of the situations below. Act it out in pairs.

- You have to give an important presentation at work tomorrow, and you're very anxious. Your partner reassures you. Go to page 38 for useful language.

  > I have to give a presentation to the sales department tomorrow, and I'm really worried.

  > There's no need to worry. Your presentations are always a big success.

  > Yes, but all the directors are going to be there, and …

- Think of something surprising that happened to you. Tell your partner about it. Your partner reacts with surprise. Go to page 48 for useful language.

  > I had a real surprise last night. My father gave me a fantastic birthday present.

  > Are you serious? What did he give you?

  > You'll never guess. He gave me …

- You heard your partner had an accident earlier today. Ask about the situation and express concern and relief. Go to page 58 for useful language.

  > I heard you had a car accident this morning. Are you all right?

  > Yes, I'm OK. I need a new car, though.

  > What a relief! I was really worried about you.

B Change roles and repeat the role play.

UNIT OBJECTIVES
- discuss your changing tastes in music
- talk about TV shows and movies
- refuse invitations and respond to refusals
- write a movie review
- talk about changing tastes

ENTERTAIN US

7

START SPEAKING

A What kind of performance is this? How are the people feeling about it?

B What makes a performance enjoyable? disappointing? awful?

C When did you last go to a concert or another live performance? Describe what it was like. For ideas, watch Brenda's video.

Did you and Brenda have similar experiences?

7.1 A 50-YEAR PLAYLIST

LESSON OBJECTIVE
- discuss your changing tastes in music

1 VOCABULARY: Music

A 🔊 2.02 **GROUP WORK** Listen and repeat the words. Name a musician, band, or song for each kind of music. You can go online to learn more about the kinds of music.

| classical | country | EDM | folk | heavy metal |
| hip-hop | jazz | pop | reggae | rock |

B **GROUP WORK** Which kinds of music do you like or dislike? Is there one kind of music you all like?

C ▶ Now go to page 147. Do the vocabulary exercises for 7.1.

2 LANGUAGE IN CONTEXT

A Look at the picture of Hugo and his son Logan. They're talking about music. What kind of music do you think each one likes?

B 🔊 2.03 Read and listen. They are planning the music for Hugo's 50th birthday party. What kinds of music do they mention?

C 🔊 2.03 Read and listen again. Answer the questions.
1. How is Hugo planning to choose the songs?
2. Which is bigger, his digital music collection or his CD collection?

🔊 2.03 Audio script

Logan So, have you chosen the songs for your playlist yet?

Hugo No, but I've decided to choose music from different stages of my life.

Logan Cool. So, first – your teenage years, I guess. What did you use to listen to then?

Hugo **Pop** and **rock** … and **heavy metal**. I used to listen to a lot of heavy metal. I still listen to it sometimes.

Logan I know. I hear it every time I'm in the car with you! What about **folk**?

Hugo Folk? No way! But I used to like **country** when I was in my 30s.

Logan I've never heard you play country music.

Hugo Yeah. I'm not into it anymore, but I'll put some on my playlist.

Logan What other stuff did you listen to?

Hugo Not much. Actually, I listen to more music now than I used to, thanks to downloading and streaming. I didn't use to buy much music in the past because it was harder to get.

Logan Are you kidding? You have tons of CDs.

Hugo That's nothing. My digital collection is much bigger. Anyway, I don't listen to CDs much anymore. Only the heavy metal ones – in the car – just for you!

D **PAIR WORK** Imagine you're planning a playlist for a big family party. Decide what kinds of music to play so there's something for everyone.

INSIDER ENGLISH

We can use the informal expression *thanks to* + something or someone. It means *because of*.

3 GRAMMAR: used to

A Circle the correct answers. Use the sentences in the grammar box to help you.
1 In affirmative sentences, use **use to** / **used to** and the base form of a verb.
2 In negative sentences, use *didn't* with **use to** / **used to** and the base form of a verb.
3 In questions, use *did* with **use to** / **used to** and the base form of a verb.

> **used to**
>
> What did you **use to listen** to then?
> I **used to like** country music.
> I **didn't use to buy** much music.

B Choose the correct answers.
1 I **used to / didn't use to** like jazz, but I don't like it anymore.
2 I **used to / didn't use to** like EDM, but now I love it.
3 I **used to / didn't use to** listen to a lot of classical music. I still do, sometimes.
4 I **used to / didn't use to** have a lot of country music, but now I don't.

C ▶ Now go to page 135. Look at the grammar chart and do the grammar exercise for 7.1.

D Complete the questions with *you*, the correct form of *used to*, and the verbs in parentheses ( ). Check your accuracy. Then ask your partner the questions.
1 When you were 13, who _____ (listen) to music with?
2 What kind of concerts _____ (go) to?
3 Which singers _____ (like)?
4 Where did you _____ (buy) music?
5 Did you _____ (play) an instrument? Which one?

> ✓ **ACCURACY** CHECK
>
> Be careful not to confuse *usually* and *used to*. Don't use them in the same sentence.
>
> I usually ~~used to~~ listen to hip-hop. ✗
> I usually listen to hip-hop. ✓
> (present habit)
> I used to listen to heavy metal. ✓
> (past habit)

4 SPEAKING

A Think about how your musical tastes have changed. What kind of music did you use to like? Which artists did you use to listen to? What do you listen to now? Who are your favorite artists? Make notes.

B GROUP WORK Describe your changing musical tastes. How much do you have in common?

> I used to love rock music. When I was 13, rock was all I listened to. Now I like pop music. My favorite artist is Camila Cabello.

67

7.2 THE BEST ENTERTAINMENT

LESSON OBJECTIVE
- talk about TV shows and movies

1 VOCABULARY: TV shows and movies

A 🔊 2.04 PAIR WORK Listen and repeat the words. Which can describe movies? Which can describe TV shows? Which can describe both?

animated movie	comedy	documentary	drama	game show
horror	musical	reality show	romantic comedy	science fiction
soap opera	talk show	thriller		

B PAIR WORK Give an example of each kind of movie or show in exercise 1A.

C ▶ Now go to page 147. Do the vocabulary exercises for 7.2.

2 LANGUAGE IN CONTEXT

A Read the article. What do *the small screen* and *the big screen* mean?

Big screen or small screen?

You sit down after a long day and open an app on your smartphone. What are you going to watch this time? Maybe an episode of your favorite **game show** or **soap opera**? Your roommates are on the couch, using a tablet to binge-watch episodes of a popular **drama** series. Your friend texts you about the **documentary** she's watching on her laptop.

Many viewers think that personal devices are as good as TVs. We watch a lot of movies and TV shows on the "small screen" instead of the "big screen." But is it the same? If you like **science fiction**, you probably love special effects – the way monsters look or the way spaceships fly through the air. But on a phone, the effects aren't as exciting as they are in the theater. Watching a **horror** movie at home isn't as frightening as watching it in a dark theater. (Although maybe that's a good thing!)

Do you like watching shows on your device as much as watching on a big screen? Maybe it depends on the genre. Nothing is as much fun as watching reality shows on one big screen with your friends – and laughing together.

B Read again. How does the article suggest watching shows and movies in different ways gives people a different experience?

C Guess the meaning of these words from context. Match the words (1–5) to the definitions (a–e).

1. episode ___   a. set of television broadcasts using the same characters but in different situations
2. series ___   b. a style of TV show or movie
3. binge-watch ___   c. people who watch TV or movies
4. viewers ___   d. one of the parts of a television or radio program
5. genre ___   e. watch a lot of episodes in a short amount of time

D PAIR WORK Do you like watching TV shows and movies on a small screen or a big screen? Does it matter to you? What are the pros and cons of each option? For ideas, watch Angie's video.

Do you and Angie agree on how you like to watch TV shows and movies?

3 GRAMMAR: Comparisons with (not) as … as

A Circle the correct answers. Use the sentences in the grammar box to help you.
1. *as … as* means **the same as / different from**.
2. *not as … as* means **more than / less than**.

> **Comparisons with (not) as … as**
>
> Many viewers think that personal devices are **as good as** TVs.
> Nothing is **as much fun as** watching reality shows with your friends.
> Watching a horror movie at home is**n't as frightening as** watching it in a dark theater.
> Do you like watching on your device **as much as** watching on a big screen?

B Rewrite the sentences with (*not*) *as … as* so that they mean the same. Then think of a TV series for one or more of the sentences.
1. The first season is better than the second season.
   The second season _____*isn't as good as*_____ the first season.
2. The first season and the second season are both good.
   The second season _____ the first season.
3. The second season has more special effects than the first season.
   The first season _____ the second season.
4. I liked watching the first season more than the second season.
   I _____ the second season _____ the first season.

C ▶ Now go to page 135. Look at the grammar chart and do the grammar exercise for 7.2.

D [PAIR WORK] Talk about two movies you've watched that have a similar story or the same characters. Compare them using (*not*) *as … as*. Do you and your partner have the same opinion?

4 SPEAKING

A Look at the shows and movies in exercise 1A. Choose your three favorites kinds of shows and movies (for example, documentaries, comedies, and thrillers). For each kind, choose your favorite movie or show.

B [PAIR WORK] Talk about your favorite shows. Why do you think your favorites are the best and the others aren't as good? Do you like the same shows?

> My favorites are science fiction, thrillers, and reality shows. My favorite science fiction movie is …

> Oh, I like science fiction, too! But my favorite movie is …

7.3 A NEW BAND

LESSON OBJECTIVE
- refuse invitations and respond to refusals

1 FUNCTIONAL LANGUAGE

A 🔊 **2.05** Look at the picture. What do you think is happening? Then read and listen. What does Cody invite Mari to do? Why does Mari say she can't go?

2.05 Audio script

A Hey, Mari. Did I tell you I'm learning to play the banjo?
B Yeah, actually, you've mentioned it a few times.
A But you haven't seen my new banjo. I have a picture of it on my phone …
B We should drink our coffee before it gets cold. **Maybe after that.**
A OK. Well, anyway, I know I haven't told you this: I started a country band with a few students in my music class.
B A band? That's cool, Cody. Country isn't my favorite, but I bet you guys are great.
A Well, we're not perfect. But we think we'll get better if we play in front of an audience. So, I was wondering, would you like to hear us play? We're having our first concert on Friday night.
B Um, **I'd love to, but** I can't make it on Friday. I have … other plans. **But thanks for asking.**
A **Oh, that's too bad.** Are you free on Saturday?
B **I'm sorry. Unfortunately,** I'm going to be kind of busy all weekend.
A **I understand.** Well, **let me know if your plans change**.

B Complete the chart with expressions in bold from the conversation above.

Refusing invitations	Responding to a refusal
Maybe ¹_____ . / Maybe later.	Oh, that's ⁶_____ .
I'd ²_____ , but …	I ⁷_____ .
But thanks ³_____ .	Let me know if ⁸_____ .
I'm ⁴_____ . ⁵_____ , …	Let me know if you change your mind.

C **PAIR WORK** Choose the correct response to each sentence. Then practice the conversations with your partner.

1 A Do you want to go to a movie on Friday night?
  B a Let me know if your plans change.   b I'm sorry. Unfortunately, I have to work.
2 A I'm sorry I can't go to your soccer game on Saturday.
  B a I understand.   b I'd love to.
3 A Do you want to come over for dinner tonight?
  B a But thanks for asking.   b I'd love to, but I already have plans.
4 A I'd love to go shopping on Saturday, but I have too much to do.
  B a Let me know if you change your mind.   b I'm sorry. Unfortunately, I can't.

2 REAL-WORLD STRATEGY

> **SOFTENING COMMENTS**
> You can use *kind of* or *sort of* before adjectives to soften your comments so the other person won't feel uncomfortable.
> *Are you free on Saturday?*
> *I'm sorry. Unfortunately, I'm going to be **kind of** busy all weekend.*

A   Read the information in the box about softening comments. Which expression does Mari use?

B   🔊 2.06 Listen to a conversation between Victor and his friend Nate. What does Victor want to do? Why does Nate say "no" for Friday? Why does he say "no" for Saturday?

C   🔊 2.06 Listen again. What adjective does Nate use to describe heavy metal concerts? Which phrase does he use to soften his comment?

D   PAIR WORK   Practice the conversation with a partner and add phrases to soften the comments. More than one answer is possible. Change roles and practice again.

   A Do you want to see a documentary later?
   B No thanks. I think documentaries are boring.
   A How about a thriller?
   B I'm sorry, but I'm tired.
   A I understand. Let me know if you change your mind.

E   ▶ PAIR WORK   Student A: Go to page 158. Student B: Go to page 160. Follow the instructions.

3 PRONUNCIATION: Saying /m/ in *I'm*

A   🔊 2.07 Listen. Focus on the /m/ sound in *I'm*.
   1 Sorry. I can't go. **I'm** going to a concert that night.
   2 **I'm** kind of busy this week.

B   🔊 2.08 Listen. Which speaker (A or B) says the /m/ sound? Write *A* or *B*.
   1 ___ **I'm** sorry. I can't.
   2 ___ **I'm** going on a business trip that week.
   3 ___ I'd love to but **I'm** kind of busy tomorrow.
   4 ___ **I'm** sorry you can't go. Can we meet next week?

C   Practice the sentences in B with a partner. Does your partner say the /m/ sound in *I'm* clearly?

4 SPEAKING

A   Think of a few events that you could invite someone to. Use an idea below or your own idea.

> a night out   a party   a sporting event
> a concert   a special event

B   PAIR WORK   Invite your partner to an event. Your partner refuses your invitation. Respond to his or her refusal. Change roles and repeat.

- Do you want to go to a karaoke club tonight?
- I'd love to, but I'm kind of busy.
- OK. Let me know if your plans change.

7.4 NOT JUST FOR KIDS

LESSON OBJECTIVE
- write a movie review

1 READING

A Look at the picture. What kind of movie or TV show do you think the family is watching?

B READ FOR GIST Read the article. What is its main argument?
   a No one knows why adults like animated movies.
   b Adults and kids like animated movies for many reasons.
   c Adults don't like animated movies.

C IDENTIFY SUPPORTING DETAILS Read the article again. What details explain why these things help adults enjoy animated movies?
   1 technology
   2 real-life topics
   3 humor
   4 famous actors
   5 endings

Animation for All Ages

Animation used to be just for kids, but today, a growing number of animated movie audiences are adults without children. What makes people of all ages enjoy animated movies these days?

Hi-tech actions Today's animated characters often look very realistic thanks to technology. The characters can walk, talk, dance, and sing almost as realistically as people can. They are also better able to show their feelings through their facial expressions, so audiences of all ages feel the characters' emotions are real and important.

Real-life situations These days, animated characters deal with real-life topics, such as moving to a new place, failure and success, friendship, growing up, and growing old. These are topics that adults can understand – even if the story is about a cat, dog, robot, or dinosaur.

Adult humor Writers include humor that both children and adults enjoy, and there are often "secret jokes" that only adults find amusing.

Well-known actors Many famous actors record the voices for animated movies nowadays. This gives star power to animated movies. Adults enjoy hearing their favorite actors bring animated characters to life.

Happy endings The biggest reason people of all ages enjoy animated movies just might be the endings. They usually end in a positive way, and everyone loves a happy ending.

We all like to laugh and have an adventure with the characters in a movie, and animated movies make that possible in a colorful and magical way.

D GROUP WORK THINK CRITICALLY Do you think it's a good idea for writers to use adult humor in animated movies? Why or why not?

2 WRITING

A Read Mateo's review of *Toy Story*. Is everything in the review positive? Why or why not?

MOVIE CLASSICS

Home News Reviews Sign in

Reviews & Ratings for

Toy Story

★★★★☆

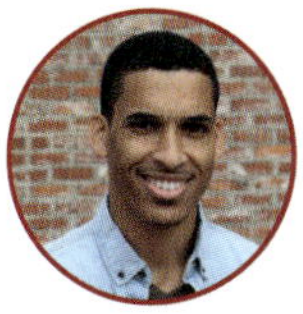

One of my favorite movies ever

Author: AnimationFanMateo

[1]I didn't use to like animated movies. But after I saw *Toy Story*, I became a fan. It's one of my favorite movies ever. The story is interesting from beginning to end. [2]If you haven't seen it, it's about toys that come alive when they're alone. Six-year-old Andy's favorite toy is Woody, a cowboy. Woody is also the leader of the other toys. But then a cool, new toy arrives – a space action figure named Buzz Lightyear. He has a lot of fancy features, and Andy is fascinated. Woody hates Buzz and tries to get rid of him, but after some adventures together, the two toys become friends. [3]*Toy Story* is as dramatic as a movie with real actors, and Woody and Buzz have the same feelings as ordinary people. Their voices are perfect, especially Tom Hanks as the voice of Woody. The story has a lot of jokes for adults, so it's fun for the whole family. My only complaint is that the animation looks a little old now. Animation technology has improved a lot since 1995.

[4]But it will always be a great movie!

GLOSSARY

dramatic *(adj)* full of action and excitement

B WRITING SKILLS **Read about organizing ideas in a movie review. Match parts 1–4 in Mateo's review with the sections below.**

___ Give a brief description of the story.

___ Give a final statement with your opinion and/or a recommendation.

___ Introduce the movie and give your feeling or opinion about it.

___ Describe positive and/or negative things about the movie.

REGISTER CHECK

When we describe a movie to a friend in a text message, we usually don't worry about organization. Notice how the order of ideas in the texts is different from the order Mateo used in his more formal review.

I just saw Toy Story again.

Yeah? I've never seen it.

Really? It's famous. The main character is the voice of Tom Hanks.

Cool! Tom Hanks is always good.

Definitely! The movie's about toys that come to life. It has some good jokes.

WRITE IT

C **Write a review of a movie you have seen. Organize your ideas in the same order Mateo used in his review.**

D PAIR WORK **Exchange reviews with a partner. Have you seen the movie your partner describes? Do you agree with his/her opinions? If you haven't seen it, would you like to?**

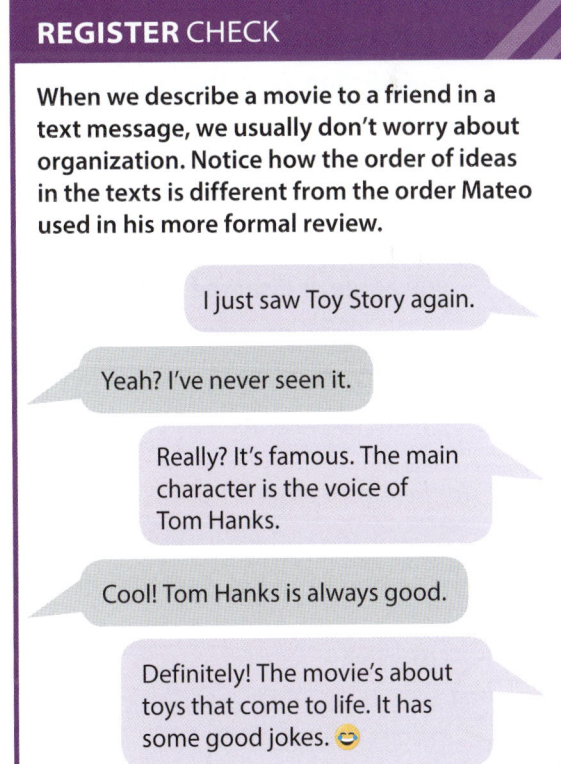

7.5 TIME TO SPEAK
Changing tastes

LESSON OBJECTIVE
- talk about changing tastes

FIND IT

A **DISCUSS** With a partner, talk about some music, movies, and TV shows you used to like five years ago. Then talk about what you like today. You can go online to find out more details about entertainment five years ago.

B **DECIDE** Which profile below describes you, and which one do you think describes your partner? Compare your ideas.

Rock: Your tastes never change.

Onion: You keep all of your old tastes and also get some new ones.

Tree: You keep some of your old tastes but lose others. You also get new tastes.

Chameleon: Your tastes keep changing completely.

C **PREPARE** In your opinion, how common is each profile in your class? With your partner, make a prediction. Rank the profiles from the most common to the least common.

D **PRESENT** Tell the class about your ranking. Then everyone in the class reveals their profile. What is the most common profile in the class? The least common? Was your prediction correct?

E **AGREE** As a class, compare the opinions below with what you learned in part D. How much do you agree or disagree with them?
- We all get bored with things eventually.
- Everyone loves to discover new things.
- Our tastes depend on our age.
- Our tastes change because trends change.
- Our tastes don't change much.

To check your progress, go to page 155.

USEFUL PHRASES

DISCUSS
I used to like … , but now I don't like it so much.
I've always liked …
My favorite … is/was …

PREPARE / PRESENT
I think everyone / most people / some people …
I don't think many people / anyone …

AGREE
I think this is true.
I disagree.
I think this is partly true.
I agree that … , but I disagree that …

UNIT OBJECTIVES
- talk about what you've been doing
- talk about progress
- catch up with people's news
- write a post about managing your time
- decide on better ways to use your time

GETTING THERE

8

START SPEAKING

A What are the people in the picture doing? Do you spend a lot of time doing this? Do you enjoy it?

B Talk about other things you do:
- only because you like to.
- only because you have to.
- because you have to but also like to.

C Imagine each day is two hours longer. With this extra time, would you do things you *want to do*, *have to do*, or both? Say what you would do. For ideas, watch Andres's video.

What would Andres do with his extra time?

8.1 SAYING AND DOING

LESSON OBJECTIVE
- talk about what you've been doing

1 LANGUAGE IN CONTEXT

A **GROUP WORK** Look at the sayings. What do they mean? You can go online to learn more about these sayings.
1 Work hard, play hard.
2 No pain, no gain.
3 You only live once.
4 Variety is the spice of life.
5 Actions speak louder than words.

B 🔊 2.09 Read and listen to three people talking about their lives. What is each person doing these days?

C 🔊 2.09 Read and listen again. Match a saying in exercise 1A to each person. There are two extra sayings.

What have you been doing lately?

Vanessa: ___ I have an opportunity to work in Mexico next year. I think it'll be an interesting experience, but it's going to be a challenge because I need to be able to speak the language. So, I've only been doing one thing lately – studying Spanish. It's a difficult job, so I haven't been going out at all. But that's OK. It'll be worth it.

Rodney: ___ At work, I've been designing a new app. It's not easy, but I'm getting there. I think it will be a big success as well as a personal achievement for me. It's not the only thing in my life, though. I'm on a soccer team, and we're doing really well. Soccer practice is a nice change after sitting in front of a computer all day. Now I just need to make time for family and friends!

Min-hee: ___ I've been doing lots of things lately! I've been painting pictures of nature – that's a fun project. I've also been learning to make sushi. It's a long process, but I'm getting better at it. And of course, I always have chores, like doing the dishes or the laundry. Yeah … it's a challenge to fit in everything I want to do. But that's what makes life interesting!

2 VOCABULARY: Describing experiences

A 🔊 2.10 Listen and say the words. Then find and underline these nouns in the text in exercise 1C.

| achievement | challenge | change | chore | job |
| opportunity | process | project | success | |

INSIDER ENGLISH

We use *It's worth it* and *It'll be worth it* to show that something is useful or enjoyable even though it takes a lot of effort.

B **PAIR WORK** Ask and answer the questions.
1 What is an annoying chore you have to do at home?
2 What's your biggest achievement?
3 What is one change that has happened in your life that was good?
4 Who has given you a good opportunity in the past? What was it?

C ▶ Now go to page 148. Do the vocabulary exercises for 8.1.

D **PAIR WORK** Look at the sayings in exercise 1A. Which one do you agree with the most? Why? For ideas, watch Brenda's video.

Which saying does Brenda talk about?

3 GRAMMAR: Present perfect continuous

A Circle the correct answer. Use the sentences in the grammar box to help you.

To make the present perfect continuous, use *have* + **be** / **been** + verb + *-ing*.

Present perfect continuous

What **have** you **been doing**?
I**'ve been painting** pictures of nature.
I **haven't been going out** at all.

 Use *have*, *haven't*, *has*, or *hasn't* in short answers. Do not use *been*.
Have you been going out?
Yes, I have. / No, I haven't.

B Complete the conversations with the correct form of the words in parentheses ( ). Then check your accuracy.

1 A What _____ lately? (you / read)
  B _____ a lot of travel blogs. (I / read)
2 A _____ recently? (you / eat out)
  B No, _____ .
    _____ at home. (I / cook)
3 A How _____ to class these days? (you / get)
  B _____ me to class. (my sister / drive)
4 A Where _____ ? (you / study)
  B _____ at the library lately. (I / study)

ACCURACY CHECK

Remember to use the correct form of *have* with the present perfect continuous.

~~I'm having~~ been studying a lot lately. ✗
I've been studying a lot lately. ✓

C **PAIR WORK** Practice the conversations from exercise 3B. Change the answers so they're true for you.

What have you been reading lately? *I've been reading some new comic books.*

D ▶ Now go to page 136. Look at the grammar chart and do the grammar exercise for 8.1.

4 SPEAKING

A Think of some activities your friends or family have been doing lately. Use the topics below or your own ideas.

child care   classes   hobbies   housework   school   work

B **PAIR WORK** Talk about what your friends or family have been doing recently.

My sister has been taking karate classes.

C **GROUP WORK** Work with another pair. Talk about the activities you discussed in your pairs. Whose activities are the most difficult? Whose are the most interesting?

8.2 STARTED, BUT NOT FINISHED

LESSON OBJECTIVE
- talk about progress

1 LANGUAGE IN CONTEXT

A   Look at the picture. What is he doing? What do you do when you're out in a city?

B   Read Monroe's social media post. What is he working on? Why is he asking his friends for advice?

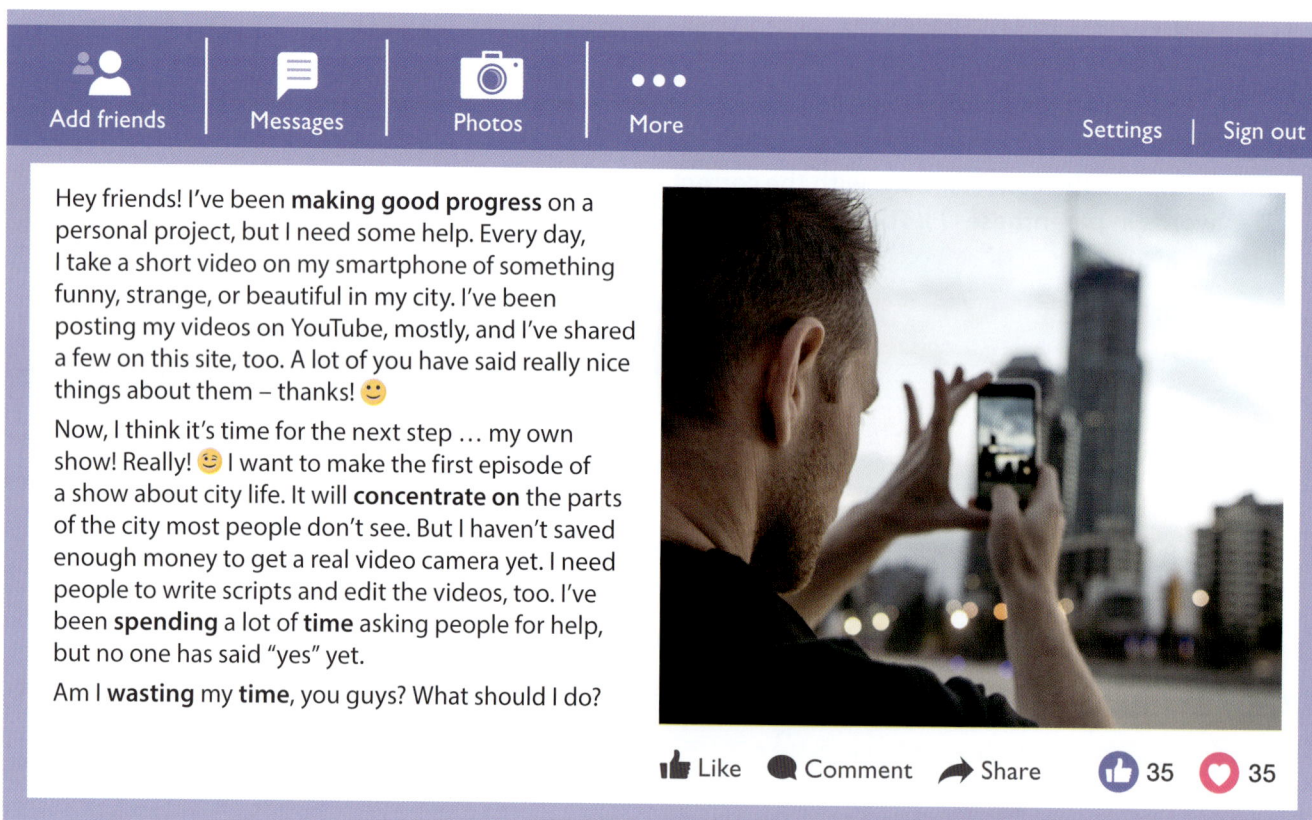

Hey friends! I've been **making good progress** on a personal project, but I need some help. Every day, I take a short video on my smartphone of something funny, strange, or beautiful in my city. I've been posting my videos on YouTube, mostly, and I've shared a few on this site, too. A lot of you have said really nice things about them – thanks! 🙂

Now, I think it's time for the next step … my own show! Really! 😊 I want to make the first episode of a show about city life. It will **concentrate on** the parts of the city most people don't see. But I haven't saved enough money to get a real video camera yet. I need people to write scripts and edit the videos, too. I've been **spending** a lot of **time** asking people for help, but no one has said "yes" yet.

Am I **wasting** my **time**, you guys? What should I do?

C   Read again. What jobs does Monroe need help with?

2 VOCABULARY: Describing progress

A   🔊 2.11 PAIR WORK Look at the pairs of sentences. Which pairs have a similar meaning? Which have an opposite or different meaning? You can use a dictionary or phone to help with words you don't know. Then listen and check.

1 A I've been **making good progress**.   B I've been **getting nowhere**.
2 A I've been **having problems with** that.   B I've been **having trouble with** that.
3 A I haven't **had time** to do that.   B I haven't **had a chance** to do that.
4 A I've been **doing my best**.   B I've been **taking it easy**.
5 A I've been **spending** a lot of **time** doing that. B I've been **concentrating on** that.
6 A I've **wasted** a lot of **time**.   B I've **saved** a lot of **time**.

B    Now go to page 148. Do the vocabulary exercises for 8.2.

C   PAIR WORK Read the last paragraph of Monroe's post again. How does he feel right now? Talk about times when you have felt like that.

3 GRAMMAR: Present perfect vs. present perfect continuous

A Circle the correct answers. Use the sentences in the grammar box to help you.

1. Use the **present perfect** / **present perfect continuous** to focus on the results of a finished activity.
2. Use the **present perfect** / **present perfect continuous** for an unfinished activity that started in the past.

Present perfect vs. present perfect continuous	
Present perfect	**Present perfect continuous**
I've **shared** a few videos on this site.	I've **been making** good **progress** on a personal project.
A lot of you **have said** nice things.	I've **been posting** my videos.
I **haven't saved** enough money.	I've **been spending** a lot of **time** asking people for help.

B Complete the paragraph with the verbs in parentheses ( ). Use the present perfect or the present perfect continuous.

Recently, I ¹ _have been trying_ (try) to find a larger apartment. It's not easy. I ² _____ (look) at ads for a few weeks, and I ³ _____ (visit) two places so far. I ⁴ _____ (think) about which one to rent, but I ⁵ _____ (not decide) yet. Actually, I'm not really sure I want to move. I ⁶ _____ (live) in my present apartment for just eight months, so maybe I should stay here a little longer.

C PAIR WORK Talk about something you've been thinking about spending money on. Say what you've looked at so far and what you've found out.

D ▶ Now go to page 136. Look at the grammar chart and do the grammar exercise for 8.2.

4 SPEAKING

A Think about something you've been working on lately, but haven't finished. Use one of the topics below or your own ideas.

| art | clubs | family | hobbies |
| school | volunteering | work | |

B PAIR WORK Talk about the things you've been working on. What have you been doing? What have you done so far? What haven't you done yet?

> I've been spending a lot of time on work for college. I've been concentrating on a project for my psychology class. So far, I've only written about two pages. I've been having trouble finding the information I need.

79

8.3 HOW HAVE YOU BEEN?

LESSON OBJECTIVE
- catch up with people's news

1 FUNCTIONAL LANGUAGE

A 🔊 2.12 Look at the picture. The women haven't seen each other for a long time. What do you think they're talking about? Then read and listen to their conversation. What topics do they mention?

🔊 2.12 Audio script

A It's great to see you again, Juliet. **It's been a long time**.

B I know. **I haven't seen you since** last spring. That was the last time I was here in Mexicali for work.

A I'm so happy you could meet me today. So, **what have you been up to**?

B Oh, **the same as usual**. Working, going to the gym, seeing friends. **What have you been doing**?

A **I've been really busy.** I got a new job in January, so …

B Hey, congratulations!

A Thanks. It's great, but there's one problem. We start work at 8:00, so I've been getting up at 6:00 every morning. Can you believe it?

B No! I remember you hated getting up early in college. By the way, how's your brother, Antonio? **What's going on with him**?

A **Not much**. He's on vacation right now. But listen. Why don't we go and have lunch together, and you can tell me all your news? I know a great Chinese restaurant.

B Really? I love Chinese food, but … we're in Mexico!

A Didn't you know that Mexicali is famous for its Chinese restaurants?

B Complete the chart with expressions in bold from the conversation above.

Saying how long it's been	Asking about someone's news	Answering
1 _____ a long time.	What 3 _____ up to?	The same 6 _____.
I 2 _____ last spring. / for a long time.	What have you 4 _____?	7 _____ (really) busy.
	5 _____ him?	Not 8 _____.
	How have you been?	

C 🔊 2.13 Choose the correct responses. Then listen and check.

1 Wow! It's been a long time. a Yeah. What have you been doing? b The same as usual.
2 What have you been up to? a What have you been doing? b Not much.
3 What's going on with Peter? a He's really busy. b It's been a long time.
4 I haven't seen you for a long time. a I know. How have you been? b The same as usual.

2 REAL-WORLD STRATEGY

A 🔊 2.14 Listen to more of Rosa and Juliet's conversation. What does Rosa suggest? What does Juliet ask?

B 🔊 2.14 Read the information in the box about using *That would be* to comment on something. Then listen again. What comment does Juliet make?

> **USING *THAT WOULD BE* TO COMMENT ON SOMETHING**
>
> You can use *That would be* (or *That'd be*) and an adjective to comment on a suggestion or possibility.
>
> *Why don't we go and have lunch together? I know a great Chinese restaurant.*
>
> *Really? **That would be great!** I love Chinese food.*

C 🔊 2.15 Listen and complete the conversation with an adjective. Then practice with a partner.

  A Lenny got another speeding ticket. His parents are thinking about taking away his car.

  B That would be _____ ! He loves his car.

D ▶ PAIR WORK Student A: Go to page 158. Student B: Go to page 160. Follow the instructions.

3 PRONUNCIATION: Saying /ɑ/ and /æ/ vowel sounds

A 🔊 2.16 Listen and repeat the two different vowel sounds.

  /ɑ/ got   Lenny got another speeding ticket.
  /æ/ haven't   I haven't seen you since last spring.

B 🔊 2.17 Listen. Write A for words with /ɑ/. Write B for words with /æ/.

  1 ___ can   4 ___ problem
  2 ___ haven't   5 ___ job
  3 ___ concentrate   6 ___ chance

C PAIR WORK Practice the words from exercise 3B with a partner. Does your partner say the /ɑ/ and /æ/ sounds?

4 SPEAKING

A PAIR WORK Imagine you are friends who haven't seen each other in a long time. Ask and answer the questions below. You can answer with your own information or make something up.

- How've you been?
- What have you been up to?
- What's going on with … ?

B PAIR WORK Continue the conversation. Suggest something you can do together, and agree on one of the ideas.

> Why don't we go get coffee? I would love to catch up. There's a nice espresso place on the corner.

> Really? That would be great! I could use a coffee.

8.4 A TIME-SAVING TIP

LESSON OBJECTIVE
- write a post about managing your time

1 LISTENING

checking email

paying bills online

doing homework

A Look at the pictures. Which activity takes the most time? Which one takes the least amount of time?

B 🔊 2.18 **LISTEN FOR EXAMPLES** Listen to the podcast. What two small activities does Naomi talk about?

C 🔊 2.18 **GUESS MEANING FROM CONTEXT** Listen again. What do these words mean?

1. wisely — a in a boring way — b in a smart way — c in an exciting way
2. technique — a a place to go — b a difficult process — c a way of doing something
3. responded — a answered someone — b asked something — c didn't understand someone
4. tasks — a times you have to be somewhere — b things you have to do — c places you go to work
5. as well as — a and — b but — c so

2 PRONUNCIATION: Listening for weak forms of *didn't*

A 🔊 2.19 Listen to the extracts from the podcast. Focus on how the speaker says the words in bold.
1. It **didn't** take very long.
2. Then I **didn't** need to put those tasks on my to-do list.

B 🔊 2.20 Listen. Which speaker (A or B) says *didn't* like the speakers in A? Write *A* or *B*.
1. ___ I didn't know how much time I was wasting.
2. ___ I could have answered the emails right away, but I didn't.
3. ___ I didn't realize paying my bills online was so easy.
4. ___ It didn't take as much time as I thought.

C Check (✓) the statement that is true.
- ☐ In fast speech, English speakers often drop the /d/ sound at the beginning of *didn't*.
- ☐ In fast speech, English speakers often drop the /t/ sound at the end of *didn't*.

3 WRITING

A Read the post Matthew wrote on the Tools for Life podcast website. What has he achieved since the podcast? Why didn't he do these things in the past?

Home   News   Radio   **Podcasts**   Community   Sign in

Tools *for* Life
▶ Episode 201: Interview with Naomi Moore

🔊 Subscribe
🔈 Listen

Comments

Matthew, Chicago
6 hours ago

After I heard this podcast, I knew I had to try Naomi's technique. I don't have many problems with emails, but I do have a lot of homework! Up to now I've had a lot of trouble managing all the work for my different classes. To be honest, sometimes I don't prepare for class as much as I should because I'm tired or busy, or have something better to do. But I always felt worried and stressed about it.

So I sat down and made a to-do list. Even that was a little frightening! I put all the jobs into two groups: short jobs (that I could do in less than five minutes) and long jobs. I immediately started with a few short jobs – I put away my papers, cleaned my desk, and things like that. I felt much happier right away. I had so much energy, I worked on one of my "long jobs" afterward – I wrote an outline for a research paper that's due next week.

So far, this has been working well! I feel more positive about what's on my to-do list. From now on, I'm going to try to study a little every day, and I'll probably finish my research paper early next week. If you're stressed about organization, definitely try Naomi's plan!!

👍 Like 7   💬 Reply   ⤴ Share   🚩 Report

B PAIR WORK THINK CRITICALLY How has this technique changed Matthew's life? Do you think he'll continue to make improvements? Why or why not?

C WRITING SKILLS Read the information about time expressions and match the time expressions (1–4) with ones of the same meaning (a–d). Then find and underline some of the time expressions in Matthew's post.

Use time expressions to talk about actions and experiences in the present, past, and future.

1 immediately ___
2 so far ___
3 before ___
4 in the future ___

a up to now
b from now on
c right away
d in the past

REGISTER CHECK

We often put time phrases at the beginning of sentences in more formal writing. In informal writing, we often put them at the end.

Formal: *From now on, I'm going to try to study a little every day.*
Informal: *I'm going to try to study a little every day from now on.*

WRITE IT

D Write a post about how you manage your time and the things you have to do. If you already use Naomi's technique (or a similar one), describe your experiences. If you don't use a time-management technique, describe how you've been managing up to now and say what you might do in the future to manage your time better.

E PAIR WORK Exchange posts with a partner. Would you like to use any of your partner's time-management ideas?

8.5 TIME TO SPEAK
Building a better life

LESSON OBJECTIVE
- decide on better ways to use your time

A **PREPARE** Look at the words below. Which things make you happy, and which ones don't? Write them in the pyramid above, with the things you like best at the top and things you like least at the bottom.

| chores | commuting | exercise | family | free-time activities |
| friends | learning | rest | travel | work |

B **DECIDE** Share your pyramid with your partner. Discuss how you've been spending your time lately and compare it with the information in your pyramid. Then each decide on two things you'd like to spend more time on and two things you'd like to spend less time on.

C **DISCUSS** In groups, share the things you want to spend more time on and less time on. Give each other advice on how to make these changes in your lives. Your ideas can be big, small, serious, or funny. Be creative!

D **PRESENT** Tell the class about the best advice you got from your group in part C.

E **AGREE** As a class, choose the three most creative ideas you heard in part D.

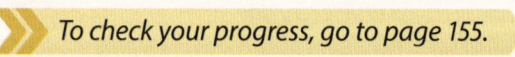
To check your progress, go to page 155.

USEFUL PHRASES

PREPARE
… makes me happy.
I enjoy …
I don't really like …
I'm not interested in …

DECIDE
I've been spending a lot of time …
I haven't had (much) time to …

DISCUSS
I want to spend more/less time …
You could … Or you could …
What about … ing … ?

MAKE IT WORK

9

UNIT OBJECTIVES
- talk about college subjects
- discuss rules for working and studying at home
- express confidence and lack of confidence
- write the main part of a résumé
- decide how to use your skills

START SPEAKING

A   Where do you think this man is working? Do you know anyone that works from an unusual place? Why?

B   What kind of job do you think this man does? What other jobs allow people to telecommute?

C   Discuss the pros and cons of working like this. Would you like it? Why or why not?

D   Do you think the man is telecommuting because he *chooses to* or because he *has to*? How much choice do most people have about where or how they work or study? For ideas, watch Angie's video.

REAL STUDENT

Does Angie have the same ideas you do?

85

9.1 BUILDING A FUTURE

LESSON OBJECTIVE
- talk about college subjects

1 VOCABULARY: College subjects

A 🔊 2.21 **PAIR WORK** Listen and say the words. Give an example of something students learn about in each college subject.

architecture   biology   business
chemistry   computer science economics
education   engineering   law
medicine   physics   political science

B **PAIR WORK** Which are your favorite subjects? Which are you not interested in? Why?

C ▶ Now go to page 149. Do the vocabulary exercises for 9.1.

2 LANGUAGE IN CONTEXT

A **PAIR WORK** What jobs do you think the subjects in exercise 1A are useful for? Why?

B 🔊 2.22 Read and listen to the conversation between two cousins. Have they thought about their future jobs? What are they going to do?

🔊 2.22 Audio script

Ian So, when will you start training as a mechanic?

Luca Well, actually, I'm going to get a degree in automotive **engineering** instead.

Ian Why do you need to get a degree? I thought you were going to work in your dad's garage.

Luca I am. But Dad says I have to get a degree first. Anyway, what about you?

Ian I'm going to create my own program of study. I want to take courses in **business**, **education**, and maybe **biology**.

Luca Wow, that's an interesting mix! But don't you have to choose a major?

Ian No. It's like I'm creating my own major. Here, this is from the college website: "Applicants must take 120 credits of any subject to get a degree."

Luca Interesting. So, what kind of job do you want to get after that?

Ian For now, I'm going to take classes I like and see how it goes. I don't have to choose a job yet.

Luca True. Well, with a degree like that, I guess you'll be ready for anything!

GLOSSARY
degree (n) a qualification you get for finishing college
major (n) the most important part of your study in college

C 🔊 2.22 Read and listen again. How is Ian's program different from Luca's?

D **PAIR WORK** Would you like to create your own major? Why or why not? For ideas, watch Andrea's video.

INSIDER ENGLISH
We use *see how it goes* to say we will allow a situation to develop for some time before we make a decision.

REAL STUDENT

What kind of program of study does Andrea want?

3 GRAMMAR: Modals of necessity: *have to, need to, must*

A Circle the correct answers. Use the sentences in the grammar box to help you.
1. Use *have to*, *need to*, or *must* to say something is **necessary** / **not necessary**.
2. Use *don't have to* or *don't need to* to say something is **necessary** / **not necessary**.
3. After *have to*, *need to*, or *must*, use the **base form** / ***-ing*** form of the verb.

> **Modals of necessity: *have to, need to, must***
>
> I **have to get** a degree first.
> I **don't have to choose** a job yet.
> Applicants **must take** 120 credits of any subject to get a degree.
> Why do you **need to get** a degree?
> Don't you **have to choose** a major?

B Complete the sentences with the correct forms of the words in parentheses ( ). Use the simple present. Then tell a partner if you agree with the sentences.
1. You _____ (not have to / work) hard to be successful.
2. When you _____ (need to / shop) for clothes, it's best to order them online.
3. You _____ (need to / think) about what job you want in the future and then choose what to study.
4. I _____ (have to / do) a lot of chores, but most of them are a waste of time.

C ▶ Now go to page 137. Look at the grammar chart and do the grammar exercise for 9.1.

D Complete the sentences with your own ideas. Then share with a partner.
1. When I was in school, I had to _____ .
2. Now, I don't need to _____ .
3. To be successful, college students need to _____ .
4. In my country, students don't have to _____ .

4 SPEAKING

A Think of a job you want to have. What do you need to learn to get this job? Make a list of three subjects. Think about how you could learn these subjects.

B PAIR WORK Compare your lists and talk about how you will learn these subjects. What do you think will happen when you learn them?

> I want to be an architect. I'm really interested in cool buildings.

> You probably need to take art classes.

C GROUP WORK Join another pair. Make a plan for your group to learn your new subjects. Whose subjects are more interesting? Whose subjects seem harder? Can you think of creative ways to use your new knowledge?

9.2 HOUSE RULES

LESSON OBJECTIVE
- discuss rules for working and studying at home

1 LANGUAGE IN CONTEXT

A Look at the picture of a self-employed woman. What do you think is good about working from home? What's difficult?

B Read the posts on an internet forum. What two things does Rina want help with?

C Read again. Summarize what Theo, Lynn, and Kosuke suggest.

Posted at 10:02 a.m.

Rina I just started my own small business and am working from home. I need to make some rules for myself. Any suggestions?

Theo You have to imagine you're going to an office. Get up, get dressed, and have the same working hours every day. You can take short breaks, of course, but you can't waste time. For example, you shouldn't do chores during working hours because you'll never get your work done. And you must not miss your deadlines!

Lynn Make time for yourself. You can't spend all of your time on work. Sometimes, it's hard to stop working when your office is in your home.

Rina Thanks! I see it's going to be important to manage my time. Now, any tips on how to manage my files? I work for a lot of different employers, and my wages are different for each contract.

Kosuke There are a lot of great computer programs to help you with that kind of thing.

Rina Thanks, Kosuke. May I email you? I'd love to chat more about those programs.

Kosuke Of course! My #1 rule for working at home: Get help when you can!

GLOSSARY
deadline *(n)* a time or day by which something must be done

2 VOCABULARY: Employment

A 🔊 2.23 Find and <u>underline</u> six of these words in the posts in exercise 1C. Then write all of the words in the correct places in the chart and discuss what they mean. You can use a dictionary or your phone to look up words you don't know. Then listen and check.

| apply | career | contract | employer | fire | hire |
| manage | profession | retirement | salary | wage | working hours |

Nouns	Verbs

B ▶ Now go to page 149. Do the vocabulary exercises for 9.2.

C **GROUP WORK** Which problem do you think is worse for people who work at home – not working enough or working too much? Why?

88

3 GRAMMAR: Modals of prohibition and permission

A Circle the correct answers. Use the sentences in the grammar box to help you.
1. Use *can't* or *must not* to say you **are / aren't** allowed to do something.
2. Use *can, may,* or *could* to say you **are / aren't** allowed to do something.

> **Modals of prohibition and permission**
>
> Prohibition: *can't, must not*   Permission: *can, may, could*
> You **can't waste** time.   You **can take** short breaks.
> You **must not miss** your deadlines. **May** I **email** you?

> ! *Must not* does not have the same meaning as *don't have to*. *Must not* means you <u>can't</u> do something. *Don't have to* means you <u>can</u> do something, but it's <u>not necessary</u>.

B Circle the correct answers. Check your accuracy. Then practice the conversation with a partner. Do you agree with Mario or Sarah about working from home on Fridays?

Mario I heard that we can work from home on Fridays now. ¹*Can / Must* we work any hours we want?
Sarah No, we ²*may / can't*. We have to work from 9:00 a.m. to 5:00 p.m.
Mario I guess we ³*can / must not* take breaks, though.
Sarah Yeah, but you have to log in and ⁴*can / can't* stop working for more than 15 minutes at a time – except at lunchtime. And the boss's email also says, "You ⁵*could / must not* use your computer for personal use." Our computers know everything.
Mario And they tell the boss! But it's still great that we ⁶*can / could* work from home.
Sarah I don't know. I think we're going to have to work harder than in the office.

> ✓ **ACCURACY CHECK**
>
> You can use *could* to ask for permission, but not to give someone permission.
> Could I email you? ✓
> ~~Yes, you could email me.~~ ✗

D ▶ Now go to page 137. Look at the grammar chart and do the grammar exercise for 9.2.

E Complete the sentences with your own ideas.
1. When you study at the library, you must not _____ .
2. If you study with me at my house, you can't _____ , but you can _____ .
3. Can I _____ after class?

4 SPEAKING

A Make a list of rules for working or studying at home. Think of as many ideas as you can. Be creative!

B ⬛ PAIR WORK   Compare your lists. Then choose your three best ideas.

> You can't have a lot of snacks in the house when you work from home. You'll eat all day and not get anything done!

> True. But you can take breaks for meals. And you need to eat away from your desk.

C ⬛ GROUP WORK   Present your three ideas to another pair. Which ideas are the most helpful?

89

9.3 A NEW CHALLENGE

LESSON OBJECTIVE
- express confidence and lack of confidence

1 FUNCTIONAL LANGUAGE

A 🔊 2.24 **PAIR WORK** Look at the picture of a jujitsu class. Say why someone might be worried about starting jujitsu. Then read and listen to two coworkers talking about the class. What is the woman worried about? How does the man respond?

🔊 **2.24 Audio script**

A   I heard you're giving jujitsu lessons to some of our coworkers.
B   I am. We're starting next week. Why don't you join us?
A   Me, doing jujitsu? **I'm not sure I can handle** that!
B   Why not?
A   **I don't think I'm strong enough**.
B   It's not about being strong, it's about technique. And if you're worried about falling …
A   Well, yeah. **That concerns me** a little!
B   Honestly, **that won't be a problem**. You'll learn to fall safely. And it's a beginners' group.
A   OK. And who's in the group?
B   Well, if you join us, you'll have to fight with your boss!
A   Well, **that doesn't bother me**. **I think I can handle** that!

B Complete the chart with expressions in bold from the conversation.

Expressing confidence	Expressing lack of confidence
That won't [1]_____ .	I'm not sure [4]_____ that.
That doesn't [2]_____ .	I don't think I'm strong [5]_____ .
I think [3]_____ that.	That [6]_____ a little.

C **PAIR WORK** For each sentence, choose a response from the chart in exercise 1B to say how you feel. Then practice the conversations with a partner.

1 The pilot is sick. You need to fly the plane and land it!
2 We're inviting 15 people to the barbecue. Can you make all the food?
3 For your English test, you'll need to write five sentences in the simple past.
4 On the team-building course, you'll have to hike 25 miles (40 km) in the mountains.

2 REAL-WORLD STRATEGY

A 🔊 2.25 Listen to the conversation. What does Robin invite Tim to do? Does he accept?

B 🔊 2.25 Read the information in the box about focusing on reasons. Then listen again. What's the reason why Tim doesn't like mountain biking?

> **FOCUSING ON REASONS**
> You can use *The thing is* to focus on the reason why you don't want to or can't do something.
> *Me, doing jujitsu? I'm not sure I can handle that!* **The thing is**, *I'm not very strong.*

C Complete the conversation with a reason why you can't go swimming. Then practice the conversation with a partner. Who gave the best reason?
   A Would you like to go swimming with me on Sunday morning?
   B Thanks for the offer, but I can't. _____

D ▶ PAIR WORK Student A: Go to page 158. Student B: Go to page 160. Follow the instructions.

3 PRONUNCIATION: Grouping words

A 🔊 2.26 Listen and repeat. Focus on how words are grouped.
   A I don't think / I'm strong / enough.
   B It's not about / being strong, / it's about / technique.

B 🔊 2.27 Group the words in the conversation. Mark the groups with a /. Then listen and check.
   A Would you like to go swimming with me on Sunday morning?
   B Thanks for the offer, but I can't. I'm taking my sister to breakfast for her birthday.
   A OK. Well, I go every Sunday morning. What about the next Sunday?

C PAIR WORK Work with a partner. Practice the conversation in B with a partner. Does your partner say the word groups correctly?

4 SPEAKING

A Think of some challenging sports or outdoor activities that people can do in or near your city. Make notes.

B PAIR WORK Use your ideas to plan a weekend challenge for a group of people. Choose one activity for Saturday morning and one for Saturday afternoon.

C GROUP WORK Tell other pairs about your plan. They say whether or not they can handle the activities and say if they'd like to join your group.

> So, in the morning we're going to go skateboarding at the skate park.

> That won't be a problem. I used to skateboard when I was a kid.

> I'm not sure I can handle that. The thing is, my legs aren't very strong.

9.4 A JOB SEARCH

LESSON OBJECTIVE
- write the main part of a résumé

1 READING

A **RECOGNIZE TEXT TYPES** Look at the two texts. What is each one from? Choose from the words in the box. You can use a dictionary or your phone to help with words you don't know.

> a cover letter   a guidebook   a job ad
> a job application   a passport application   a résumé

CareerQuest.com

Local Jobs | Search Jobs | Events | Résumé Help | Join | Log In

Description:
We're looking for someone reliable and intelligent to join our growing team. The perfect applicant is ready for a new challenge. This is an excellent opportunity if you're interested in a "people profession." Salary is based on experience.

Responsibilities:
You will help us design our programs and increase our business. You must be able to deal with difficult customers calmly. Working hours are usually from 9:00 a.m. to 5:00 p.m., but you also have to work two evenings a week.

Qualifications:
You need to have a two-year or four-year degree in education, business, or similar. You should have at least two years of work experience. You need strong communication skills and basic computer skills, and you must write well. You need to work well in a group and by yourself.

APPLY NOW

GLOSSARY
applicant (n) a person who applies for a job
qualifications (n) skills or experiences that prepare you to do a job or activity

---

Jacob Bradley

- 298 Willow Street, Denver, Colorado 80123
- 303-555-2910
- jbradley23@metmail.com

PROFESSIONAL PROFILE
I have a degree in education with one year of experience as a teacher's assistant at a high school. I'm bilingual (English and Spanish). My biggest accomplishment so far is starting an after-school technology program for teens. I'm also a soccer coach, and I play on a basketball team. I learn new things quickly and get along well with people of all ages.

EXPERIENCE

B **READ FOR DETAILS** Read both texts. Answer the questions.
1. What kind of person does the employer want to hire?
2. If the person is hired, when will he or she have to work?
3. Compare Jacob's profile with the qualifications needed. Do you think he should apply for the job?

C **PAIR WORK** **THINK CRITICALLY** Look at the first text again. What do you think the job is? You can think of several possibilities.

2 WRITING

A Read the rest of Jacob Bradley's résumé. What are the four main sections? What jobs has he had? Which one does he still have?

EXPERIENCE

Teacher's Assistant, Fairmount High School, Denver, CO
- Help plan and teach business and English classes to students in grades 10–12
- Organize classroom projects and day trips for the students

Barista, Carlo's Coffee, Denver, CO
- Prepared hot and cold drinks for customers
- Cleaned machines, work areas, and customer seating areas

EDUCATION
- Bachelor of Arts in Education, University of Colorado Boulder

SKILLS
- Fluent in English and Spanish; beginner-level Japanese
- Experienced in MS Office, Adobe Photoshop, web design
- Excellent time-management and communication skills

ACTIVITIES
- Coach, Soccer for Kids (neighborhood program)
- Member, Hoops Community Basketball

B **WRITING SKILLS** Read about how to write a résumé. Then look at Jacob's résumé in exercise 2A and check (✓) the things he has done. What has he not done?

- [ ] Use present verbs to describe a current job and past verbs to describe past jobs.
- [ ] Include dates for your past jobs, and put the most recent one first.
- [ ] Use bullet points and incomplete sentences (with no subject).
- [ ] List your degrees or certificates. Include dates, and put the most recent ones first.
- [ ] List skills that are useful for jobs. They can be skills you learned or personal skills.
- [ ] List activities and interests that show you are active, creative, or good with people.

REGISTER CHECK

In résumé writing, people often use parallel structures in bulleted lists.

Simple present verbs	Simple past verbs	Nouns to describe positions/people
– Help plan and teach …	– Prepared hot and cold drinks …	– Coach, Soccer for Kids …
– Organize classroom projects …	– Cleaned machines …	– Member, Hoops Community …

 WRITE IT

C Write the main part of a résumé. Begin with EXPERIENCE and end with ACTIVITIES. You can include real information or make it up. Follow the rules in exercise 2B and use parallel structures under each heading.

D **PAIR WORK** Exchange résumés with a partner. Ask your partner about one item from each of their resume sections: Experience, Education, Skills, and Activities. Do you have anything surprising in common?

9.5 TIME TO SPEAK
Design your perfect job

LESSON OBJECTIVE
- decide how to use your skills

A **DISCUSS** With a partner, talk about the skills and interests you need for your job – or a job you'd like to do. Compare them with your partner's job.

> In engineering, you have to be good at math and physics. And you need to be interested in technology and computers.

> In accounting, you have to be good at math, but you don't need to know about physics. You also …

B **RESEARCH** Now tell your partner about skills and interests you have, which you <u>don't</u> need for the job you chose in part A. Together, think of other jobs you could do in order to use these skills. You can go online to find the names of jobs you don't know in English.

> I'm good at cooking. And I really like writing.

> OK. So, you could be a journalist who writes about food and restaurants.

C **PREPARE** With your partner, design a real or imaginary job for each of you that uses as many of your skills and interests as possible. Invent a title for your job.

D **PRESENT** Tell the class about your partner's job and why it would be perfect for him/her.

E **AGREE** The class chooses: (a) the most useful job, (b) the most amusing job, and (c) the coolest job.

To check your progress, go to page 155.

USEFUL PHRASES

DISCUSS
You have to be good at …
You need to know a lot about …
You have to be interested in …

RESEARCH / PREPARE
You could make/help/sell/design …
You could be a / work in a …

PRESENT
My partner's job is …
It would be perfect for him/her because …

REVIEW 3 (UNITS 7–9)

1 VOCABULARY

A Complete the chart with the words and phrases below. Then write a category name for each group.

> career · challenge · drama · EDM · education
> hip-hop · jazz · opportunity · physics · political science
> reality show · retirement · soap opera · success · wage

_____	_____	_____	_____	_____
classical	game show	achievement	chemistry	profession

B Add at least two more words or phrases to each group.

2 GRAMMAR

A Circle the correct words to complete the conversation.

A ¹*Can / Must* I change the channel? I really don't like scary movies.

B Me either. I ²*usually liked / used to like* horror movies a lot when I was a teenager, but not anymore. New horror movies are not ³*as good as / as better as* old ones.

A I agree. By the way, have you ⁴*seen / been seeing* any good movies recently?

B Well, I ⁵*don't go / haven't been* to the movies in such a long time. ⁶*I work / I've been working* so hard lately. ⁷*I visited / I've been visiting* clients almost every day. I think ⁸*I've visited / I've been visiting* about 20 clients this month.

A You ⁹*need to / must* have some fun. Your social life is ¹⁰*as important as / more important as* your job. Anyway, you ¹¹*didn't use / didn't used* to be so serious about work in the past.

B I know, but in the past, I wasn't a father, so I ¹²*didn't have to / hadn't to* worry about the future … And hey, I do have a social life – watching TV with you!

B **PAIR WORK** Has your taste in movies changed since you were younger? What kinds of movies did you use to watch? What do you watch today?

3 SPEAKING

PAIR WORK Talk to your partner about one of these topics. Answer your partner's questions and give as many details as possible.

- Choose a real or invented thing you have been doing a lot lately that makes you happy. Talk to your partner about it. Give and get details.
- Choose a real or invented thing you have been doing that you're not happy about. Why have you been doing it?

> I've been learning to surf. I've been taking lessons since the beginning of summer. I've already made some progress, but I have to practice a lot more …

4 FUNCTIONAL LANGUAGE

A Complete the conversation with the phrases below.

a long time	be a problem	been up to	have you been	I'd love to
if you change	I haven't seen you	I'm not sure	I understand	I've been
kind of	not much	thanks for asking	the thing is	too bad

A Dmitri? Wow. Is that you?
B Raheem! [1]_____ since we graduated.
A Yeah. It's been [2]_____.
B What have you [3]_____?
A [4]_____. Working, playing tennis … What about you? What [5]_____ doing?
B [6]_____ really busy. I went back to school, so I've been working and studying.
A Nice! Hey, do you still play tennis? I'm on my way to the gym now. Come with me, and we can play together.
B [7]_____ I can handle that. I haven't played for about three years.
A That won't [8]_____. We can take it easy.
B [9]_____, I broke my arm three years ago, and I stopped playing. But [10]_____.
A [11]_____. Look, some friends are coming over for dinner on Saturday. Would you like to join us?
B [12]_____, but I can't. Actually, I'm going to be [13]_____ busy this weekend. I have to study for my exams.
A That's [14]_____. Let me know [15]_____ your mind.

5 SPEAKING

A PAIR WORK Choose one of the situations below. Act it out in pairs.

■ You have a job interview tomorrow, but you don't feel very confident about it. Talk to your partner and describe how you feel. Go to page 90 for useful language.

> I don't think I'm prepared for my job interview tomorrow.

> Why not? You have so much experience.

> That won't be a problem. The thing is, I don't know much about the company …

■ You and your partner were classmates a year ago. You haven't seen each other since that time. Talk about what the two of you have been doing. Go to page 80 for useful language.

> It's been a long time. What have you been doing?

> The same as usual. I've been …

■ You're painting your apartment this weekend. Invite your partner to have lunch and then help you with the job. Go to page 70 for useful language.

> I'm painting my apartment this weekend. Would you like to come for lunch and help me?

> I'm sorry. Unfortunately, …

B Change roles and repeat the role play.

WHY WE BUY

10

UNIT OBJECTIVES
- say what things are made of
- talk about where things come from
- question or approve of someone's choices
- write feedback about company products
- design a commercial

START SPEAKING

FIND IT

A   Imagine you're in this store. Would you buy any candy? What kinds? You can go online to learn the words for different kinds of candy in English.

B   How did you decide which candy to buy, and how much? Do you think the child is choosing his candy for the same reasons? Do you think adults and children make decisions about what to buy for the same reasons? Why or why not?

C   Think of something you bought recently. Explain why you decided to buy it. For ideas, watch Andrea's video.

REAL STUDENT — *What did Andrea buy? Were any of her reasons similar to yours?*

97

10.1 GREEN CLOTHES

LESSON OBJECTIVE
- say what things are made of

1 VOCABULARY: Describing materials

A 🔊 2.28 **PAIR WORK** Listen and say the words for materials. Then look at the picture. Which of these materials do you see? What other things do we wear that use these materials?

| cotton | glass | leather | metal | plastic |
| polyester | stone | wood | wool | |

B 🔊 2.29 Listen and say the adjectives. Which are opposites? Which describe something the man is wearing?

| artificial | fragile | hard | heavy | light |
| natural | soft | strong | warm | waterproof |

C ▶ Now go to page 150. Do the vocabulary exercises for 10.1.

2 LANGUAGE IN CONTEXT

A Read the text from a clothing company's website. What questions does it ask? Which ones can you answer?

B Read again. Which material is more environmentally friendly: cotton or polyester? Why?

INSIDER ENGLISH

We use *-friendly* with a noun to say that something is not harmful or that it's appropriate for a specific group of people. Common expressions with *-friendly* are eco-friendly, budget-friendly, family-friendly, customer-friendly, and earth-friendly.

Eco Stitch

○ Women | ○ Men | ○ Kids | ○ Sale | ○ About us

🛒 Shopping cart
Search

Are your clothes "green"?

For many of the things we buy, like paper products and cars, we know what's green and what's not. That knowledge helps us make eco-friendly choices. Our goal at Eco Stitch is to help you do the same with your clothing.

Unless you're wearing that **wool** sweater your grandmother knitted, you might not know what your clothes are made of. The names of the materials are written on the labels, but have you ever looked at them? Most people are interested in how fashionable the clothes are, not whether they're **cotton** or **polyester**.

Even if you know what materials you're wearing, do you know how eco-friendly they are? Cotton is taken from plants, and because it's **natural**, many people think it is more environmentally friendly than polyester, which is **artificial**. However, a lot of chemicals are used by most cotton farmers, and large amounts of water are needed, too. Meanwhile, polyester is often made from recycled **plastic** bottles. It's also **warmer** and **lighter** than cotton, so less material is needed!

We're here to help you make the best choices for you.

LEARN MORE.

GLOSSARY
green *(adj)* environmentally-friendly
eco-friendly *(n)* good for the environment

C **PAIR WORK** Do you know what materials your clothes are made of? Is it important to you? For ideas, watch Angie's video.

REAL STUDENT

Do you and Angie wear similar things?

3 GRAMMAR: Simple present passive

A Circle the correct answers. Use the sentences in the grammar box to help you.
1 In the passive, we **always** / **sometimes** say who or what does the action.
2 For the simple present form of the passive, use *is* or *are* + **a simple present verb** / **a past participle**.

> **Simple present passive**
>
> Cotton **is taken** from plants.
> Large amounts of water **are needed**.

> ❗ We can use *by* to show who does the action.
> *A lot of chemicals **are used** by cotton farmers.*

B ▶ Now go to page 138. Look at the grammar chart and do the grammar exercise for 10.1.

C **PAIR WORK** Complete the sentences with the simple present passive of the verbs in parentheses ( ). Then discuss whether each sentence is true for your country.
1 Warm clothes _____ for more than half of the year. (need)
2 A lot of clothes _____ in supermarkets. (sell)
3 Jeans _____ more often than other kinds of pants. (buy)
4 Hats _____ by a lot people. (wear)
5 Most coats _____ of waterproof material. (make)
6 Most of the labels on clothes _____ in English. (write)

4 SPEAKING

A **PAIR WORK** Think of ways the materials below are used. Make notes. You can go online to learn more.

> cotton   glass   plastic   wood

B **PAIR WORK** Are the materials in exercise 4A good or bad for the environment? To explain why, say how each material is used.

> Plastic is really bad. So many things are made of plastic – like bottles. And they're just thrown away.

> That's true, but some bottles are recycled. And plastic bottles are lighter than glass bottles, so it takes less energy to transport them on trucks.

C **CLASS ACTIVITY** Compare your ideas with others in the class. What did you learn about the materials?

10.2 GLOBAL OR LOCAL?

LESSON OBJECTIVE
- talk about where things come from

1 LANGUAGE IN CONTEXT

A PAIR WORK Look at the picture. What products and food items do you see? Guess where they came from.

B 🔊 2.30 Read and listen. Lucy, an economics student, is interviewing Monty. Where does Monty think his laptop, coffee, and sandwich come from? Are his ideas the same as yours?

🔊 2.30 Audio script

Lucy Thanks for helping me with my project, Monty. So, my first question is, do you know where your laptop comes from?

Monty Well, it's an American brand, but it probably wasn't made in the US. I guess it was designed there and then manufactured in China. But I didn't think about that when I bought it. I just wanted a good laptop for a good price.

Lucy I understand. And how about your coffee?

Monty I guess the coffee beans were imported. They weren't grown here in Canada, that's for sure! They were probably shipped from Brazil. I think that's where some of the best coffee comes from, and this is really good.

Lucy Yeah. And how about your sandwich?

Monty Well, I know it's fresh because it was made right in front of me. I'm not sure about the things in it, though. The tuna was probably caught and frozen weeks ago, but maybe the tomatoes were grown here. I hope so. It's good when fruit and vegetables are produced locally.

Lucy OK, thanks very much. I think I'll get one of those sandwiches now. Talking about food always makes me hungry!

C 🔊 2.30 Read and listen again. Why did Monty buy his laptop? What does he know for sure about his sandwich?

GLOSSARY
brand (n) a product that is made by a particular company

2 VOCABULARY: Production and distribution

A 🔊 2.31 Listen and repeat the verbs. Find and <u>underline</u> eight of these verbs in the interview in exercise 1B. Then answer the questions.

| catch | deliver | design | export | freeze | grow | import |
| manufacture | pick | produce | ship | store | transport | |

Which words are about:
1 moving products from one place to another?
2 creating and making things?
3 getting fish? getting fruit?
4 keeping things for a long time?

B ▶ Now go to page 150. Do the vocabulary exercises for 10.2.

C PAIR WORK Talk about …
1 three kinds of food people grow or pick in your country.
2 three things that companies in your country design or manufacture.
3 three things your country exports and three things it imports.

3 GRAMMAR: Simple past passive

A Circle the correct answers. Use the sentences in the grammar box to help you.
1. For the simple past form of the passive, use *was* or *were* + **a past participle** / **a simple past verb**.
2. In questions and negative sentences, **use** / **do not use** *did* or *didn't*.

> **Simple past passive**
>
> The tuna **was caught** weeks ago. My laptop **wasn't made** in the US.
> The coffee beans **were imported**. The beans **weren't grown** in Canada.

B Complete the paragraphs with the simple past passive of the verbs in parentheses. Check your accuracy. Then discuss with a partner: How do the two people feel about imported things? Who do you agree with more?

> **ACCURACY CHECK**
>
> Do not use the base form of a verb after *be* with the passive. Use the past participle.
>
> The coffee was ~~export~~ from Brazil. ✗
> The coffee was exported from Brazil. ✓

I bought some roses this morning. The flower shop owner told me they ¹_____ (grow) on a rose farm in Ecuador. After they ²_____ (cut), they ³_____ (store) in a refrigerated truck and ⁴_____ (take) to the airport. Then, after landing in Miami, they ⁵_____ (transport) by truck to her shop. Isn't that cool?

My coat ⁶_____ (make) in this city. It ⁷_____ (not, import). I like to support local companies. And because my coat ⁸_____ (produce) locally, it ⁹_____ (not, ship) across the world. That's important to me because a lot of resources, like gas, ¹⁰_____ (save).

C ▶ Now go to page 138. Look at the grammar chart and do the grammar exercise for 10.2.

D Complete the sentences with simple past passive verbs and your own ideas. You can go online to get more ideas. Then share them with a partner.
1. My phone _____.
2. Most of the food I eat _____.
3. A lot of the cars in my country _____.

4 SPEAKING

A GROUP WORK Make a list together of five things you have with you. Guess what country they came from. You can go online to check where these types of things usually come from.

> OK, let's start with Carrie's bag. The company is American, so I guess it was made in the US.

> Are you sure? Maybe it was designed in the US and made in India. Does it have a label?

B CLASS ACTIVITY Share what you found out in exercise 4A with the class. Which things were made the furthest away? Were you surprised about where any of the things were made? Why? Which items were you not able to find out about?

101

10.3 WHAT TO BUY?

LESSON OBJECTIVE
- question or approve of someone's choices

1 FUNCTIONAL LANGUAGE

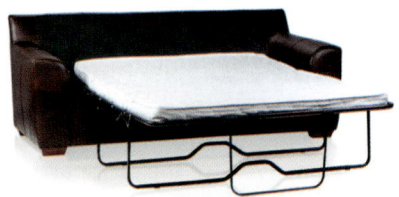
sofa bed

futon

air mattress

A 🔊 2.32 Look at the pictures. Which one do you think is the most comfortable? Then read and listen. Which two things do Ryan and Andrea talk about? Which one will Ryan get?

> 🔊 2.32 Audio script
>
> **A** Hey, Andrea. Look at this picture. What do you think of this sofa bed? It's on sale.
>
> **B** A sofa bed? **Why would you want to buy that?**
>
> **A** My friend Faruk is visiting me from Istanbul. And I don't have a place for him to sleep.
>
> **B** I see. But **do you really need a sofa bed**? You already have a couch.
>
> **A** Yeah, but it's too small to sleep on. And Faruk will be here for a week. I want him to be comfortable. And after that, it'll be good for other friends who come to stay.
>
> **B** True, but how often do people stay with you?
>
> **A** Well, not very often, actually. You know, I could get an air mattress.
>
> **B** **Now that's a good idea.** It's a lot cheaper, and you can just keep it in the closet when you aren't using it.
>
> **A** OK, you convinced me. I'll get an air mattress.
>
> **B** **That's what I would do.**

B Complete the chart with expressions in bold from the conversation.

Questioning someone's choices	Approving of someone's choices
¹_____ to buy/get that?	Now that's ³_____.
²_____ a sofa bed?	That's what ⁴_____.
Are you sure you want to get that?	I think you made the right choice.

C 🔊 2.33 Put the conversation in the correct order (1–4). Then listen and check.

___ Yeah, but it's not great. I could borrow my sister's camera, I guess.

___ That's what I would do.

___ Are you sure you want to get that? Your phone has a camera, right?

___ I'm going to buy this new camera.

2 REAL-WORLD STRATEGY

A 🔊 2.34 Darcy and Tara are shopping for gifts for their sister. Listen to their conversation. What does Tara want to buy? What does Darcy think about it?

B 🔊 2.34 Read the information in the box about changing your mind. Then listen again. What does Tara change her mind about? Why?

> **CHANGING YOUR MIND**
> You can say *Now that I think about it* or *On second thought* when you change your mind.
> OK, you convinced me. I'll get an air mattress.
> That's what I would do. But, **now that I think about it**, if you get the sofa bed, you could give me your couch!

C Complete the conversation with an expression from exercise 2B and a type of food. Then practice with a partner.

A I'm going to have the black bean chili for lunch.
B Are you sure you want to get that? It's really spicy.
A ¹_____, I'll have ²_____.
B I think you made the right choice.

3 PRONUNCIATION: Saying /u/, /ʊ/, and /aʊ/ vowel sounds

A 🔊 2.35 Listen and repeat the different vowel sounds.

/u/ you   /ʊ/ would   /aʊ/ couch

B 🔊 2.36 Put the words in the correct categories. Then listen and check.

could	Faruk	good
now	too	true

/u/	/ʊ/	/aʊ/

C Practice the words from exercises 3A and 3B with a partner. Does your partner say the vowel sounds correctly?

4 SPEAKING

A Think of something you want to buy. Use one of the categories below or your own idea.

| clothing | food | furniture | sporting goods | technology |

B **PAIR WORK** Tell your partner what you want to buy. Your partner questions or approves of your choice. Take turns.

> I'm going to buy a bike helmet.
> Do you really need a new helmet?
> Yes, I do. Mine broke in two pieces!

C **CLASS ACTIVITY** Tell the class what your partner wanted to buy and what you thought about it. Did your partner agree with your opinion?

10.4 NOT JUST CUSTOMERS – FANS

LESSON OBJECTIVE
- write feedback about company products

Cacao beans are used to make Cocobar's products.

Jon is a fan of Cocobar's chocolate.

1 LISTENING

A **PAIR WORK** Look at the pictures and read the captions. What's a fan? Talk about some companies that have a lot of fans.

B 🔊 2.37 **LISTEN FOR GIST** Listen to the podcast with host Rachel. What do business owners Erica and Tianyu say about their relationship with customers?

C 🔊 2.37 **IDENTIFY SPEAKERS** Listen again. Who gives this information? Write *R* for Rachel, *T* for Tianyu, or *E* for Erica. Sometimes more than one answer is possible. Then listen one more time and give answers for each item.

1 ___ where the beans are from
2 ___ where the products are produced
3 ___ how they want customers to feel about the products
4 ___ why fans are important to the business
5 ___ the kind of feedback fans give

D **PAIR WORK** **THINK CRITICALLY** What are some reasons why people might be fans of the company Cocobar? Think about one of your favorite companies. Why are you a fan?

2 PRONUNCIATION: Listening for contrastive stress

A 🔊 2.38 Listen to extracts from the podcast. Focus on the underlined words. Are they stressed more or less than the other words?

1 I know your products are made from cacao beans that are <u>imported</u> from Peru, but they're <u>produced</u> locally with other natural ingredients.
2 We don't want them to just <u>like</u> our products – we want them to <u>love</u> our products.

B 🔊 2.39 Listen. Underline two words in each sentence that receive the most stress.

1 Some business owners care about customer reviews, but every business owner should.
2 I started making chocolate as a hobby, but it quickly became a business.
3 If our chocolate is a little more expensive, that's because it's also much higher quality.

C Check (✓) the statement that is true.

☐ We often place additional stress on words with similar ideas.
☐ We often place additional stress on words with different ideas.

104

3 WRITING

A Read the feedback that fans posted on two company websites. What products do the fans give feedback about? Is the feedback positive, negative, or a little bit of both?

Jon
36 posts

I ordered two boxes of Cocosations last week. The chocolate bars were delivered this morning, and my mom and I immediately tried them. They're fantastic! The caramel in the middle is not too sweet, and it goes well with the dark chocolate on the outside. We noticed a little salt was included in the caramel, and that's the magic touch. Salted caramel is very popular now. Although I usually buy Cocomax bars, I'll probably buy Cocosations from now on. This is another great product from my favorite candy company – thanks, Cocobar!

Adriana
4 posts

I'm a big fan of SUPERSPORT watches. I used to have a SUPERSPORT P1, but I lost it, so yesterday I went out and bought the new SUPERSPORT P2. I notice the screen of the new watch is made of glass. In the old model, the screen was made of hard plastic. I'm not sure glass is a good idea. It's true that the old plastic screen looked a little cheap. However, it was stronger than the glass screen, and that's very important for a sports watch. Otherwise, the P2 is really good and looks cool.

GLOSSARY
feedback *(n)* an opinion from someone about something that you have done or made
otherwise *(adv)* except for what you have just said; in other ways

REGISTER CHECK

But and *though* are informal ways to show contrasts in writing. *However* and *although* are often used in more formal writing.

Informal
I used to have a SUPERSPORT P1, **but** I lost it.
I used to have a SUPERSPORT P1, **though** I lost it.

Formal
I used to have a SUPERSPORT P1. **However**, I lost it.
Although I used to have a SUPERSPORT P1, I lost it.

B **WRITING SKILLS** You can use *however* and *although* to contrast ideas. Read the sentences and underline the contrasting ideas in each sentence.

1 Although I usually buy Cocomax bars, I'll probably buy Cocosations from now on.
2 It's true that the old plastic screen looked a little cheap. However, it was stronger than the glass screen.

C Think of two products you're a fan of that are made by two different companies. Write feedback for each product. Describe the products and say what you like about them and what you don't like or how you think the companies can improve the products. Use *however* and *although* to contrast ideas.

D **PAIR WORK** Exchange feedback. What products did your partner write about? Are the posts positive, negative, or a mixture of both?

10.5 TIME TO SPEAK
Shopping psychology

LESSON OBJECTIVE
- design a commercial

Seven Reasons Why We Buy

- Pleasure
- Fear
- Needs
- Looks good
- Makes life easier
- Self-improvement
- Saves money

A DISCUSS Look at the picture of the seven reasons why we buy. In groups, think of some examples of things that are bought for each reason.

B DISCUSS People often buy things for more than one reason. Look at the things in the box. What are some reasons people buy these things?

> fast food   phone/internet plans   toothpaste

C RESEARCH Talk about commercials you've seen for the things in part B. You can go online to watch some commercials. Which reasons for buying do the commercials make you think about? Are they the same as the reasons you discussed in part B?

D PREPARE Imagine you work for an advertising company. With your group, choose a product that is used by most people. Think about reasons why people might want to buy it. Then, as a group, think of an idea for a commercial for the product.

E PRESENT Describe your commercial to the class.

F AGREE The class chooses the best commercial.

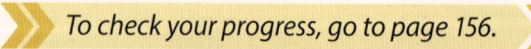
To check your progress, go to page 156.

USEFUL PHRASES

DISCUSS
… are bought for / because / in order to …

RESEARCH / PREPARE
You see a (person/ thing). They (do something). And then … At the end, …

UNIT OBJECTIVES
- talk about how to succeed
- talk about imaginary situations
- give opinions and ask for agreement
- write a personal story
- talk about a person you admire

PUSHING YOURSELF

11

START SPEAKING

A Where do you think this woman is? Why do you think she's there? What challenges do you think she's dealing with?

B Talk about something you did that was challenging. How did you feel before you did it? while you did it? after you did it?

C Why do you think people push themselves to do difficult things? For ideas, watch Andrea's video.

 *Do you agree with Andrea?*

11.1 SECRETS OF SUCCESS

LESSON OBJECTIVE
- talk about how to succeed

1 LANGUAGE IN CONTEXT

A Read the article by Ross Rivera. What is *failure*? Does Ross think it is a good or bad thing? Why?

B Read again. What qualities does the article say are good for employees to have?

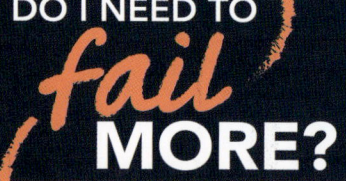

DO I NEED TO fail MORE?

As a technology writer, I spend lots of time making sure each article is as good as my last one. I've had a lot of success in my career. But could this be a bad thing?

I write about a lot of tech companies that fail, but people in the industry actually see failure as normal and an important part of later success. Evan Williams and Noah Glass, for example, once **set up** a podcasting company that didn't **work out**. They **got over it** – and joined some friends to start Twitter. A lot of international companies also agree that you have to **work at** success. Managers often promote employees who **keep up** the hard work and don't **give up** during bad times. That really makes someone **stand out** from the crowd.

I've been thinking about how I can fail more, and I think I **figured it out**. I like my writing job and don't want to **give it up**, so I'm moving on … to writing music reviews! And if that doesn't work out … well, I just hope failure is good for me.

– Ross Rivera

Evan Williams

C **PAIR WORK** Do you think the change Ross is going to make is a good idea? Why or why not?

INSIDER ENGLISH

We say *I'm moving on* to mean *I'm starting something new* or *I'm ready for something new*.

2 VOCABULARY: Succeeding

A 🔊 2.40 Find the expressions in the text and complete them with the correct preposition. Then listen and check.

1 set _____
2 work _____
3 get _____ something
4 work _____ something
5 keep _____
6 give _____
7 stand _____
8 figure something _____
9 give something _____

B ▶ Now go to page 151. Do the vocabulary exercises for 11.1.

C **PAIR WORK** Which of these statements do you agree with the most? Why?

1 If your job is making you unhappy, give it up, and set up your own business.
2 It's good to stand out and not be like everyone else.
3 If you want to be successful, never give up – keep up the hard work, no matter what.
4 If something goes wrong, don't get upset – get over it.

> I don't think it's a good idea to give up your job. You can do something fun on weekends instead.

3 GRAMMAR: Phrasal verbs

A Circle the correct answers. Use the sentences in the grammar box to help you.
1 **All / Some** phrasal verbs have an object.
2 We can **always / sometimes** put the object after the two words of a phrasal verb.
3 We can **always / sometimes** put the object between the two words of a phrasal verb.

> **Phrasal verbs**
>
> If that doesn't **work out**, I hope failure is good for me.
> They **set up** a company. They **set** it **up**.
> I **figured out** the answer. I **figured** it **out**.
> I don't want to **give up** my job. I don't want to **give** it **up**.
> They **got over** the failure. They **got over** it.

> *Give up* can have an object or it can have no object.
> You have a good job. Don't **give** it **up**.
> Keep trying. Don't **give up**.

B ▶ Now go to page 139. Look at the grammar chart and do the grammar exercise for 11.1.

C PAIR WORK Rewrite each sentence using *it*. Compare with your partner. Then discuss who might say these things (your boss? teacher? friend?).

1 You should **set up** a new company.
   You should set it up.
2 You can **figure out** the solution.
   _____
3 We're **working at** the solution.
   _____
4 Don't **give up** your job.
   _____
5 You'll **get over** the disappointment.
   _____
6 **Keep up** the good work.
   _____

D Complete the sentences with your own ideas. Then share them with a partner.
1 I'll never give up …
2 I'd like to figure out …
3 If you want to stand out, you can …

4 SPEAKING

A Think of a time in the past when something didn't go well for you, a friend, or a family member. It can be true or you can make it up. What effects did the failure have? Were any of the effects positive? Take notes.

B GROUP WORK Share your ideas with the group. What happened after the failures? Did any of the failures lead to successes?

> My teammate passed the ball to me in a really important soccer game – but I missed it, and we lost the game.

> That sounds really tough! How did you deal with that?

> Well, at first I was embarrassed. But I practiced harder for the next game.

11.2 NOW THAT'S INTERESTING!

LESSON OBJECTIVE
- talk about imaginary situations

1 LANGUAGE IN CONTEXT

A Look at the picture. What do you know about crocodiles? How dangerous are they? Why?

B 🔊 2.41 Read and listen to an interview with a successful businesswoman. What unusual and surprising question does Miles ask?

C 🔊 2.41 PAIR WORK Read and listen again. How does Selma decide what she would do? Why does she use that approach?

🔊 2.41 Audio script

Miles So, let's get right to it. Why do you think you've been so successful? Is it because you've taken risks?

Selma I think that's a big part of it – yes.

Miles Would you risk *everything* for money and success? Even your life?

Selma My life? In what kind of situation?

Miles Well, … would you swim across a river full of crocodiles if I offered you a million dollars?

Selma Now that's interesting! Let's see … if I succeeded, the reward would be fantastic. That much money would have a big effect on my life. But I'd have to consider the risk carefully – and think about how to reduce it. So, I'd find out about the number of crocodiles in the river. Um … I'd research ways to protect myself. If I spent $100,000 on a "crocodile-proof" suit, I'd still make $900,000!

Miles You're really thinking about this *seriously* …

Selma In business, you have to consider all of the options – compare the advantages and disadvantages – and then decide if the risk is worth it.

Miles And if your research showed the risk was high?

Selma I wouldn't do it. I wouldn't be able to spend a million dollars if I ended up inside a crocodile!

2 VOCABULARY: Opportunities and risks

FIND IT

A 🔊 2.42 Listen and repeat the words. Which words are nouns? verbs? both nouns and verbs? You can use a dictionary or your phone to help you. Then find and underline nine of the words in the conversation in exercise 1B.

advantage	consider	disadvantage	effect	goal	option
purpose	research	result	reward	risk	situation

B  Now go to page 151. Do the vocabulary exercises for 11.2.

C GROUP WORK Are you a risk-taker? What risks do you take? Which ones do you avoid? Why? For ideas, watch Angie's video.

Is Angie a risk-taker?

3 GRAMMAR: Present and future unreal conditionals

A Circle the correct answers. Use the sentences in the grammar box to help you.
1. In the *if* clause, use **would + verb / the simple past** to describe an imagined situation.
2. In the main clause, use **would + verb / the simple past** to describe a predicted result.

> **Present and future unreal conditionals**
>
> **Would** you **swim** across a river full of crocodiles **if** I **offered** you a million dollars?
> **If** I **succeeded**, the reward **would be** fantastic.
> **If** I **spent** $100,000 on a "crocodile-proof" suit, **I'd** still **make** $900,000!
> I **wouldn't be** able to spend a million dollars **if** I **ended up** inside a crocodile!

B  Now go to page 139. Look at the grammar chart and do the grammar exercise for 11.2.

C Complete the sentences with your own ideas. Check your accuracy. Then share your answers with a partner.
1. If I had to run a marathon, I _____.
2. I would save money if I _____.
3. I _____ if I had to give up one thing.
4. If my friends _____, I would be excited.
5. If I were really strong, I _____.
6. My parents would be happy if _____.

> ✓ **ACCURACY CHECK**
>
> Do not use *would* in the *if* clause. Use the simple past.
>
> If the risk ~~would be~~ high, I wouldn't do it. ✗
> If the risk were high, I wouldn't do it. ✓

D [PAIR WORK] Ask and answer the questions.
1. Which sport would you choose if you wanted to play a new one?
2. If you started a new business, what would it be?
3. Where would you fly if you owned a plane?

4 SPEAKING

A Think of three different activities to complete the question below. They can be silly, serious, easy, or extreme. Be creative! Take notes.
Would you … if I offered you a million dollars?

B [PAIR WORK] Compare your activities. Choose your two favorite "Would you …" questions.

C [GROUP WORK] Work with another pair. Ask and answer your questions from exercise 4A. Say what you would need to know before deciding.

> Would you walk on a tightrope if I offered you a million dollars?

> I think I would. First, I'd find out …

11.3 IT'S NOT WORTH IT

LESSON OBJECTIVE
- give opinions and ask for agreement

1 FUNCTIONAL LANGUAGE

A 🔊 **2.43** Look at the photo of the man. How does he feel, and why? Then read and listen to two people talking about him. What are his problems? What do his friends think he should do?

> 🔊 **2.43 Audio script**
>
> **A** Milo just texted me again from his office. He's really unhappy with work.
> **B** I know. But I guess it's hard to give up a good job.
> **A** **Yeah, especially when** it pays so well. But he has to work long hours, he's stressed, and he can't stop thinking about work, even on the weekends.
> **B** That's not good.
> **A** And he's a hard worker. He really pushes himself. But he thinks he's getting nowhere. If I had his job, I'd leave. **Don't you think**?
>
> **B** **Yeah, I agree with you**. It's not worth it.
> **A** But I wouldn't leave right away. I'd find a new job before I left.
> **B** Hmm, not me. I wouldn't stay at a job if I didn't like it. And I wouldn't go out and get another job immediately. It would be a chance to start something new, **right**? I mean, Milo doesn't like his job, so maybe he should think about a new career.
> **A** **Good point**. He needs to find something he likes.

B Complete the chart with expressions in bold from the conversation.

Asking for agreement	Agreeing
Don't you ¹_____?	³_____ it pays so well.
…, ²_____?	Yeah, I ⁴_____ with you.
…, you know?	Good ⁵_____.
Don't you agree?	I see what you mean.

C 🔊 **2.44** Put the conversation in the correct order (1–4). Then listen and check.

___ Good point. I should call them today, right?

___ I applied for that job two weeks ago, but I haven't heard from the company yet.

___ I would. You need to show them you're really serious about the job.

___ I think you should call them. Then they'll know you're interested. Don't you agree?

2 REAL-WORLD STRATEGY

A 🔊 **2.45** Listen to a conversation between Noah and Callie, two of Milo's colleagues. What did they both notice?

B 🔊 **2.45** Read the information in the box about softening an opinion. Then listen again. Which opinions do Noah and Callie soften?

> **SOFTENING AN OPINION**
> You can use *I guess* or *I feel like* to soften an opinion.
> **I guess** it's hard to give up a good job. / **I feel like** it's hard to give up a good job.

C Complete another conversation with expressions from exercise 2B. More than one answer is possible. Then practice with a partner.

A That exam was really strange. _____ there were some errors in the questions.
B Yeah, I see what you mean. _____ we should ask the teacher about it. Don't you agree?

3 PRONUNCIATION: Saying /ʃ/ and /dʒ/ sounds

A 🔊 **2.46** Listen and repeat. Focus on the sounds of the letters in bold.

1 /ʃ/   pu**sh**es   He really pu**sh**es himself.   2 /dʒ/   **j**ust   Milo **j**ust texted me.

B 🔊 **2.47** Which words have the /ʃ/ sound, and which have the /dʒ/ sound? Put the words in the correct categories. Then listen and check.

| especially | job | should | | /ʃ/ | /dʒ/ |
| fashion | eject | | | | |

C **PAIR WORK** Practice saying the words in exercises 3A and 3B with a partner. Does your partner say the /ʃ/ and /dʒ/ sounds correctly?

4 SPEAKING

A **PAIR WORK** Together, choose one of these topics to discuss. Choose opposite sides of the argument.

> 1 Technology is driving people apart. **vs.** Technology is bringing people together.
> 2 Get a degree or certificate before getting a job. **vs.** You don't need a degree. Get a job and learn while you work.
> 3 Pets are good for people. **vs.** Pets are a lot of trouble.

B On your own, think about opinions and points that support your side of the argument in exercise 4A. Take notes.

C **PAIR WORK** Give your opinions. Try to get your partner to agree. You can use expressions to soften some of your opinions. When you're finished, tell the class which topic you chose and whether you agreed in the end.

> Technology is definitely driving people apart. Everyone just looks at their screens all the time. No one talks anymore.

> True, but they're still communicating.

11.4 OUTSIDE THE COMFORT ZONE

LESSON OBJECTIVE
- write a personal story

1 READING

A **IDENTIFY POINT OF VIEW** Read the article. Then read about point of view (POV) below. Which POV does the writer use? Why do you think she uses it?

☐ First person: The writer talks about herself and her own experiences.
☐ Second person: The writer speaks directly to the reader.
☐ Third person: The writer talks about other people's experiences.

B **NOTE TAKING** Read the article again. What is your "comfort zone"? Is it good or bad? Why? How does the article suggest "leaving your comfort zone"? Take notes. Then compare your notes with a partner.

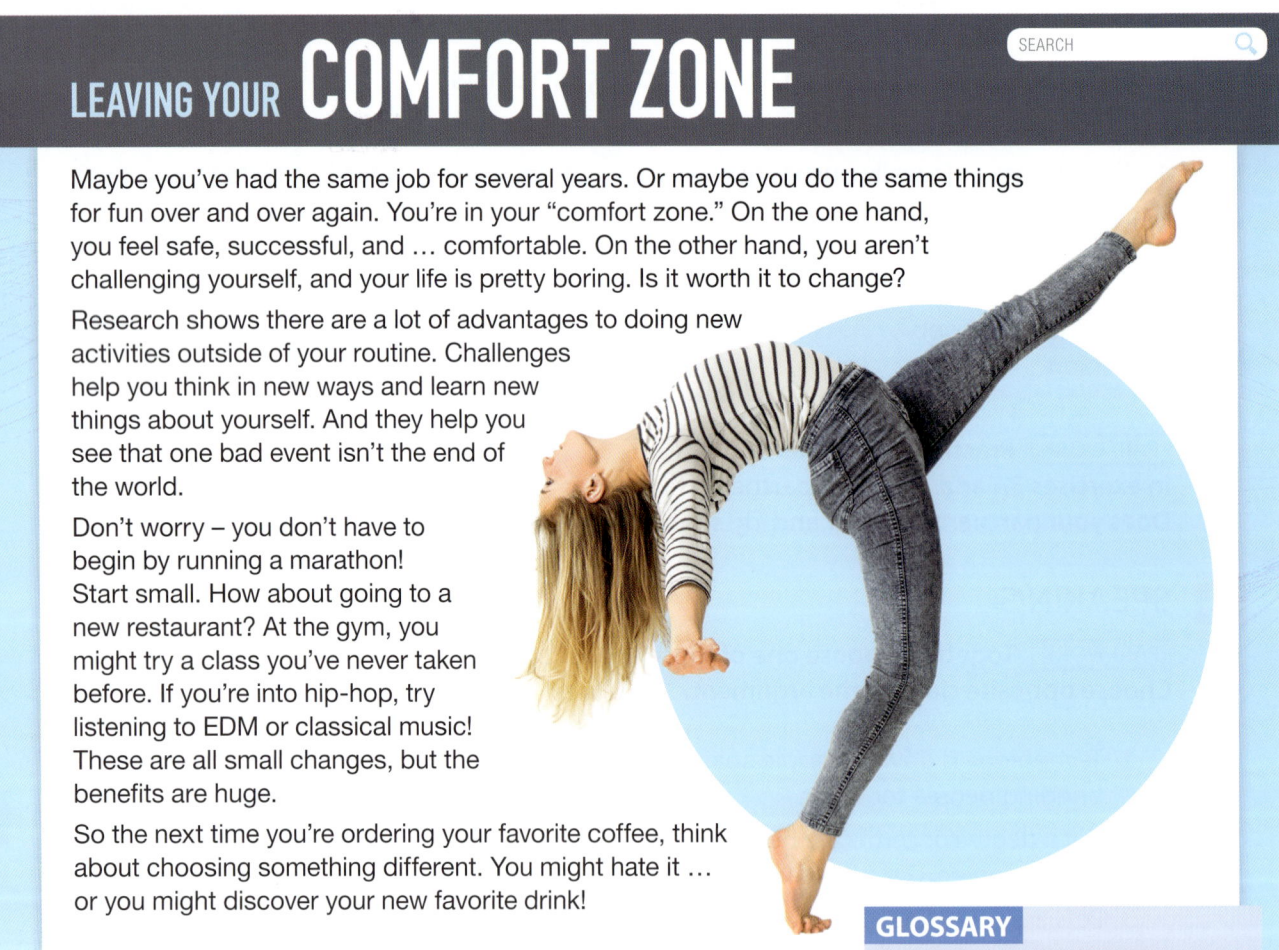

LEAVING YOUR COMFORT ZONE

Maybe you've had the same job for several years. Or maybe you do the same things for fun over and over again. You're in your "comfort zone." On the one hand, you feel safe, successful, and … comfortable. On the other hand, you aren't challenging yourself, and your life is pretty boring. Is it worth it to change?

Research shows there are a lot of advantages to doing new activities outside of your routine. Challenges help you think in new ways and learn new things about yourself. And they help you see that one bad event isn't the end of the world.

Don't worry – you don't have to begin by running a marathon! Start small. How about going to a new restaurant? At the gym, you might try a class you've never taken before. If you're into hip-hop, try listening to EDM or classical music! These are all small changes, but the benefits are huge.

So the next time you're ordering your favorite coffee, think about choosing something different. You might hate it … or you might discover your new favorite drink!

GLOSSARY
benefit *(n)* something that helps you

C **PAIR WORK** What is your comfort zone? Are you doing things that are outside that comfort zone? How does it make you feel?

D **THINK CRITICALLY** How far is "too far" to push yourself out of your comfort zone? Is there a risk to changing things in your life?

2 WRITING

A Look at the pictures and read Marty's story. What was his fear? How did he overcome it?

Conquering a fear

I have a surprising secret: I used to be really frightened of escalators. Yes, escalators: those moving stairs you see everywhere. It's actually a very common fear. For years, if I saw an escalator, I would do anything to avoid it. If I did get on, my heart would beat really fast. My friends told me that very few people fall off escalators. "I know," I'd say, "but I don't want to be that one!"

Then one day I thought, "Enough! I'm going to deal with this now." I decided to start with a short escalator and then try the longer ones. At first, it wasn't too bad. The hardest part was facing an escalator in a subway station that went deep underground. That first step was awful! I was sure I was going to fall, but I held on and didn't give up. And the more I practiced, the easier it got. Now I ride those moving stairs with confidence!

I learned something useful from this. On the one hand, it's good to push yourself out of your comfort zone. On the other hand, you don't want to push yourself too far, too fast. Take it slow! You might surprise yourself.

B **WRITING SKILLS** Read about comparing facts and ideas. Then underline the two opposite ways of thinking in Marty's story.

We use *On the one hand, …* and *On the other hand, …* to compare two different facts or two opposite ways of thinking about a situation.

On the one hand, I was afraid to ride escalators. On the other hand, I was tired of being afraid.

C Write a story about a time when you pushed yourself out of your comfort zone. It can be true, or you can make it up. Use *on the one hand* and *on the other hand* to compare facts or ideas. Give advice to the reader.

D **PAIR WORK** Exchange stories. Would your partner's advice work for you?

REGISTER CHECK

First-person stories often contain a lot of personal details and feelings. Articles in the third person often contain more facts and neutral information. Notice the differences between a sentence in Marty's story and a sentence that could be in an article about Marty.

My friends told me that very few people fall off escalators.

According to the National Institutes of Health, there are only 10,000 escalator injuries per year in the US that result in emergency room visits.

11.5 TIME TO SPEAK
Success stories

LESSON OBJECTIVE
- talk about a person you admire

Indra Nooyi

Neil DeGrasse Tyson

Angela Merkel

Lin-Manuel Miranda

Misty Copeland

A **DISCUSS** Look at the pictures. What do you know about these people? What areas have they been successful in? Tell a partner.

B **RESEARCH** Look at the categories of successful people below. In groups, make a list with one successful person from each category. You can go online for ideas. What were some of the challenges these people faced? What did they do to succeed?

| athletes | businesspeople | entertainers | politicians | scientists |

C **DISCUSS** Imagine these people are going to help you achieve success in different parts of your life. Who would you want to:
- teach your class?
- help you do something you're afraid to try?
- show you how they do their job?
- teach you a new skill?
- give you advice about money?

D **DECIDE** Look at the magazine. Who would you put on the cover? Choose the person your group admires most from part C.

E **PRESENT** Share your choice with the class. Explain what skills or knowledge this person can offer and how their struggle for success helped them. Answer any questions about the person.

F **AGREE** As a class, choose the best person for the cover.

SUCCESS MAGAZINE

To check your progress, go to page 156.

USEFUL PHRASES

DISCUSS
I know him/her!
He/She is …
I would want … to …
because …
That would be …

DECIDE
I'd put … on the cover because …
… is a good choice because …
I wouldn't choose … because …

PRESENT
We chose … because …
We felt that …
We admire … for his/her …

UNIT OBJECTIVES

- talk about accidents
- talk about extreme experiences
- describe and ask about feelings
- write an anecdote about a life lesson
- plan a fun learning experience

LIFE'S LITTLE LESSONS

12

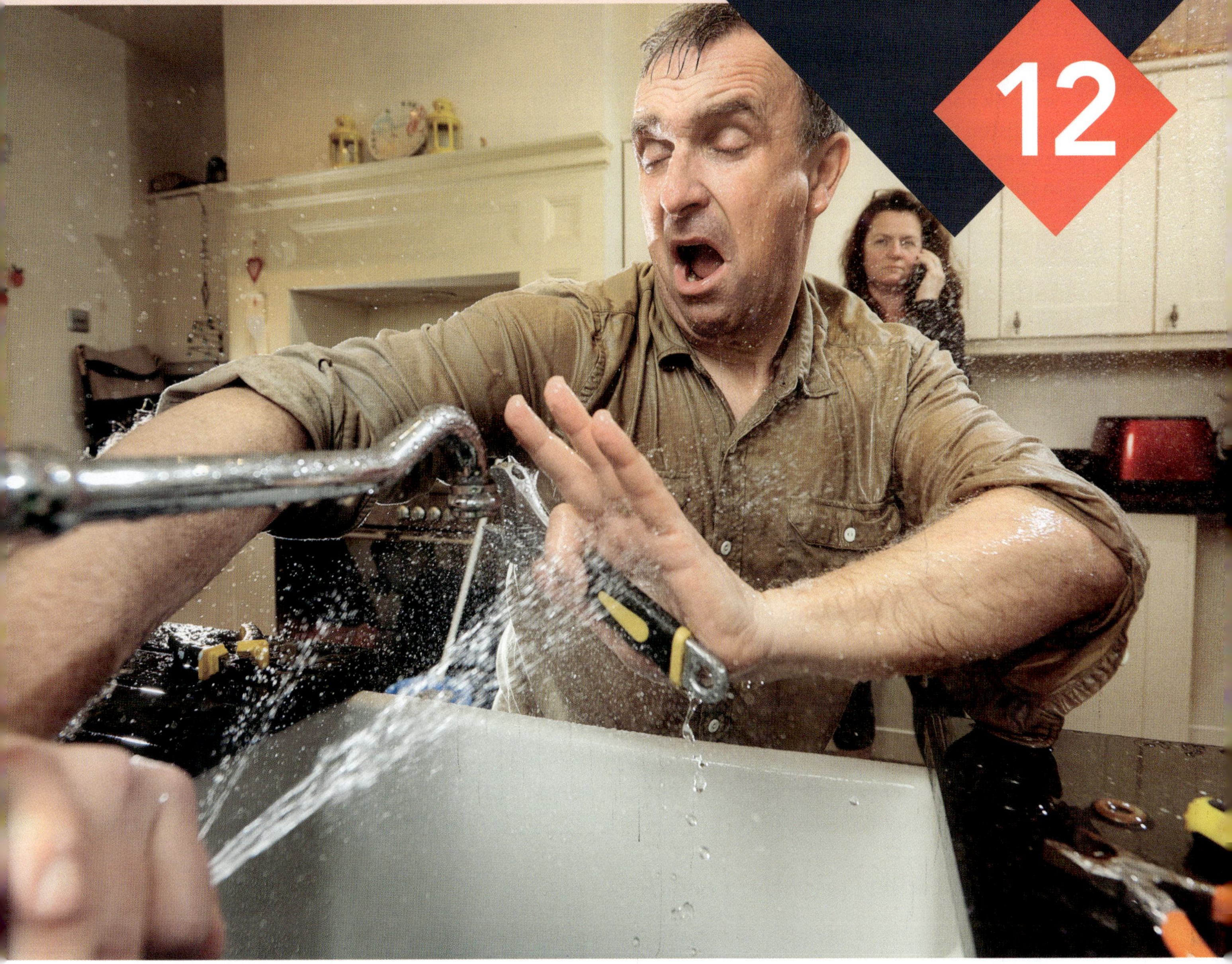

START SPEAKING

A Look at the picture. What do you think is happening?

B What might have happened in the five minutes before this accident? Make up a story.

C Who do you think learned a lesson in this picture? What lessons do you think he or she learned? For ideas, watch Andrea's video.

Does Andrea think the same thing as you?

12.1 IT WAS AN ACCIDENT!

LESSON OBJECTIVE
- talk about accidents

1 LANGUAGE IN CONTEXT

A 🔊 2.48 Look at the picture. What do you talk about at mealtimes? Then read and listen to Lorena, Talya, and Mark's conversation. What do their stories have in common?

🔊 2.48 Audio script

Lorena When I was a kid, I picked up the ketchup bottle from the dinner table and started shaking it to mix it up. The lid came off, and ketchup spilled everywhere! You've never seen anything like it! Everyone was mad at me. I felt bad about it, but it was also funny. Anyway, it was an accident!

Talya I know what you mean. One time, I was in a restaurant somewhere with my parents. My dad was cutting his steak, and suddenly his knife slipped, and his peas flew everywhere. He was so embarrassed, but my mom said, "It's not what happens – it's how you deal with it." So we laughed, got up from the table, and quickly picked up all of the peas.

Mark That reminds me … I was eating in a restaurant once, and I knocked something off my plate. I looked on the floor but couldn't see anything. Then the woman at the next table reached into her open purse on the floor and pulled out a chicken leg! She said nothing. She didn't blame me – she just gave me the chicken leg. I'm sure she never left her purse open in a restaurant again!

B 🔊 2.48 Read and listen again. Answer the questions.
1. What feelings did Lorena have about her ketchup accident?
2. What lesson did Talya learn from her father's accident?
3. Where did Mark's chicken leg go?

INSIDER ENGLISH

We use *You've never seen anything like it* to mean that something was incredible or very unusual.

2 VOCABULARY: Describing accidents

A 🔊 2.49 [PAIR WORK] Listen and repeat the verbs. Which verbs are actions and which are feelings? Then find and underline ten of these verbs in the conversation in exercise 1A.

be mad at	blame	damage	destroy	fall out
feel bad (about)	knock off	leave on	leave open	pick up
pull out	shake	slip	spill	

B ▶ Now go to page 152. Do the vocabulary exercises for 12.1.

C [PAIR WORK] Describe an accident you had or saw during a meal, and say how people reacted. For ideas, watch Celeste's video.

What accident did Celeste see?

3 GRAMMAR: Indefinite pronouns

A Circle the correct answers. Use the sentences in the grammar box to help you.
1 Indefinite pronouns with *every-* describe **some** / **all** members of a group.
2 Indefinite pronouns with *some-* / *any-* are usually used in questions and negative sentences.
3 Indefinite pronouns with *no-* mean "**only one**" / "**none**."

> **Indefinite pronouns**
>
> Ketchup spilled **everywhere**. I was in a restaurant **somewhere**.
> **Everyone** was mad at me. You've never seen **anything** like it!
> I knocked **something** off my plate. She said **nothing**.

B ▶ Now go to page 140. Look at the grammar chart and do the grammar exercise for 12.1.

C **PAIR WORK** Complete the sentences with indefinite pronouns. Check your accuracy. Then say if the sentences are true for you or if you agree.
1 I didn't have _____ for breakfast this morning.
2 _____ once borrowed my headphones and damaged them.
3 _____ ever leaves their windows open at night here. It's too cold.
4 I spilled _____ on my clothes earlier today.
5 _____ has accidents, but they shouldn't feel bad about them.
6 I once lost my keys. They fell out of my pocket _____.

ACCURACY CHECK

Be careful with the spelling of *no one*. It is **not** one word like the other indefinite pronouns.

~~Noone~~ saw me spill my drink. ✗
No one saw me spill my drink. ✓

D Complete the sentences with your own ideas. Then share with a partner.
1 I damaged _____ by accident, but nobody _____.
2 I looked everywhere for _____, but _____.
3 Once, I spilled _____ at someone's house. Everybody _____.

4 SPEAKING

A Think about a time when you had a small or amusing accident. What happened? How did you feel? What did you learn from the accident? Take notes.

B **GROUP WORK** Describe your accident and say what you learned. Listen to the other stories and ask questions to find out more. Whose accident was the funniest? Who learned the most valuable lesson?

> I got a new phone a few weeks ago, but I didn't buy a case for it right away. I was walking home when I dropped my phone on the sidewalk.

> Oh, no! Was there glass everywhere?

> Yeah, there was. Luckily, someone lent me their phone for the day. I learned my lesson: get a case for your phone.

12.2 LEARNING UNDERWATER

LESSON OBJECTIVE
- talk about extreme experiences

1 LANGUAGE IN CONTEXT

A Look at the picture. Would you like to do this? Why or why not?

B Read Bryce's social media post. How long has he been taking his diving course? What has he learned?

C Read the post again. Which two things made Bryce feel good today?

Profile | Wall | Friends

I'm exhausted … but day two of my diving course was terrific! Last night, I said that I was feeling miserable after a difficult start. But today, I'm thrilled. Elena (my instructor) told me that I had done really well. She said that I was concentrating on my dives, and that had made a huge difference because I'd stayed calm today.

I definitely didn't feel calm this morning when Elena told us we were going to learn to deal with air problems. Then she said we would be at a depth of 45 feet (15 meters), so we couldn't swim to the surface quickly. She said we would have to work as a team and share air. We practiced a few times just below the surface of the water. And then we went down deep. I was terrified. But in the end, everything was fine. And while we were down there, hundreds of tiny fish swam past us. It was a magnificent sight. Suddenly, I realized I was enjoying myself.

So, the five things I've learned about diving are: concentrate, stay calm, work as a team, practice, and enjoy it. That's good advice for whatever you're doing, I guess.

2 VOCABULARY: Describing extremes

A 🔊 2.50 Find and <u>underline</u> eight of the words in the post in exercise 1B. Then match all of the words to the synonyms. One item has two words that mean the same. Listen and check.

| boiling | enormous | exhausted | freezing | huge | magnificent |
| miserable | starving | terrific | terrified | thrilled | tiny |

1 _____ very beautiful or good
2 _____ , _____ very big
3 _____ very cold
4 _____ very good
5 _____ very happy
6 _____ very hot
7 _____ very hungry
8 _____ very sad
9 _____ very scared
10 _____ very small
11 _____ very tired

B ▶ Now go to page 152. Do the vocabulary exercises for 12.2.

FIND IT

C **PAIR WORK** Think of a surprising situation you have heard about recently. You can go online to read recent news stories. Describe it with extreme adjectives.

> Did you know four hikers got lost on Mount Elbrus last year? Fortunately, they were rescued!

> They must have been miserable! Were they freezing?

3 GRAMMAR: Reported speech

A How do these words change in reported speech? Write them below. Use the sentences in the grammar box to help you.

is / are → _____ / _____   can → _____
will → _____   did → _____   have done → _____

Reported speech

Direct speech	Reported speech
"It**'s** difficult."	She said (that) it **was** difficult.
"They**'re do**ing well."	She said (that) they **were do**ing well.
"They **did** well."	She said (that) they **had done** well.
"They**'ve done** well."	She said (that) they **had done** well.
"They **can** do it."	She said (that) they **could** do it.
"It **will** be difficult."	She said (that) it **would** be difficult.
"It**'s going to** be easy."	She said (that) it **was going to** be easy.

B PAIR WORK Change the comments to reported speech. Then cover the sentences on the right and practice with a partner. You say a sentence on the left, and your partner says, "He/She said … " Take turns.

1 "We can't have a break."   She said that we _____.
2 "We're going to start early."   She told us we _____.
3 "It will be a long day."   She said it _____.
4 "You took too many risks."   She told me that I _____.
5 "It's an important rule."   She said it _____.
6 "You've worked hard."   She told us that we _____.

C ▶ Now go to page 140. Look at the grammar chart and do the grammar exercise for 12.2.

4 SPEAKING

A PAIR WORK Think of an extreme experience you had. Use one of the ideas below or your own ideas. Tell your partner about your experience and say how you felt. Change roles.

> a challenging activity   a fun day out   a long trip
> extreme or unusual weather an amazing place

B PAIR WORK Work with a different partner. Tell him or her about your last partner's experience.

> David went rock climbing last week. He said that he had never tried it before. He said that he had been terrified, but he would do it again.

C PAIR WORK Go to the person your partner talked about. Tell him or her what your partner said about him or her. Did your partner get all the details correct?

12.3 A HOTEL NIGHTMARE

LESSON OBJECTIVE
- describe and ask about feelings

1 FUNCTIONAL LANGUAGE

A 🔊 **2.51** Look at the picture. What do you think is happening? How do you think the people feel? Then read and listen. What was the problem? How was it solved?

🔊 2.51 Audio script

A So, what happened to you last weekend? I got your text. You said you were at a hotel on the coast, or somewhere, and you were having problems …

B Yeah, one big problem! I reserved a room online with a hotel-booking website, not directly with the hotel. And when I got to the hotel, there was no reservation!

A Oh, no! **You must have been furious**.

B **Actually, I was shocked**. Then I was mad at myself for not checking with the hotel before I got there.

A So, what happened?

B Well, first they said I should call the booking company. But then they checked the computer and told me there were no rooms available anyway. **What a nightmare**!

A Yeah. What did you do?

B I called the booking company and told them about the problem. They apologized and said they'd find me another hotel while I waited. Then they told me they had a room – in a five-star hotel! And I didn't have to pay anything more.

A **I bet that made you feel good**.

B Yeah. **I couldn't stop smiling**. It turned into a dream vacation!

B Complete the chart with expressions in bold from the conversation.

Describing your feelings	Asking about or guessing others' feelings
1 _____	4 _____
2 _____	5 _____
3 _____	I bet that made you feel bad.
It was a horrible/fantastic experience.	How did that make you feel?

C **PAIR WORK** Circle the correct response. Then practice with a partner.

1. **A** I finally passed my driver's test.
   B a How did that make you feel? b I bet that made you feel bad.
2. **A** You must have been excited about the news.
   B a What a nightmare! b Actually, I was shocked.
3. **A** The airline lost my bags.
   B a It was a horrible experience. b You must have been furious.
4. **A** How did you feel after the exam?
   B a I bet that made you feel good. b Great! I couldn't stop smiling.

2 REAL-WORLD STRATEGY

A 🔊 2.52 Listen to Jimmy telling Mi-young about a presentation. Why did it start late? How did that make Jimmy feel?

B 🔊 2.52 Read the information in the box about ending a story. Then listen again. What expression does Jimmy use to end his story? How did his story end?

> **ENDING A STORY**
>
> You can use *In the end* or *After all that* to end a story. The expressions often show there were some problems before the situation ended.
>
> Yeah. I couldn't stop smiling. **After all that**, it turned into a dream vacation!

C **PAIR WORK** Tell your partner about a time when you had some problems, but things ended in a good way. Use one of the expressions from the box to end your story. Take turns.

D ▶ **PAIR WORK** Student A: Go to page 158. Student B: Go to page 160. Follow the instructions.

3 PRONUNCIATION: Saying -ed at the end of a word

A 🔊 2.53 Listen. Focus on the sound of the *-ed* at the end of each word in bold.

/id/ waited   /t/ shocked   /d/ happened

B 🔊 2.54 Match the words below with the correct sound for their *-ed* endings. Then listen and check.

called	checked	decided	/id/	/t/	/d/
exhausted	knocked	looked			
passed	reserved				

C Practice the conversation with a partner. Does your partner say the *-ed* endings correctly?

A What a day. I'm exhausted.
B Why what happened?
A You know that project I've been working on? Well my boss decided that we needed to do the whole thing over. And the thing is he waited until we were almost done to tell us!
B What a nightmare! I hope he apologized at least.

4 SPEAKING

A Choose one of these expressions and think of an experience that goes with it. Use a personal experience or make one up. Include your feelings about what happened. Take notes.

- What a nightmare!
- What an exhausting day!
- What a great experience!
- What a fantastic trip!

B **PAIR WORK** Tell your partner about your experience. Your partner asks about or guesses how you felt. Change roles and repeat.

> My friend and I were hiking last weekend, and we got lost.

> Oh, no! Weren't you scared?

12.4 LESSONS LEARNED?

LESSON OBJECTIVE
- write an anecdote about a life lesson

1 LISTENING

A **PREDICT** You are going to hear Tasha Roberts give a talk. Look at the pictures. What do you think she's going to talk about?

B 🔊 **2.55** **LISTEN FOR MAIN IDEAS** Listen to the talk. Were your ideas in exercise 1A correct? What other example does Tasha give? What's the main point she illustrates with these examples?

C 🔊 **2.55** **LISTEN FOR DEFINITIONS** Listen again. Tasha defines some words in her talk. Complete the definitions as you listen. You will need to change the form of some of the words.
1 *Constantly* means something happens _____.
2 *Temporarily* means something happens _____.
3 A *creature of habit* is someone who _____.
4 An *intention* is something that you _____.

D **PAIR WORK** **THINK CRITICALLY** Which statement below do you think Tasha would agree with? Why? Which one do you agree with?
You can easily learn from your mistakes.
You can learn from your mistakes, but it's difficult.
You can't learn from your mistakes.

2 PRONUNCIATION: Listening for 'll

A 🔊 **2.56** Listen. Focus on the difference in the uncontracted and contracted forms.
You will be able to stop telling that same bad joke!
You'll be able to stop telling that same bad joke!

B 🔊 **2.57** Listen. Focus on the words in bold. Circle the vowel sound you hear.
1 /u/   /ʊ/   **You'll** know how to make little lessons turn into life lessons.
2 /i/   /ɪ/   **We'll** soon go back to our old habits.
3 /eɪ/ /e/   **They'll** learn from this experience.

C **Circle the correct word to complete the statement.**
When the *'ll* comes after a vowel sound, that vowel sound is often *shortened* / *lengthened*.

3 WRITING

A Read Gavin's anecdote. What wrong lesson did he learn? What did he learn in the end?

When I was ten, my teacher told me I had to write a report about volcanoes and make a model volcano. I delayed working on the project until the day before my presentation, and then I told my parents after dinner. At first, they were mad at me, and I felt really bad, but then they said they'd help me. We researched volcanoes online and went to a craft store just before it closed to buy things to make the volcano. We worked on it until midnight, and I wrote the report. The next day, I gave a terrific talk. All of my classmates said I had made a cool volcano, and the teacher took a picture of me with it.

This taught me that I could wait until the last minute and still do a magnificent job. But it was the wrong lesson to learn, and I spent the next ten years trying to unlearn it. In high school and college, everything was harder, but because of my volcano, I told myself I could wait until the last minute. I failed a lot before I learned how to manage my time well. I think now that it would have been better if my parents had let me fail when I was ten. I would have learned a valuable lesson a lot earlier.

B **WRITING SKILLS** Read about using expressions with similar meanings. Then find expressions in exercise 3A that have similar meanings to 1–5 and write them in the correct place.

We often use different expressions with similar meanings to make our writing more interesting and to avoid repeating the same words.

1. This taught me = _I learned_
2. delay = _____
3. until the day before X = _____
4. terrific = _____
5. presentation = _____

C Write an anecdote about an important lesson you learned. Think of a time when you changed your behavior based on something that happened in the past. Write at least two paragraphs. Use different expressions with similar meanings to avoid repeating the same words.

> **REGISTER CHECK**
>
> In writing anecdotes, we often use longer sentences with conjunctions. It is similar to how we speak when we tell someone a story.
>
> *At first*, they were mad at me, *and* I felt really bad, *but* then they said they'd help me.

D **PAIR WORK** Exchange stories. Talk about the lessons you learned. Have you learned the same lesson? How would you change your behavior based on your partner's lesson?

> The lesson you learned is such a good one. Managing your money is important. I would like to be better at that!

> I know what you mean! I liked your lesson about being nice to servers in restaurants. I learned that, too, when …

12.5 TIME TO SPEAK
Skillful fun

LESSON OBJECTIVE
- plan a fun learning experience

paddle-boarding

go-karting

karaoke

bowling

FIND IT

A **RESEARCH** With a partner, talk about fun activities you've done where you learned or practiced some skills. Look at the pictures to help you think of ideas. You can go online to learn the names in English of activities you like. Then choose the activity you've done that you enjoyed the most.

B **DISCUSS** Move around the class and tell others about the activity you chose in part A. Explain why it was fun, and try to persuade them that they'll enjoy it, too. Listen to what others say about their activities.

C **DECIDE** Work in groups. Tell the group about an activity you heard about in part B (<u>not</u> your own activity) that sounded fun. Say what the person told you about it. The group chooses the best activity.

D **PRESENT** Tell the class about the activity your group chose in part C. Try to persuade your classmates that they'll enjoy it.

E **AGREE** Imagine the class is going to do one of the activities from part D together. Choose something that would be good for everyone. Avoid anything that anyone would be scared to do.

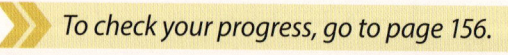
To check your progress, go to page 156.

USEFUL PHRASES

PREPARE
Once, I went/did/tried …
It was terrific!
At first, I was terrified, but then …

DECIDE
… told me that …
He/She said that …
I think it sounds fun.
I'd like to try it.

AGREE
Nobody else wants to …
… said he/she was terrified of …
Most of us would like to …

REVIEW 4 (UNITS 10–12)

1 VOCABULARY

A Which word or phrase doesn't belong in each set? Circle it.

1 Materials:	cotton	glass	plastic	polyester	ship
2 Describing materials:	artificial	light	option	soft	strong
3 Production:	design	freezing	grow	pick	produce
4 Distribution:	deliver	export	knock off	transport	store
5 Opportunities:	advantage	goal	purpose	reward	warm
6 Accidents:	blame	damage	destroy	leather	spill
7 Extremes:	huge	manufacture	starving	terrific	tiny

B Look at the words you circled in exercise 1A. Add them to the correct set.

C Add two more words or phrases that you know to each category.

2 GRAMMAR

A Complete the paragraph with the correct form of the verbs in parentheses ( ).

"The planet will get hotter in the next 100 years," said many scientists in 2017. In fact, they said that the planet [1]_____ (become) 3°C hotter before 2100. That is a major problem, and what we consume has a huge impact. Everyone [2]_____ (be) worried about the planet, but no one [3]_____ (know) how to solve the problem. We often consume fruits and vegetables that [4]_____ (produce) in other parts of the country. Those items [5]_____ (transport) by trucks or planes, and that increases pollution. If everyone [6]_____ (buy) their food from local farmers, the world [7]_____ (be) less polluted. Another problem is the use of chemicals. In the past, not so many chemicals [8]_____ (use) by farmers. Certainly, people [9]_____ (consume) more organic food if it [10]_____ (not be) so expensive.

B PAIR WORK What did you have for breakfast this morning? Where do you think those food items were produced? How far do you think they were transported?

3 SPEAKING

PAIR WORK Talk to your partner about the questions below. Ask for and give details.

- What is something you said you would do this year that you have actually done?
- What is something you said you would do but haven't done?

> This year I said I'd exercise more often. I've been doing my best to go to the gym at least three times a week. And I won't give up.

> I said I'd give up my job and set up my own company. I've been doing a lot of research, and I'm considering different options, but I'm still working at my old job.

4 FUNCTIONAL LANGUAGE

A **Use the words and phrases below to complete the conversation.**

> actually • are you sure • don't you agree
> feel angry • right • that's what
> think about it • what a • what you mean
> would agree

A I need to find a new apartment quickly.
B But your apartment is so nice and comfortable. ¹_____ you want to move?
A The thing is, I don't really get along with my roommate. He's so messy, ²_____?
B Yeah, I ³_____ with you.
A It's impossible to share a place with a person like that, ⁴_____?
B I see ⁵_____.
A And last week he had friends over, and there were dozens of dirty glasses on the kitchen table. ⁶_____ nightmare!
B I bet that made you ⁷_____.
A Angry? ⁸_____, I was furious!
B Why don't you talk to him about it again? ⁹_____ I'd do.
A Yeah, now that I ¹⁰_____, he's usually a pretty good listener. I'll have a talk with him tonight.

5 SPEAKING

A **PAIR WORK** Choose one of the situations below. Act it out in pairs.

- Tell your partner about something you're thinking of buying. Your partner questions or approves of your choice. Go to page 102 for useful language.

> I just saw a fantastic suitcase on sale for only $99.99.
>
> Why would you want to buy a new suitcase? You aren't planning to travel this year.
>
> Well, it's on sale, and …

- Discuss with your partner. Which is better: working for a big, global company or setting up your own company? Give your opinions. Try to get your partner to agree. Go to page 112 for useful language.

> I think it's better to set up your own business. You can be more creative, and you'll probably make more money. You know what I mean?
>
> That's a really good point, but you have to consider the risks …

- Talk to your partner about a good or bad experience you had on your last vacation. Your partner asks about or guesses how you felt. Go to page 122 for useful language.

> It was an amazing trip, but on the last day, I overslept and missed the plane back.
>
> I bet that made you feel horrible. And what did you do then?
>
> I called the airline company, and they said that I would have to wait for the next flight …

B **Change roles and repeat the role play.**

GRAMMAR REFERENCE AND PRACTICE

1.1 INFORMATION QUESTIONS (page 3)

Information questions		
Question words	To ask about …	Examples
Where	places	Where do you live?
When	times	When's your birthday?
Why	reasons	Why did you try to call me earlier?
What	things	What's your email address?
		What color do you like the best?
Which	a specific group of things or people	Which floor is your apartment on?
Who	people	Who's your boss?
Whose	who things belong to	Whose phone is this?
How	ways to do things	How do you make chocolate cake?

A Complete the questions with the words in the box. Then match them with the answers.

How	What	When	~~Where~~	Which	Who	Whose	Why

1. _____Where_____ can we get some coffee?   d   a Oh, they're mine. Thanks.
2. _____ does the movie start?   b At 6:30, I think.
3. _____ keys are these?   c Because it's too hot in here.
4. _____ would you like to drink?   d There's a café on the corner.
5. _____ are all the windows open?   e Just some water, please.

1.2 INDIRECT QUESTIONS (page 5)

Indirect questions			
Questions within questions		Questions within statements	
Do you have any idea	where he was born?	I'd like to know	where he was born.
Can you tell me	if she plays any sports?	I want to find out	if she plays any sports.
Do you know		I wonder	

A Put the words in the correct order to make indirect questions.

1. have / Do / idea / where / born / you / your roommate / was / any / ?
   Do you have any idea where your roommate was born?

2. know about / my cousins / I wonder / if / anniversary party / my parents' / .
   _____

3. and Eva / you / married / know / if / Ramiro / are / Do / ?
   _____

4. to / retire / when / like / my boss / I'd / know / is going to / .
   _____

5. people / I / those / want / are / to / who / find out / .
   _____

129

2.1 PRESENT PERFECT WITH EVER, NEVER, FOR, AND SINCE (page 13)

Present perfect with *ever* and *never* (for experience)	Present perfect with *for* and *since*

Have you **ever played** video games?
  Yes, I **have**. I'**ve played** them many times.
  No, I **haven't**. I'**ve never played** them.
Has he **ever traveled** to another country?
  Yes, he **has**. He'**s traveled** to ten countries.
  No, he **hasn't**. He'**s never traveled** anywhere.
	How long **has** your car **been** outside?
	  It's **been** outside **for** two years.
	How long **have** you **had** your comic books?
	  I'**ve had** them **since** I was 12.
	Have you **ridden** your bikes lately?
	  No. We **haven't ridden** them **since** college.

A Make complete sentences or questions in the present perfect from these words. Add *for* or *since* when needed.

1. you / ever / buy / car / ?
   Have you ever bought a car?
2. We / not see / Maria / a few years / .

3. They / never / clean / their garage / !

4. You / live in / the same house / 11 years / .

5. he / ever / visit / your family / ?

6. Nadia / not play / computer games / she was 16 / .

7. Roberto / has / his car / a long time / .

8. I / not eat / meat / 2015 / .

2.2 PRESENT PERFECT WITH ALREADY AND YET (page 15)

Present perfect with *already* and *yet*	
already	*yet*

I'**ve already** made folders.
She'**s already** tried the camera.
	I **haven't** tried the camera **yet**.
	He **hasn't** made folders **yet**.
	Have you tried the camera **yet**?
	  Yes, I **have**. / No, I **haven't**.
	Has he made folders **yet**?
	  Yes, he **has**. / No, he **hasn't**.

A Look at the sentences. Write sentences with opposite meanings. Use the words in parentheses ( ).

1. I haven't used my new computer yet. (already / three times)
   I've already used my new computer three times.
2. Ken hasn't downloaded any apps yet. (already / ten new apps)

3. My parents haven't seen my apartment yet. (already / twice)

4. I've already ridden my new bike. (not / yet)

5. Vicky has downloaded new apps. (not / any apps / yet)

6. I've already chosen my online profile photo. (not / yet)

3.1 ARTICLES (page 23)

Articles

Use *a / an* ...

when something isn't definite: *Is there **a ferry** in your city?*

with jobs: *I'm studying to be **an engineer**.*

Use *the* ...

for something you've mentioned before: *How often does **the ferry** run?*

for something your listener knows: *He works in **the city**.*

with ordinals: *What time does **the first** ferry leave?*

with superlative adjectives: *Where can I find **the most unusual** sculptures?*

for only one thing: *Don't sit in **the sun** too long.*

Don't use an article ...

with noncount nouns or plural nouns: *Where can I play **music**? I like to draw **monuments**.*

when you talk about something in general: ***Hostels** are usually cheap.*

for the names of countries*, cities, and continents: *I'm from **Russia**. I live in **Moscow**.*

for the names of parks, streets, single mountains, and lakes: ***Central Park** is on **Fifth Avenue**.*

*but: the United States (the US), the United Kingdom (the UK), the Philippines

A Complete the sentences with *a, an, the,* or – (no article).

1. There's ___a___ Russian embassy in my city. I think ___the___ embassy is on ___–___ Fourth Avenue.
2. I'm _____ engineer, and I design _____ bridges and _____ tunnels.
3. There's _____ sculpture of a horse near _____ river. Have you seen it?
4. You can get _____ information about _____ city at your hotel. Then you can email me _____ information.

3.2 MODALS FOR ADVICE (page 25)

Modals for advice

Affirmative statements	Negative statements	Yes/no questions	Information questions
You **should take** the subway.	You **shouldn't take** the bus.	**Should** I **take** a bus? Yes, you **should**. No, you **shouldn't**.	**Which** line **should** I **take**?
You **could get** the train to Terminal 3.	X	**Could** I **take** a train? Yes, you **could**. No. That's not possible.	**How should** I **book** my ticket?
I'd walk. It's not too far.	I **wouldn't take** that route.	**Would** you **take** the subway? Yes, I **would**. No, I **wouldn't**.	**What would** you **do**?
shouldn't = should not	wouldn't = would not	I'd = I would	

A **Match the questions (1–5) with the responses (a–e). Then practice with a partner.**
1 Should I meet you at the airport? ___
2 How do I get to the library from here? ___
3 Do you know when the bus leaves? ___
4 Would you take a train to Chicago? ___
5 What is the best time to take the ferry? ___

a You should go in the morning.
b No. I'd check the schedule online.
c Yes. Let's meet in the parking lot.
d You could take the subway to Oak Street.
e No, I wouldn't. It takes too long. I'd fly.

4.1 BE GOING TO AND WILL FOR PREDICTIONS (page 35)

be going to and *will* for predictions
She**'ll** be shocked. = She**'s going to** be shocked.
She **won't** like it. = She**'s not going to** like it.
I think they**'ll** be late. = **I think** they**'re going to** be late.
I don't think he**'ll** retire soon. = **I don't think** he**'s going to** retire soon.
NOTE: *We don't use* will *to make a prediction about something when there is evidence. Instead, we use* be going to.
The sky is dark. It**'s going to** rain. NOT The sky is dark. ~~It'll rain~~.

A **Put the words in the correct order to make sentences.**
1 embarrassed / be / He'll / really / . _____
2 be / it / I / think / fascinating / will / . _____
3 to / disappointed / going / They / are / be / . _____
4 won't / surprised / She / be / probably / . _____
5 will / don't / be / I / amusing / think / it / . _____
6 going / enjoy / He / to / it / not / is / . _____

4.2 WILL FOR SUDDEN DECISIONS; PRESENT CONTINUOUS FOR FUTURE PLANS (page 37)

will for sudden decisions	Present continuous for future plans
I**'ll deal** with renting tents, OK?	**Are** we **staying** with your cousin?
OK, and I**'ll check** places to stay.	They**'re staying** with Leo's cousin.
Just a minute. I**'ll check** online.	They**'re not staying** in a hotel.

A **Circle the correct words to complete the sentences. Then check (✓) the correct column.**

	Sudden decision	Future plan
1 Thanks for inviting me to the movies. *I'll pay / I'm paying* for the tickets.		
2 *He'll drive / He's driving* to Miami next weekend to visit his parents.		
3 Do you want to come with us? OK, *I'll book / I'm booking* a room for you.		
4 *We'll meet up / We're meeting up* at the Hilton Hotel at 6:30.		
5 *I'll take / I'm taking* my kids to the zoo tomorrow. They're very excited.		
6 The traffic isn't moving! What's going on? *I'll check / I'm checking* on my phone.		

5.1 SIMPLE PAST (page 45)

Simple past	
Sentences, *yes/no* questions, short answers	**Information questions**
The ring **disappeared** in the sand. She **didn't find** it. **Did** she **find** the ring? 　Yes, she **did**. / Yes. She **found** it. 　No, she **didn't**. / No. She **didn't find** it.	**Where did** she **search**? **How did** she **find** it? **Who helped** her? **What happened** next?

A Choose the correct verb for each sentence. Use the simple past.

| discover | drop | make | not ask | return | tell |

1 She _____ her new coffee cup on the floor.
2 _____ you _____ Marina's books to her?
3 I _____ my favorite jacket in the back of my closet.
4 He _____ a wonderful dinner for us when he got home.
5 _____ they _____ you about their trip to Bolivia?
6 I _____ him for his email address.

5.2 PAST CONTINUOUS AND SIMPLE PAST (page 47)

Past continuous and simple past	
Event in progress	**Action that interrupts**
While/When I **was looking** at some art, The subway doors **were closing** **While/When** you **were talking** to Joe, It **was raining** a lot	the subway **came**. when I **looked** up. your earring **fell off**. when we **left** the restaurant.
NOTE: The order can change. The subway came **when/while** I **was looking** at some art. **When** I **looked** up, the subway doors **were closing**.	

A Write sentences. Use the simple past and past continuous of the verbs.

1 I / give my friend a ride to the airport / when / my car break down
   I was giving my friends a ride to the airport when my car broke down.

2 When / I wash the dishes, / my ring fall off
   _____

3 When / I look up, / the train leave the station
   _____

4 Finn lose his phone / while / he walk in the park
   _____

5 While / they have a picnic, / it start to rain
   _____

6.1 QUANTIFIERS (page 55)

Quantifiers	
With count nouns	**With noncount nouns**
Almost all of the walls have graffiti.	**Almost all of** the graffiti looks ugly.
There are **so many** walls with graffiti.	There's **so much** graffiti.
There are **several** walls with graffiti.	There's **a little** / **very little** / **so little** graffiti.
There are **a few** / **very few** / **so few** walls with graffiti.	There's **almost no** graffiti.
There are **almost no** walls covered with graffiti.	There's **almost none**.
There are **almost none**.	

A   Complete the sentences with the correct words from the box.

| few | little | many | much | no | several |

1 This store isn't usually busy. I don't know why there are so _____ people here.
2 I didn't bring much food. I just brought a _____ sandwiches.
3 This bus is crowded. There are almost _____ seats left.
4 I'm not sure exactly how long the trip is, but I think it takes _____ hours.
5 It's been very dry recently. There's been very _____ rain.
6 Be quiet! There's no need to make so _____ noise!

6.2 PRESENT AND FUTURE REAL CONDITIONALS (page 57)

Present real conditionals

The present real conditional shows the usual result of a present situation. It can describe something that is generally true, a fact, or a habit.

Condition (*if/when* clause)	Result (main clause)
If there **is** a lot of garbage in the street,	people often **leave** more trash there.
When you **speak** angrily to noisy neighbors,	they **don't stop** making noise.

Future real conditionals

The future real conditional shows the likely result of a possible future situation.

Condition (*if* clause)	Result (main clause)
If you **explain** your feelings clearly,	they **will understand**.
If she **talks** to him calmly,	he**'ll** probably **listen**.
If you **make** a special area for graffiti,	people **won't paint** on other buildings.
'll = will won't = will not	

A   Complete the sentences with the correct form of the verbs in parentheses ( ).

Present situations:
1 When crime _____ (not be) a problem, neighborhoods _____ (be) safe.
2 If I _____ (drive) to work, I _____ (listen) to the traffic report before I leave.

Future situations:
3 If my sister's neighbors _____ (play) music loudly this weekend, she _____ (get) angry.
4 There _____ (be) less trash if people _____ (recycle).

7.1 USED TO (page 67)

used to				
You can use *used to* for actions that happened regularly in the past but do not happen now, and for states that were true in the past but are not true anymore.				
	Affirmative	**Negative**	**Questions**	**Short answer**
I / You / He / She / We / They	**used to buy** CDs.	**didn't use to like** pop music.	**Did** you **use to listen** to pop music? What **did** you **use to like**?	Yes, I **did**. No, I **didn't**.

A Complete the sentences with the verbs in parentheses ( ) and the correct form of *used to*.

1. _____Did_____ you _____use to go_____ to school with Terry Johnson? (go)
2. That company _____ famous all around the world. (be)
3. I _____ to the radio, but I don't have a radio now. (listen)
4. He _____ chocolate, but now he loves it. (not eat)
5. Who _____ she _____ married to? (be)
6. I _____ my friends at the local coffee shop. (meet)

7.2 COMPARISONS WITH *(NOT) AS … AS* (page 69)

Comparisons with *(not) as … as*					
We can use *as … as* to say that two things are the same or similar. *not as … as* means the first thing is less than the second thing.					
Subject	**Verb**	**as**	**Adjective**	**as**	
The new series	is isn't	as	good funny	as	the first series.
Subject	**Verb**	**as**	**Adverb**	**as**	
I	train don't train	as	hard often much	as	my brother does.
Subject	**Verb**	**as**	**Noun**	**as**	
My old phone	had didn't have	as	many ringtones much memory	as	my new one.

A Are the sentences true (*T*) or false (*F*)? Change one or two words in each false sentence to make it true.

1. _F_ Tablet screens are as big as TV screens. _____Tablet screens aren't as big as TV screens._____
2. ___ Birds can fly as fast as planes. _____
3. ___ Movies aren't as long as series. _____
4. ___ Buses don't have as many seats as movie theaters. _____
5. ___ Shoes aren't as expensive as socks. _____
6. ___ A lake has as much water as an ocean. _____

8.1 PRESENT PERFECT CONTINUOUS (page 77)

Present perfect continuous

Use the present perfect continuous for an action or event that started in the past and continues into the present time.

What **have** you **been doing**?	**Have you been going out** lately?
I**'ve been painting** pictures recently.	Yes, I have.
I **haven't been going out** lately.	No, I haven't.
What **has** she **been doing**?	**Has** he **been playing** soccer recently?
She**'s been making** sushi lately.	Yes, he has.
She **hasn't been eating out** recently.	No, he hasn't.

A Complete the conversation with the present perfect continuous of the verbs in parentheses ( ).

A What ¹____are____ you ²____doing____ at work these days? (do)
B I ³_____ software. (design)
A That's interesting. ⁴_____ you ⁵_____ with other people? (work)
B Yes, I ⁶_____ . I ⁷_____ with a guy in our Japan office. (work)
A Will you have the opportunity to go to Japan?
B I think so. My boss ⁸_____ a trip for me, but it won't happen this month. (plan)
A So, ⁹_____ you ¹⁰_____ any fun lately? (have)
B No, I ¹¹_____ ! I ¹² _____ at all, but I have some free time this weekend. (not go out) Let's meet up!

8.2 PRESENT PERFECT VS. PRESENT PERFECT CONTINUOUS (page 79)

Present perfect vs. present perfect continuous

Present perfect	Present perfect continuous
I**'ve cleaned** the bathroom.	I**'ve been cleaning** the bathroom.
I**'ve made** some cookies.	I**'ve been making** cookies. That's why the kitchen is a mess.
She**'s worked** for the company for 24 years.	She**'s been working** for the company for three months.
So far, we**'ve watched** four episodes of the series.	I**'ve been going** to the gym three times a week.
We**'ve watched** that movie twice.	

A Complete the sentences with the verbs in parentheses ( ). Use the present perfect or the present perfect continuous.

1 I ____'ve been riding____ my mountain bike a lot recently. (ride)
2 My essay is going well. I _____ six pages so far. (write)
3 We just got here. We _____ long. (not wait)
4 Sorry about my dirty clothes. I _____ on my car. (work)
5 I was born in this town. I _____ here since 1998. (live)
6 She's getting better on the guitar. She _____ every day. (practice)
7 You can't look at my painting. I _____ it. (not finish)
8 He knows how to make cookies. He _____ them before. (make)

9.1 MODALS OF NECESSITY: *HAVE TO, NEED TO, MUST* (page 87)

Modals of necessity: *have to, need to, must*

| I **have to** / **need to take** enough courses to get a degree. | Why do you **have to** / **need to get** a degree? |
| I **don't have to** / **don't need to choose** a job yet. | Do you **have to** / **need to choose** a major? Yes, I do. / No, I don't. |

NOTE: We mainly use must *in formal situations.*
Students **must enroll** in four classes each semester.

A Complete the sentences with the correct form of the words in parentheses ( ).
1 He _____ call the office in San Francisco right away. (need to)
2 You _____ buy us a gift, but it was very nice of you. (not have to)
3 The college _____ reply within ten days. (must)
4 How much homework _____ you _____ do last night? (have to)
5 She _____ make a decision now. (not need to)
6 _____ we _____ have a degree to get a job at that company? (have to)

9.2 MODALS OF PROHIBITION AND PERMISSION (page 89)

Modals of prohibition and permission

Use *can't* and *must not* + the base form of a verb to say what is prohibited or what is not allowed. *Must not* is stronger than *can't*. When speaking, we often use *can't* instead of *must not*.

Prohibition: *can't, must not*	Permission: *can, may, could*
You **can't waste** time. We **can't leave** work early. You **must not do** chores around the house. They **must not take** their laptops out of the building.	You **can** / **may** take short breaks. They **can** / **may** work from home on Fridays. **Can** / **Could** / **May** I email you? Yes, you **can** / **may**. No, you **can't** / **may not**.

A Cross out the word or phrase that does not work in each sentence.
1 The official company handbook says: "You ~~can~~ / must not / can't have drinks at your desk because they might spill."
2 We need to be in the office four days a week, but we can / may / could work from home on Fridays.
3 A Can / Must / Could I use your laptop?
   B Sure. No problem.
4 A May I come to work a few minutes late tomorrow?
   B Yes, you can / could / may.
5 Employers can't / must not / couldn't hire people without experience.
6 You can / can't / may have the meeting in my office tomorrow. There's enough room for everyone.

We often use *please* when asking for permission.
*Can I **please** come to work late tomorrow?*
*Can I come to work late tomorrow, **please**?*
Don't use *could* in statements. This shows a possibility, not permission.

10.1 SIMPLE PRESENT PASSIVE (page 99)

Simple present passive

We use the passive when we're more interested in the action, or in the person or thing receiving the action – and less interested in, or don't know, the person or thing doing the action. We can use *by* to say who or what is doing the action.

The furniture **is made** in this factory.	
The chairs **are used** in restaurants.	Where **are** the beds **sold**?
The price **isn't written** on the label.	**Are** the beds **sold** in the US?
The beds **aren't sold** in the US.	**Yes**, they **are**. / **No**, they **aren't**.
The meals **are cooked** by a famous chef.	

A Write the sentences in the passive.

1 They make all the furniture from wood.   *All the furniture is made from wood.*
2 You cook the dish in the oven.   _____
3 They sell the snacks at local supermarkets.   _____
4 Where do you find these plants?   _____
5 Do they play the sport in Mexico?   _____
6 You don't eat the dish in summer.   _____
7 They use this technology in hospitals.   _____
8 You don't see the animals during the day.   _____

10.2 SIMPLE PAST PASSIVE (page 101)

Simple past passive

My laptop **was designed** in the US.	**Was** the fruit **picked** and **frozen** right away?
This dress **was designed by** my friend.	Yes, it **was**. / No, it **wasn't**.
The coffee beans **were imported**.	**Were** the computers **shipped** from China?
My laptop **wasn't made** in the US.	Yes, they **were**. / No, they **weren't**.
The coffee beans **weren't grown** in Canada.	Where **were** the computers **shipped** from?
	Who **were** the computers **shipped by**?

A (Circle) the correct active or passive verb.

1 I *bought / was bought* a tablet online. It *shipped / was shipped* to me right away.
2 These pictures *painted / were painted* by my sister. She *trained / was trained* really well.
3 My house *built / was built* more than 100 years ago. I have no idea who *built / was built* it.
4 These shoes *made / were made* locally, but those *imported / were imported* from Italy.
5 She *sent / was sent* the birthday card on Tuesday, and it *delivered / was delivered* the next day.
6 I *caught / was caught* this fish last summer and *froze / was frozen* it right away.

11.1 PHRASAL VERBS (page 109)

Phrasal verbs		
No object	**With object, separable**	**With object, inseparable**
Things hardly ever **work out** the first time. You need to **stand out**. Don't **give up** when it gets tough.	They **set up** a company. (They **set** it **up**.) I **figured out** the answer. (I **figured** it **out**.) **Keep up** the hard work. (**Keep** it **up**.) **Give up** candy and you'll feel better. (**Give** it **up**.)	**Get over** the problem. (**Get over** it.) **Work at** something you're good at. (**Work at** it.)

A Complete the sentences. Put the second word of the verb and *it* in the correct order.

1. When did you set _____it up_____ ? — up / it
2. I just can't figure _____ ? — out / it
3. She's really working _____ . — at / it
4. I've decided to give _____ . — up / it
5. You'll get _____ soon. — over / it
6. I hope you keep _____ . — up / it

11.2 PRESENT AND FUTURE UNREAL CONDITIONALS (page 111)

Present and future unreal conditionals	
The present and future unreal conditional describes the possible result of an imagined situation in the present or future.	
Condition (*if* clause)	**Result (main clause)**
If you **had** a million dollars,	what **would** you **do**?
If I **had** a million dollars,	**I'd start** a business.
If I **had** a million dollars,	I **wouldn't work**.
If I **offered** you a million dollars,	**would** you **swim** across a river full of crocodiles? Yes, I **would**. No, **I wouldn't**.

A Complete the sentences with the correct form of the verbs in parentheses ( ).

1. If Viggo ___had___ (have) a better job, he ___would be___ (be) happier.
2. Lorenzo _____ (walk) to work if he _____ (live) closer.
3. I _____ (consider) moving to Japan if I _____ (not have) a cat.
4. If we _____ (start) a business, we _____ (not see) our friends much.
5. If I _____ (be) you, I _____ (do) more research before making a decision.
6. Mara _____ (not know) what to do if her parents _____ (not help) her.

> ❗ 'd = would   wouldn't = would not
> The condition (*if* clause) can also be in the second part of the sentence. Note there is no comma when the result (main clause) is first.
> *What would happen if I won the race?*
> *You would be famous if you won the race.*

12.1 INDEFINITE PRONOUNS (page 119)

Indefinite pronouns

Indefinite pronouns are used when the noun is unknown or not important.

with *every-*	with *some-*	with *any-*	with *no-*
Everyone was mad at me.	Can **someone** pass me the ketchup?	**Anyone** can make a mistake.	**No one** / **Nobody** blamed me for the accident.
The peas flew **everywhere**.	My wallet fell out of my bag **somewhere**.	I can't find the salt **anywhere**.	There's **nowhere** to eat in this area.
I ate **everything** on my plate.	Would you like **something** to eat?	Can I help you with **anything**?	Is there really **nothing** in the fridge?

A Circle the correct indefinite pronouns.

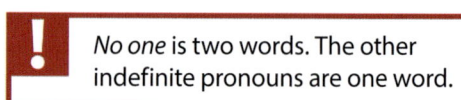 *No one* is two words. The other indefinite pronouns are one word.

1 I asked *someone / anyone* about the café, but he didn't know *nothing / anything* about it.
2 The kids want to watch *anything / something* on TV. Is there *anything / everything* good on right now?
3 Let's go *anywhere / somewhere* nice for lunch. Does *anybody / nobody* know a great restaurant?
4 *No one / Anyone* can join the company gym, and it's free. It doesn't cost *anybody / anything*.
5 I've made *something / anything* for dinner. It's *nothing / something* special, but I hope you like it.
6 *Everyone / Anyone* loves this beach. They say there's *nowhere / everywhere* like it.

12.2 REPORTED SPEECH (page 121)

Reported speech

Reported speech tells us what someone says in another person's words. In reported speech, we use a reporting verb – for example, *say* or *tell* – followed by a *that* clause.

Tense/Verb	What someone said (direct speech)	How it's reported (reported speech)
Simple present	"I **play** baseball."	She said that she play**ed** baseball.
Present continuous	"I**'m** work**ing** all day."	He said he **was** work**ing** all day.
Simple past	"I **spoke** to Ken."	He told me that he **had spoken** to Ken.
Present perfect	"I**'ve seen** the report."	She told me she **had seen** the report.
Future with *going to*	"I**'m going to** quit my job."	He said he **was going to** quit his job.
Future with *will*	"I**'ll** call you soon."	She said that she **would** call me soon.
can	"I **can** see you on Friday."	He told me he **could** see me on Friday.

A Write what the person said.

1 He said that he was thrilled with the idea.   "I'm thrilled with the idea."
2 She said she couldn't come to the party.   "I _____."
3 He told me he was going to eat out.   "I _____."
4 She told me that she wouldn't be home.   "I _____."
5 He said that he was going shopping.   "I _____."

VOCABULARY PRACTICE

1.1 DESCRIBING PERSONALITY (page 2)

A Match the adjectives (1–12) with the definitions (a–l).

1. brave ___
2. cheerful ___
3. easygoing ___
4. generous ___
5. helpful ___
6. honest ___
7. intelligent ___
8. nervous ___
9. reliable ___
10. selfish _a_
11. serious ___
12. sociable ___

a. caring only about yourself
b. often giving people money or presents
c. telling the truth
d. relaxed and not worried
e. likes to be with people and meet new people
f. worried
g. able to learn and understand things easily
h. not afraid of dangerous or difficult situations
i. willing to help
j. quiet and doesn't laugh a lot
k. happy
l. able to be trusted or believed

B Complete the sentences with the correct words. There is one extra word.

> cheerful   honest   intelligent   reliable   selfish   sociable

1. I'm sure Lucy will do well on her exams. She's really _____.
2. Max is always smiling and laughing. He's very _____.
3. Maria says what she thinks. She's always _____.
4. My uncle doesn't enjoy meeting people. He's not very _____.
5. David always does what he says he's going to do. He's _____.

1.2 GIVING PERSONAL INFORMATION (page 4)

A Cross out the word that does <u>not</u> work in each sentence.

1. Kelly is *single / married / ~~born~~*.
2. Marcos was *born / retired / raised* in Quito.
3. Leila lives *alone / with her cousin / single*.
4. My parents *raised / celebrated their anniversary / retired* last month.

B Number the sentences in the correct order (1–4).

Story 1
___ Now he's married to Nina.
___ He lived alone during that time.
___ Ivan was single until he was 34.
___ They celebrated their third anniversary last week.

Story 2
___ She was raised in Incheon.
___ Now she lives alone near her parents.
___ Ji-soo was born in Seoul.
___ She lived there with her parents and brother.

2.1 DESCRIBING POSSESSIONS (page 12)

A Match the expressions (1–12) with the definitions (a–l).

1. brand new ___
2. common ___
3. damaged ___
4. fancy ___
5. in good condition ___
6. modern ___
7. plain ___
8. outdated ___
9. special _a_
10. used ___
11. useful ___
12. useless ___

a. not ordinary or usual
b. decorative, complicated, or expensive
c. old and not useful anymore
d. completely new
e. in good shape
f. existing in large numbers
g. helping you do things
h. not helpful; doesn't work well
i. using the newest design or technology
j. not new; owned by someone else before you
k. not decorated
l. broken or harmed

B Circle the correct answers.

1. My sister usually gives me her old clothes, but today I bought a *special / brand new* coat.
2. This bag is really *modern / useful*. I can put a lot of stuff in it.
3. I think your bike is *useless / in good condition*. You should keep it.
4. My brother says DVD players are *outdated / damaged*. People watch things online now.
5. Martina bought a *used / fancy* car, but she'd prefer a new one.
6. Everyone has smartphones these days. They're very *plain / common*.

2.2 TECH FEATURES (page 14)

A Complete the sentences with the correct words.

delete	devices	folder	home screen	model
set up	storage	sync	try	work

1. I _____ my new computer by myself. Now the sound doesn't _____ .
2. I put all of my travel apps in one _____ .
3. Did you _____ the new weather app? It's pretty cool.
4. I have a picture of my cat on my _____ .
5. My old phone is fine. I don't need the newest _____ .
6. I need to _____ my phone with my computer so I can listen to my music on both _____ .
7. I need to _____ some photos because I don't have enough _____ for them all.

B Cross out the word that does not work in each sentence.

1. This is the best *device / folder / model* the electronics company has made.
2. Can you help me *sync / set up / delete* my new phone?
3. I want more *folders / home screens / storage* on my phone.
4. I need to *try / sync / delete* my photos.
5. It's easy to *delete / set up / work* an online profile.

3.1 CITY FEATURES (page 22)

A Complete the sentences with the correct words.

> bridge   clinic   embassy   fire station   hostel   monument   sidewalk   tunnel

1 Firefighters work in a _____ .
2 A large house where people can stay cheaply is a _____ .
3 People can go to a _____ for medical treatment or advice.
4 A path by the side of a road that people walk on is a _____ .
5 A _____ is a long passage under the ground or through a mountain.
6 A _____ helps people remember a famous person or important event.
7 An _____ is an official building of a government in another country.
8 People drive across a _____ to get across a river.

B Complete the sentences with words from exercise A.

1 I went to the American _____ and got a visa. Then I flew to San Francisco and stayed in a _____ for a week.
2 The _____ over the river was closed, so I drove through the _____ instead.
3 I went to the _____ to see a doctor. I got there before it opened, so I waited outside on the _____ for 15 minutes.
4 There's a large _____ in memory of the Great Fire next to the _____ where my husband works. He's a firefighter.

3.2 PUBLIC TRANSPORTATION (page 24)

A Match the words (1–10) with the definitions (a–j).

1 arrival ___
2 book ___
3 departure ___
4 direct ___
5 fare ___
6 line ___
7 reservation ___
8 route ___
9 schedule ___
10 terminal ___

a to arrange to have a seat on a plane or a hotel room at a particular time
b an arrangement to have something kept for a person or for a special purpose
c the price that you pay to travel on a plane, train, bus, etc.
d the act of coming to a place
e a particular way or direction between places
f a subway route
g a list of times when buses, trains, etc., arrive and leave
h going straight from one place to another without changing trains, buses, etc.
i a building where you can get onto a plane, bus, or ship
j the act of leaving a place

B Complete the sentences with words from exercise A.

1 Is the ticket expensive? How much is the ____fare____ ?
2 _____ is at 9:00 a.m., and _____ is at 11:30 a.m. It's a short flight.
3 We don't need to change trains. The trip is _____ .
4 I still need to _____ a flight for the trip. I hope I can get a good price.
5 What time should we leave? Can we look at the bus _____ again?
6 Did you make a _____ for dinner? The restaurant gets busy on Saturdays.

4.1 DESCRIBING OPINIONS AND REACTIONS (page 34)

A Match the *-ed* adjectives (1–8) with the definitions (a–h).

1. frightened ___
2. fascinated ___
3. annoyed ___
4. shocked ___
5. amused ___
6. embarrassed ___
7. disappointed ___
8. surprised ___

a. showing you think something is funny
b. a little angry
c. sad because something wasn't as good as you expected
d. red-faced and worried what others will think of you
e. very interested
f. afraid
g. very surprised, usually in a bad way
h. happy because something you didn't expect happened

B Complete the words with the endings *-ed* or *-ing*.

1. That movie was frighten_____ .
2. Olga isn't coming to the party. I'm so disappoint_____ .
3. My friends were really surpris_____ to see me.
4. I didn't think the joke was amus_____ .
5. We were shock_____ when we saw the price. It was really expensive!
6. I had to sing in front of 50 people. It was so embarrass_____ .
7. That noise is really annoy_____ .
8. The kids were fascinat_____ by some of the animals at the zoo.

4.2 MAKING DECISIONS AND PLANS (page 36)

A Match the expressions (1–10) with the definitions (a–j).

1. look into ___
2. check ___
3. deal with ___
4. get in touch with ___
5. arrange ___
6. forget ___
7. think about ___
8. meet up ___
9. let (someone) know ___
10. remind ___

a. make necessary plans and preparations for something to happen
b. find out about something
c. take action in order to achieve something or solve a problem
d. not remember
e. contact someone
f. give someone information about something
g. examine the facts about a situation
h. get together with people
i. make someone remember something
j. consider something

B (Circle) the correct answer for each sentence.

1. Did you *get in touch with / look into* prices for the hotel?
2. We *thought about / met up with* cost before we planned our trip.
3. How are you *dealing with / forgetting* your long work hours?
4. Did you *check Carol / let Carol know* about our plans?
5. Sara *arranged / reminded* Joe to book three hotel rooms.

5.1 LOSING AND FINDING THINGS (page 44)

A Match the verbs (1–10) with the definitions (a–j).

1 appear ___
2 disappear ___
3 discover ___
4 drop ___
5 fall off ___
6 get (something) back ___
7 leave (something) behind ___
8 locate ___
9 return ___
10 search (for) ___

a give something back
b find something for the first time
c leave a place without taking something with you
d suddenly be seen
e look somewhere carefully in order to find something
f find exactly where something is
g become impossible to see
h let something you are carrying fall
i have something again after it was lost
j suddenly go to the ground

B Circle the correct word or phrase for each sentence.

1 Sofia *dropped* / *fell off* one of her earrings on the floor.
2 Did you *return* / *get* your bag back from the airport?
3 I *searched for* / *located* my credit card everywhere.
4 The police *discovered* / *appeared* our car in another town.
5 A lot of things *returned* / *disappeared* from our office last summer.
6 He *got* / *left* his books behind in the classroom.
7 I think my hat *fell off* / *left behind* when I got on the train.
8 I lost my phone, but it *located* / *appeared* on my desk two days later.

5.2 NEEDING AND GIVING HELP (page 46)

A Choose the words that mean the same as the underlined words. Circle *a* or *b*.

1 I often get lost when I'm in a new city.
   a don't know where I am
   b ask someone for directions
2 Did Vicky give you a ride to class today?
   a tell you how to get to class
   b drive you to class in her car
3 I feel sorry for Tom. He lost his grandfather's watch.
   a am happy for
   b am sad for
4 I need to figure out which subway line to take.
   a try to understand
   b tell someone
5 Mari showed me where to get the bus on the map.
   a explained
   b listened to me explain
6 Carl was in trouble at the airport because he left his passport at home.
   a found a solution
   b had a problem
7 I'm grateful when strangers give me directions on the street.
   a appreciate it
   b feel embarrassed
8 Sonny took care of his cousin when he was sick.
   a visited his cousin
   b stayed with his cousin and helped him

B   **Match the questions (1–5) with the answers (a–e).**
1   How did you find the hotel after you got lost? ___
2   Did your aunt take care of you when you were sick? ___
3   Did you figure out the bus wasn't running? ___
4   What happened after your car broke down? ___
5   Did you hear that Sara was in trouble at work? ___

a   Yeah. I feel sorry for her.
b   A friend gave me a ride home.
c   A stranger showed me where it was on a map.
d   Yes. My neighbor warned me before I got to the bus stop.
e   Yes, she did. I was really grateful.

6.1 URBAN PROBLEMS (page 54)

A   **Complete the sentences with the correct words.**

air	concrete	graffiti	land	noise	pollution	space	traffic	trash

1   Just outside our office, there's an ugly _____ wall with _____ painted on it.
2   Tall buildings need only a little _____, but they have a lot of _____ inside them.
3   Some people eat as they're walking and throw their _____ right on the sidewalk.
4   My house isn't right next to the highway, but I can hear the _____ from the _____.
5   It's hard to breathe because of all the _____ in the _____ from cars.

B   **Use words from exercise A to complete these sentences. Sometimes more than one answer is possible.**
1   The _____ makes a lot of _____.
2   The _____ has _____ on it.
3   There's a lot of _____ in the _____.

6.2 ADVERBS OF MANNER (page 56)

A   **Complete the sentences with the adverb form of the words in parentheses ( ).**
1   Sandra speaks _____*loudly*_____ (loud) when she's on the phone.
2   Duncan speaks _____ (polite), even when he's upset.
3   It's hard to understand Jeff because he doesn't speak _____ (clear).
4   Mia draws _____ (beautiful), but she can't paint at all.
5   Does your bus driver drive _____ (safe) or _____ (dangerous)?
6   How many questions did you answer _____ (correct)?
7   Did Ida react _____ (calm) or _____ (angry) when you told her the news?
8   The city cleaned up the street _____ (complete) after the tree fell down.

B   **Cross out the word that does not work in each sentence.**
1   John and Kara drive their motorcycles *dangerously* / ~~*clearly*~~ / *safely*.
2   We need to speak *completely* / *politely* / *calmly* if we want people to listen to us.
3   Trish writes *beautifully* / *clearly* / *loudly*, so she can make the sign for our meeting.
4   When you talk *angrily* / *loudly* / *safely*, I stop listening to you.
5   Melvin answered most of the questions *correctly* / *dangerously* / *clearly*, and he passed the test.

7.1 MUSIC (page 66)

A Circle the type of music that matches the definition.
1. a type of popular music with a strong beat, often played with electric guitars and drums: classical / **rock**
2. a type of popular music from Jamaica with a strong beat: **reggae** / folk
3. modern music with a strong beat that many young people like listening and dancing to: country / **pop**
4. a form of music developed mainly in the 18th and 19th centuries: **classical** / EDM
5. music that people often play without looking at written music: **jazz** / folk
6. a style of harsh, distorted rock music played loudly on electric instruments: reggae / **heavy metal**
7. a type of pop music with a strong beat in which people often speak the words: **hip-hop** / jazz
8. music written and played in a traditional style: rock / **folk**
9. a style of popular music from the southern and western US: **country** / reggae
10. a type of dance music with a strong beat usually played at clubs and festivals: classical / **EDM**

B Cover exercise A and complete the words with the missing letters.
1. r _e_ _g_ _g_ _a_ e
2. c _ _ _ _ _ _ l
3. h _ _ _ m _ _ _
4. c _ _ _ _ y
5. j _ _ _
6. f _ _ _
7. h _ _ – _ _ _
8. r _ _ _

7.2 TV SHOWS AND MOVIES (page 68)

A Match the kinds of TV shows or movies with the emojis.
1. science fiction _e_
2. romantic comedy ___
3. horror ___
4. game show ___
5. musical ___
6. comedy ___

a. 😱
b. 💰
c. 😒😠
d. 😄
e. 👾
f. 🎵

B Complete the actor's story with kinds of TV shows or movies from exercise A.

When I was 18, I was on a ¹_____, and I won $2,000! That was my first time on TV. I really liked it, so I tried out for a small part in a TV series, and I got it. It was ²_____, and my character traveled through time. It was so cool! After that, I did a ³_____ movie. I'm not crazy about scary stuff usually, but it was better to act in it than to watch it! I think I want to try something lighter next time, though. Something fun, like a ⁴_____, where my character falls in love with a celebrity. Or maybe a regular ⁵_____, where I get all the laughs. But I don't think I'll do a ⁶_____. My singing voice isn't that great!

8.1 DESCRIBING EXPERIENCES (page 76)

A Complete the sentences with the correct words. Then change the <u>underlined</u> words so the sentences are true for you.

> challenge   change   chore   opportunity   success

1. I think <u>washing dishes</u> is a boring _____ .
2. <u>Passing my driver's test</u> was a difficult _____ .
3. <u>Tina's surprise birthday party</u> was a great _____ .
4. I'm ready for a _____ in my style. I want a new <u>hairstyle</u>.
5. I'd love to have an _____ to travel to <u>Argentina</u>.

B Circle the correct words to complete the paragraph.

I had an interesting experience at work last month. I had to work on a group ¹*project / change* with three other people. We had to design a new website for our company. It was a difficult ²*opportunity / job*, but we thought of an interesting ³*chore / process* – we each took one part of the design to work on and then showed each other our work. I designed the homepage. The new website was a ⁴*success / challenge*, so our boss was happy. I hope to have ⁵*an opportunity / a change* to work with the group in the future.

8.2 DESCRIBING PROGRESS (page 78)

A Complete the sentences with the correct words. You will use one of the words twice.

> concentrate   do   have   save   spend   take   waste

1. I'm sure we'll _____ trouble with this.
2. We have plenty of extra time. We can _____ it easy.
3. I don't _____ time for a break while I'm doing this.
4. If we want to finish this, we can't _____ time.
5. We'll have to _____ our best on this.
6. I'm sure we can do this quickly and _____ a lot of time.
7. This is very complex work. We really need to _____ on this.
8. I'll have to _____ a lot of time on this.

B Which sentences from exercise A are possible before the sentence below? Check (✓) the sentences.

" _____ . It's a really difficult job."

☐ 1   ☐ 2   ☐ 3   ☐ 4
☐ 5   ☐ 6   ☐ 7   ☐ 8

9.1 COLLEGE SUBJECTS (page 86)

A Complete the sentences with the correct words. There are four extra words.

| architecture | biology | business | chemistry | computer science | economics |
| education | engineering | law | medicine | physics | political science |

1 I'm studying _____ because I want to help sick people.
2 My cousin studied _____ in college, and now he designs buildings.
3 I didn't study _____ much. I just remember it was about energy and heat and light and stuff.
4 My younger sister wants to study _____ so she can understand plants and animals better.
5 Ruby is interested in politicians and power. Her degree is in _____ .
6 I'm studying _____ because I need to know how to buy and sell products and run a company.
7 When you study _____ , you learn about the impact of money on people, companies, and countries.
8 My degree is in _____ . I'm hoping to improve the roads and bridges in my country.

B Cover exercise A and complete the words with the missing letters.

1 I have a degree in a r c h i t e c t u r e.
2 Did you study b ___ ___ ___ ___ y in school?
3 My mother studied e ___ ___ n ___ ___ ___ s in college.
4 I'd like to take some e ___ ___ ___ a ___ ___ ___ n courses.
5 I've never studied c ___ ___ m ___ ___ ___ ___ y.
6 My parents want me to study b ___ ___ ___ ___ ___ s.
7 I'm studying c ___ ___ ___ ___ ___ r s ___ ___ ___ ___ e right now.
8 P ___ ___ ___ ___ s is a fascinating subject.

9.2 EMPLOYMENT (page 88)

A Complete the sentences with the correct words. There is one extra word.

| apply | employer | fire | hire | profession | salary | wage | working hours |

I just finished college, and now I'm going to ¹_____ for jobs as a computer tech. It's a great ²_____ , and there are a lot of jobs. The ³_____ for most jobs are from 9:00 a.m. to 5:00 p.m. I hope I can find an ⁴_____ who will ⁵_____ someone without much experience. I'd like to earn a ⁶_____ , but because it's my first job, I might need to work for a ⁷_____ and get paid by the hour.

B Circle the correct answers.

1 Sarah is already saving for her *employer / retirement* even though she's only in her twenties.
2 I don't know exactly what I want to do, but I'd like to have a *career / salary* in medicine.
3 My boss says she'll *fire / hire* anyone who steals information from the company.
4 Lydia has three new *wages / contracts* to design websites for people.
5 When you're self-employed, it's important to *manage / hire* your time well.

10.1 DESCRIBING MATERIALS (page 98)

A Circle the correct adjectives. Which sentence does not include opposites?
1 Leather is *artificial / natural*.
2 Stone is *heavy / light*.
3 Metal is *hard / soft*.
4 Glass is *fragile / strong*.
5 Cotton is *hard / soft*.
6 Polyester is *artificial / natural*.
7 Wool is *warm / waterproof*.
8 Wood is *fragile / strong*.

B Complete the sentences with some of the materials from exercise A.
1 _____Wool_____ is natural and very warm.
2 _____ can feel cold and is fragile.
3 _____ comes from trees.
4 _____ is hard, heavy, and sometimes stronger than stone.
5 _____ is natural and can help keep you dry but is not totally waterproof.

10.2 PRODUCTION AND DISTRIBUTION (page 100)

A Circle the correct word to complete each sentence.
1 What time did they *deliver / store* your package?
2 How can I *design / transport* these TVs to New York?
3 I *caught / froze* a lot of fruit and vegetables this year.
4 Do they *import / export* these cars from Japan?
5 The children *produced / picked* a lot of apples yesterday.
6 My uncle's company *manufactures / grows* furniture.

B Cross out the word that does not work in each sentence.
1 Yesterday, I *caught / froze / picked* some peas and beans.
2 He *delivered / shipped / stored* the package to your house yesterday.
3 Did your company *design / grow / manufacture* these shoes?
4 We *deliver / import / transport* our products to customers around the world.
5 My country *exports / grows / manufactures* a lot of vegetables.

11.1 SUCCEEDING (page 108)

A Match the first parts of the sentences (1–9) with the second parts of the sentences (a–i).

1 I really need to **figure** _b_
2 The two friends decided to **set** ___
3 It took me a long time to **get** ___
4 I was so tired, I just had to **give** ___
5 With his green hair, he really **stands** ___
6 You'll get your degree if you can **keep** ___
7 To become a good skier, you have to **work** ___
8 Unfortunately, my plan didn't **work** ___
9 While I was sick, I decided to **give** ___

a **out** as well as I hoped.
b **out** how to fix this.
c **out** in the photo.
d **up** the hard work until next summer.
e **up** before the end of the race.
f **up** the company six years ago.
g **up** coffee and drink only water and juice.
h **over** my bad exam results.
i **at** your technique.

B Complete the text with five of the two-word verbs from exercise A. Use the correct form.

The professor said to the class, "You'll never ¹ _figure out_ the solution to this problem. It's almost impossible!" But I decided I would be the one who did. I wanted to ² _____ in my class. So I thought, "I'm really going to ³ _____ this – all day if necessary." But at midnight I was still no closer to finding the answer. So unfortunately, I had to ⁴ _____ . I thought, "I hope nobody else in the class gets the answer, or I'll never ⁵ _____ it!"

11.2 OPPORTUNITIES AND RISKS (page 110)

A Match the expressions (1–12) with the definitions (a–l).

1 advantage ___
2 consider ___
3 disadvantage ___
4 effect ___
5 goal ___
6 option ___
7 purpose ___
8 research ___
9 result ___
10 reward ___
11 risk ___
12 situation ___

a something you want to do in the future
b a choice
c the possibility of something bad happening; to do something although something bad might happen
d the set of things that are happening at a particular time and place
e something that happens because something else has happened
f why you do something
g the study of a subject to get new information; to study a subject to get more information
h something good that you get because you have done something good
i to think about something carefully
j something good that helps you
k a change caused by something else
l something that makes a situation more difficult

B Complete the paragraph with words from exercise A.

My ¹ _goal_ is to study English in Australia for a year. I can study in Melbourne or Sydney. I'll probably take the second ² _____ . I plan to quit my job at the end of the year and go to Sydney after that. It's a ³ _____ , but I think it's worth it. It'll have a big ⁴ _____ on my life. One ⁵ _____ is that my English will be excellent when I return. A ⁶ _____ is that I won't make much money while I'm in Australia. I might ⁷ _____ getting a part-time job after I get there, but I want to spend most of my time studying. The main ⁸ _____ of my year abroad is to study as much as I can.

12.1 DESCRIBING ACCIDENTS (page 118)

A Circle the correct verbs to complete the sentences.
1 She *picked up / pulled out* the broken glass from the table.
2 I dropped and broke my phone and *felt bad about / blamed* it.
3 My ring *shook / slipped* off my finger and disappeared.
4 I *spilled / knocked off* some coffee on my new white rug.
5 My brother *damaged / destroyed* his bike, but he can still ride it.
6 Did you leave the lights *open / on*?
7 When I opened the door of my car, two bags of groceries *fell out / pulled out*.
8 Don't *leave open / shake* that box. You don't know what's in it.

B Match the first parts of the sentences (1–8) with the second parts of the sentences (a–h).
1 He left his computer ___
2 I picked up ___
3 Someone left ___
4 I hope you aren't mad ___
5 He pulled all the things ___
6 She feels really ___
7 His hand slipped, and he knocked ___
8 I picked up the bottle and ___

a the back door open.
b bad about the accident.
c the glass onto the floor.
d on by accident.
e at Susan.
f shook it.
g out of the cupboard and cleaned it.
h my keys from the floor.

12.2 DESCRIBING EXTREMES (page 120)

A Match the first parts of the sentences (1–10) with the second parts of the sentences (a–j).
1 It's the most enormous TV I've ever seen. It's ___
2 I stood in the snow and waited for two hours. I was ___
3 What time are we having dinner? I'm ___
4 We had a terrific view of Rio from the plane. It was ___
5 Aren't you too hot in that big sweater? You must be ___
6 I can't read this. The writing is ___
7 She said it was the best gift she'd ever had. She was ___
8 The kids had a great vacation, but now it's over, so they're ___
9 I haven't slept for 36 hours. I'm ___
10 I'm scared of spiders. When I see one, I'm ___

a boiling.
b thrilled.
c exhausted.
d freezing.
e huge.
f magnificent.
g miserable.
h starving.
i terrified.
j tiny.

B Complete the sentences with all possible words. Use each word once.

| boiling | enormous | exhausted | freezing | huge | magnificent |
| miserable | starving | terrific | terrified | thrilled | tiny |

1 When I opened the box and saw what was in it, I was ___terrified___ / ___thrilled___ .
2 I don't feel good. I'm _____ / _____ / _____ / _____ .
3 Look at the size of that dog! It's _____ / _____ / _____ !
4 Wow, look at that view. It's _____ / _____ .

152

PROGRESS CHECK

Can you do these things? Check (✓) what you can do. Then write your answers in your notebook.

UNIT 1

Now I can …	Prove it
☐ use adjectives to describe personality.	Write six adjectives that describe people's personalities.
☐ ask information questions.	Write three questions using different question words.
☐ give personal information.	Write four expressions we use to give personal information.
☐ use indirect questions.	Change the direct question into an indirect question: *What hobbies are you into?*
☐ make introductions and end a conversation.	Write one sentence to introduce yourself, one sentence to introduce a friend, and one sentence to end a conversation.
☐ write an email to get to know someone.	Look at your email from lesson 1.4. Can you make it better? Find three ways.

UNIT 2

Now I can …	Prove it
☐ describe possessions.	Describe the condition of your phone and your favorite pair of shoes.
☐ use the present perfect with *for* and *since*.	Complete the sentence: *I've _____ for _____.*
☐ talk about tech features.	Give your opinion about the most useful and least useful features on a phone.
☐ use the present perfect with *already* and *yet*.	Complete the sentences with your own information and *already* or *yet*. *I've _____ today. I haven't _____ .*
☐ switch from one topic to another.	Introduce a new topic of conversation, and then change the topic.
☐ write an ad for something I want.	Look at your ad from lesson 2.4. Can you make it better? Find three ways.

UNIT 3

Now I can …	Prove it
☐ talk about city features.	Name four city features in your area.
☐ use articles.	Complete the sentences with *a*, *an*, *the*, or – (no article). *I live in _____ busy neighborhood. There's _____ embassy on my street. I see _____ tourists go in and out of _____ building all day long.*
☐ talk about public transportation.	Write two things you need reservations for and three kinds of transportation that have a schedule.
☐ use modals for advice.	Choose two famous things to see in your city. Write advice about how to get there from a main train or bus station.
☐ ask for and give directions in a building.	Write a question you can ask to find the restrooms in your school. Then write the answer.
☐ write a personal statement for a job application.	Look at your personal statement from lesson 3.4. Can you make it better? Find three ways.

PROGRESS CHECK

Can you do these things? Check (✓) what you can do. Then write your answers in your notebook.

UNIT 4

Now I can …	Prove it
☐ describe opinions and reactions.	How many pairs of *-ed* and *-ing* adjectives can you think of? Make a list.
☐ make predictions with *be going to* and *will*.	Make two predictions about tomorrow.
☐ talk about decisions and plans.	Talk about a decision you need to make. Who can you get in touch with to help you with it? What do you need to look into first?
☐ use *will* for sudden decisions; use the present continuous for future plans.	Complete the conversation: A *What are you doing this weekend?* B *I _____.*
☐ offer and respond to reassurance.	Write two things you can say to offer reassurance and two things you can say to respond.
☐ write an email describing plans for an event.	Look at your email from lesson 4.4. Can you make it better? Find three ways.

UNIT 5

Now I can …	Prove it
☐ talk about lost and found things.	Write two or three sentences about something you lost. Describe how you lost it and say whether you located it again.
☐ use the simple past.	Make a list of five regular simple past verbs and five irregular simple past verbs.
☐ talk about needing and giving help.	Describe when you were grateful for someone's help. Describe a time when you took care of someone.
☐ use the past continuous and the simple past.	Complete the sentence: *While I was studying, _____.*
☐ give and react to surprising news.	Complete the conversation: A *I found a ring in the trash.* B *_____*
☐ write a short story.	Look at your story from lesson 5.4. Can you make it better? Find three ways.

UNIT 6

Now I can …	Prove it
☐ talk about urban problems.	Write six words to describe urban problems. Which are the two biggest problems where you live?
☐ use quantifiers.	Write three sentences about urban problems where you live. Use the quantifiers *almost all*, *several*, and *so much*.
☐ use adverbs of manner.	Answer the questions: *How should bus drivers drive? How do you speak in class?*
☐ use future real conditionals.	Complete the sentence: *I _____ if my neighbors talk loudly tonight.*
☐ express concern and relief in different situations.	Write three things you can say to express concern and three things you can say to express relief.
☐ write a post giving my point of view.	Look at your post from lesson 6.4. Can you make it better? Find three ways.

PROGRESS CHECK

Can you do these things? Check (✓) what you can do. Then write your answers in your notebook.

UNIT 7

Now I can …	Prove it
☐ talk about different kinds of music.	Write down as many kinds of music as you can. Say which ones are your top three favorite kinds. Say which ones you don't like.
☐ use *used to*.	Write three sentences about things you used to do at different stages of your life but don't do now.
☐ talk about TV shows and movies.	What have you watched on TV in the past week? Say what kinds of shows/movies they were.
☐ make comparisons with (*not*) *as … as*.	Choose two movies or TV shows that are similar. Say which you prefer, and explain why one isn't as good as the other.
☐ refuse invitations and respond to refusals.	Write two ways to refuse an invitation and two ways to respond to a refusal.
☐ write a movie review.	Look at your review from lesson 7.4. Can you make it better? Find three ways.

UNIT 8

Now I can …	Prove it
☐ describe experiences.	Complete the sentence with as many nouns as possible: *Cleaning the house is a difficult* _____ .
☐ use the present perfect continuous.	Write two things you have been doing lately. Write two things you haven't been doing.
☐ describe progress.	Write a short paragraph about how you've been spending your time lately. Say if you've been making good progress.
☐ use the present perfect and the present perfect continuous.	Think about a project you've been doing but haven't finished. Write about what you've done so far.
☐ catch up with people's news.	Write down two expressions to ask about someone's news and two expressions to answer those questions.
☐ write a post about managing my time.	Look at your post from lesson 8.4. Can you make it better? Find three ways.

UNIT 9

Now I can …	Prove it
☐ talk about college subjects.	Write down as many words for college subjects as you can.
☐ use modals of necessity.	Write down two things you have to do soon and two things you don't need to do.
☐ talk about employment.	What the difference between *salary* and *wage*? What's the difference between *apply*, *hire*, and *fire*?
☐ use modals of prohibition and permission.	Write three rules for studying at a library. Use *can*, *can't*, and *must not*.
☐ express confidence and lack of confidence.	Write a response to the statement saying how confident you are: A *I want you to run a marathon with me.* B _____
☐ write the main part of a résumé.	Look at your résumé from lesson 9.4. Can you make it better? Find three ways.

PROGRESS CHECK

Can you do these things? Check (✓) what you can do. Then write your answers in your notebook.

UNIT 10

Now I can …

☐ describe materials.

☐ use the simple present form of the passive.

☐ talk about production and distribution.

☐ use the simple past form of the passive.

☐ question or approve of someone's choices.

☐ write feedback about company products.

Prove it

What materials are the clothes you're wearing today made of? Are they warm? Waterproof? Light?

Write two sentences about things that are recycled and two sentences about things that aren't recycled.

Write four sentences about products in your country. Use the verbs *export*, *manufacture*, *grow*, and *design*.

Write sentences using these passive verbs and your own ideas: *was made*, *were imported*, and *was invited*.

Write two expressions you can use to question someone's choices and two expressions to approve of someone's choices.

Look at your feedback from lesson 10.4. Can you make it better? Find three ways.

UNIT 11

Now I can …

☐ talk about succeeding.

☐ use phrasal verbs.

☐ talk about opportunities and risks.

☐ use present and future unreal conditionals.

☐ give opinions and ask for agreement.

☐ write a personal story.

Prove it

Complete the sentences with the missing particles: *Don't give _____ . You can figure it _____ .*

Rewrite the sentence using *it*: Deal with your problem, and work out a solution.

Write at least four sentences about a good opportunity you had. Were there any risks? What were the advantages?

Answer the questions: *What would you buy if someone gave you $1,000? If you were a famous person, who would you be?*

Write three things you can say when you want someone to agree with you and three things you can say to agree with someone.

Look at your story from lesson 11.4. Can you make it better? Find three ways.

UNIT 12

Now I can …

☐ describe accidents.

☐ use indefinite pronouns.

☐ describe extremes.

☐ use reported speech.

☐ describe and ask about feelings.

☐ write an anecdote about a life lesson.

Prove it

Write sentences using these expressions: *damage, be mad at, knock off, feel bad about*.

Write one sentence each using these words: *everyone, somewhere, anything, no one*.

Write the extreme adjectives that mean the same as these phrases: *very big, very cold, very good, very hot, very sad, very tired*.

Change these sentences to reported speech, beginning with *Karen said that*: "Tom left for Miami on Sunday." "Rita will finish her report soon."

Write two ways to describe your feelings about a good situation and two ways to ask about someone's feelings.

Look at your anecdote from lesson 12.4. Can you make it better? Find three ways.

PAIR WORK PRACTICE (STUDENT A)

1.3 EXERCISE 2D   STUDENT A (page 7)

1 You're at a party at Mariana's home in San Francisco. Read the information in the box.

Name	Sam Prentiss (male) or Sarah Prentiss (female)
Relationship to Mariana	Friend
Job	Engineer at Domia Engineering
Home	Live in Los Angeles Visiting San Francisco this week
Interests	Basketball, music, going to restaurants

2 Introduce yourself to Student B. Then ask questions to get to know B. When you're finished, end the conversation and say goodbye.

2.3 EXERCISE 2D   STUDENT A (page 17)

Read the sentences. Your partner asks short questions to show interest. Take turns.

1 I'm really busy right now.

> You are? Why are you busy?

2 That restaurant serves great food.

3 I'm learning Chinese.

4.3 EXERCISE 2C   STUDENT A (page 39)

1 Tell Student B these things. Respond to Student B's reassurance.
- You're worried about hosting a birthday party for a friend next week.
- You haven't sent invitations, ordered food, or cleaned your house yet.
- You're not sure what kind of cake to make.

2 Listen to a few of Student B's worries about a long walking trip. Reassure him or her after each one. Then point out the good side of the situation: The weather will be good, and the mountain views will be amazing.

5.3 EXERCISE 2D   STUDENT A (page 49)

Say the surprising things below. Your partner will react by repeating the surprising words or phrases. Then your partner will say some surprising things. You react by repeating key words or phrases.

1 A friend of mine has seven TVs in his house.

2 I lost my toothbrush and then I found it later in the washing machine.

3 I know a guy who asked his girlfriend to marry him in a text message.

6.3 EXERCISE 2D   STUDENT A   (page 59)

1 **Read the information below. Tell the story to Student B. Add details.**
   - You went to a movie last night.
   - There was smoke in the movie theater (it was only burned food).
   - Someone fell down in a dark movie theater (but didn't get hurt).
   - It was a strange night, but you had fun.

2 **Listen to Student B's story. Express concern and relief when you think it's necessary.**

7.3 EXERCISE 2E   STUDENT A   (page 71)

1 **Invite your partner to one of the events below. Your partner refuses the invitation. Respond to your partner's refusal.**

   a classical music concert   a horror movie   a baseball game

2 **Your partner invites you to an event. Refuse the invitation. Then give one of the reasons below.**
   I don't really like that kind of music. I think it's sort of …
   I think those movies are kind of …
   I think that sport is sort of …

8.3 EXERCISE 2D   STUDENT A   (page 81)

1 **Imagine you are in these situations. Tell Student B about them. Listen to the reaction.**
   1 I've been thinking about not eating meat anymore.
   2 My brother wants a pet. He says he might get a snake.
   3 How about coming with me to see the new James Bond movie?

2 **Student B will tell you some things. Make comments after each one using** *That would be* **and an adjective. Use the words below or your own ideas.**

   amusing   difficult   nice   silly   strange   surprising   wonderful

9.3 EXERCISE 2D   STUDENT A   (page 91)

Ask your partner a question. Your partner says "No" and gives a reason. Then your partner asks you a question. You say "No" and give a reason using *The thing is*. **Take turns.**
   1 Could you drive me to the airport?
   2 Could you take care of my dog while I'm on vacation?
   3 I'm going to paint my apartment. Can you help me?

12.3 EXERCISE 2D   STUDENT A   (page 123)

1 **Look at the picture. Imagine this happened to you. Tell your partner about the experience. Answer your partner's questions. Use** *In the end* **or** *After all that* **to end your story.**

2 **Listen to Student B's story. Ask questions about how your partner felt.**

PAIR WORK PRACTICE (STUDENT B)

1.3 EXERCISE 2D   STUDENT B   (page 7)

1   You're at a party at Mariana's home in San Francisco. Read the information in the box.

Name	Pietro Gomez (male) or Teresa Gomez (female)
Relationship to Mariana	Coworker
Job	Teacher at Central High School
Home	San Francisco, near Mariana's house
Interests	Swimming, music, movies

2   Introduce yourself to Student A. Say you've heard a lot about A. Then ask questions to get to know A. When you're finished, end the conversation and say goodbye.

2.3 EXERCISE 2D   STUDENT B   (page 17)

Read the sentences. Your partner asks short questions to show interest. Take turns.

1   The weather forecast is bad.   *It is? What is the weather going to be tomorrow?*

2   I need a new laptop.

3   I watched a great movie last night.

4.3 EXERCISE 2C   STUDENT B   (page 39)

1   Listen to a few of Student A's worries about a party. Reassure him or her after each one. Then point out the good side of the situation: There are still several days to prepare for the party, and Student A's friend will appreciate all the work she did.

2   Tell Student A these things. Respond to Student A's reassurance.
- You're nervous about a five-day walking trip in the mountains with friends this summer.
- You're worried about wild animals and about getting lost.
- You think you aren't strong enough to walk for five days.

5.3 EXERCISE 2D   STUDENT B   (page 49)

Your partner will say some surprising things. You react by repeating the surprising words or phrases. Then you say the surprising things below. Your partner will react by repeating key words or phrases.

1   My dog ate my earphones this morning.

2   I was in the park, and a helicopter landed on the grass near me.

3   I was eating in a restaurant the other day, and I found an earring in my ice cream.

6.3 EXERCISE 2D   STUDENT B (page 59)

1 **Listen to Student A's story. Express concern and relief when you think it's necessary.**

2 **Read the information below. Tell the story to Student A. Add details.**
   - You flew to Miami last weekend.
   - The airport was crowded and hot, and everyone was annoyed.
   - You couldn't find your passport; you got worried; you found it after a while.
   - It was a difficult trip, but you got to Miami on time.

7.3 EXERCISE 2E   STUDENT B (page 71)

1 **Your partner invites you to an event. Refuse the invitation. Then give one of the reasons below.**
   I don't really like that kind of music. I think it's sort of …
   I think those movies are kind of …
   I think that sport is sort of …

2 **Invite your partner to one of the events below. Your partner refuses the invitation. Respond to your partner's refusal.**

   a country music concert   a romantic comedy   a basketball game

8.3 EXERCISE 2D   STUDENT B (page 81)

1 **Student A will tell you some things. Make comments after each one using *That would be* and an adjective. Use the words below or your own ideas.**

   awful   boring   fantastic   great   impossible   interesting   surprising

2 **Imagine you are in these situations. Tell Student A about them. Listen to the reaction.**
   1 Let's hide your brother's car keys and see what he does.
   2 I've decided to get up early every morning and go for a run. Come with me.
   3 It's our teacher's birthday tomorrow. We could give her some flowers.

9.3 EXERCISE 2D   STUDENT B (page 91)

Your partner asks you a question. You say "No" and give a reason using *The thing is*. Then ask your partner a question. Your partner says "No" and gives a reason. Take turns.
   1 Can we have a meeting after the lunch break?
   2 I have a surfboard that I never use. Do you want it?
   3 Why don't we have a barbecue this weekend?

12.3 EXERCISE 2D   STUDENT B (page 123)

1 **Listen to Student A's story. Ask questions about how your partner felt.**

2 **Look at the picture. Imagine this happened to you. Tell your partner about the experience. Answer your partner's questions. Use *In the end* or *After all that* to end your story.**